Fred Schlereth,

With best wishes

You were an important source of inspiration
for this work (see pp. ix, 6-8, 55-71).

STUDIES IN
COMPUTATIONAL SCIENCE

Parallel Programming Paradigms

PER BRINCH HANSEN

Prentice Hall, Englewood Cliffs, New Jersey 07632

Library of Congress Cataloging-in-Publication Data

Brinch Hansen, Per
    Studies in computational science: parallel programming paradigms
/Per Brinch Hansen
        p.   cm.
    Includes bibliographical references.
    ISBN 0-13-439324-4
    1. Parallel programming (Computers) I. Title.
    QA76.642.B76   1995
    005.2--dc20   94-47128
                                  CIP

Publisher: Alan Apt
Production Editor: Mona Pompili
Cover Designer: Tom Nery
Copy Editor: Thomas Brinch Hansen
Production Coordinator: Lori Bulwin
Editorial Assistant: Shirley McGuire

 © 1995 by Prentice Hall, Inc.
A Simon & Schuster Company
Englewood Cliffs, New Jersey 07632

The author and publisher of this book have used their best efforts in preparing this book. These efforts include the development, research, and testing of the theories and programs to determine their effectiveness. The author and publisher shall not be liable in any event for incidental or consequential damages in connection with, or arising out of, the furnishing, performance, or use of these programs.

Printed in the United States of America

10 9 8 7 6 5 4 3 2 1

ISBN   0-13-439324-4

PRENTICE-HALL INTERNATIONAL (UK) LIMITED, *London*
PRENTICE-HALL OF AUSTRALIA PTY. LIMITED, *Sydney*
PRENTICE-HALL CANADA, INC., *Toronto*
PRENTICE-HALL HISPANOAMERICANA, S.A., *Mexico*
PRENTICE-HALL OF INDIA PRIVATE LIMITED, *New Delhi*
PRENTICE-HALL OF JAPAN, INC., *Tokyo*
SIMON & SCHUSTER ASIA PTE. LTD., *Singapore*
EDITORA PRENTICE-HALL DO BRASIL, LTDA., *Rio de Janeiro*

In memory of my mother
Elsebeth Brinch Hansen, née Ring

Preface

The Main Goal

This book is my attempt to understand the nature of parallel scientific computing from a programmer's point of view. It describes a collection of *structured multicomputer programs for computational science.*

The book is written for computer scientists and programmers with no prior knowledge of parallel scientific computing. I assume that you know Pascal and elementary calculus. The numerical methods are explained in the text.

My own background is in parallel programming languages. Since I am not a numerical analyst, I have only studied each method in sufficient detail to be able to understand and program it. There is very little discussion of the problems of numerical errors. However, as an outsider I have the advantage of looking at computational science with fresh eyes, to question the way it is programmed and published, and suggest a better way.

Programming Methodology

The unifying idea behind my programs is the concept of a *programming paradigm—a class of programs that solve different problems, but have the same control structure.* I discuss five programming paradigms for all-pairs computation, tuple multiplication, divide and conquer, Monte Carlo trials, and cellular automata.

For each paradigm, I develop a *parallel generic program*, which implements the common control structure. The paradigm is then used to solve two different problems. The generic program includes a few unspecified data types and procedures that vary from one instance of the paradigm to another. A *parallel application program* is obtained by replacing these types and procedures with the corresponding types and procedures from a sequential program that solves the same problem.

The application programs solve *realistic problems in science and engineering*: linear equations, n-body simulation, matrix multiplication, all-pairs shortest paths, sorting, fast Fourier transforms, simulated annealing, primality testing, forest fire simulation, and Laplace's equation.

The programs are written for multicomputers in which processors communicate by *message passing* only. They illustrate the programming of a variety of *multicomputer architectures*, such as pipelines, trees, hypercubes, and meshes.

Programming Tools

While reading papers as a novice in scientific computing, I soon realized that "the devil is in the details." I came to the conclusion that *subtle algorithms must be presented in their entirety as well-structured programs written in a readable, executable programming language*. This insight inspired me to invent the *publication language SuperPascal* for parallel scientific computing.

The multicomputer programs are developed and presented in Super-Pascal, which extends Pascal with statements for parallel execution and message communication. The language permits unrestricted combinations of recursive procedures and parallel statements. The book includes a brief tutorial on SuperPascal and the complete text of ten SuperPascal programs.

The SuperPascal programs were tested on a sequential Sun workstation. When the parallel programs worked, I rewrote them in the *implementation language occam2* and measured their performance on a *Computing Surface*— a reconfigurable multicomputer with 48 transputers and 48 Mbytes of distributed memory.

I emphasize that this is *not* a text about SuperPascal or the Computing Surface. It is a book about the programming of *portable multicomputer algorithms*. SuperPascal is just used as a convenient notation easily understood by anyone familiar with Pascal. And I only use the Computing Surface to demonstrate the efficiency of portable algorithms on a real multicomputer.

Graduate Course

At Syracuse University, I have used the text in a *graduate course* on *The Art of Multicomputer Programming*. While I lecture on programming paradigms, I do not expect students to invent new paradigms. Instead, each student selects a standard method in numerical analysis or graph theory, writes a multicomputer algorithm in SuperPascal, and describes it in a report that is revised several times during the semester.

I have developed a *portable implementation* of SuperPascal on a Sun workstation under Unix. It consists of a compiler and an interpreter written in Pascal. These programs are in the public domain. You can obtain the SuperPascal software by *anonymous FTP* from the directory *pbh* at *top.cis.syr.edu*.

Chapter Organization

The book is divided into seven parts.

Part I is an overview of the *programming concepts* used throughout the text.

Chapter 1 describes a programming methodology for computational science based on *parallel programming paradigms* for multicomputers.

Chapter 2 introduces the *SuperPascal language* by examples.

Part II views Householder reduction and n-body simulation as instances of an *all-pairs paradigm*—a computation on every possible subset of two elements chosen from a set of n elements.

Chapter 3 explains *Householder reduction* of linear equations to a triangular form that can be solved by back substitution. Householder reduction is derived from elementary matrix algebra and illustrated by a numerical example and a Pascal algorithm.

Chapter 4 defines coarse-grain and medium-grain variants of a generic *all-pairs pipeline*. The pipeline is adapted for parallel Householder reduction by substitution of data types and sequential procedures.

Chapter 5 considers the problem of *balancing a pipeline* for Householder reduction. The performance of the balanced pipeline is analyzed and measured on a Computing Surface.

Chapter 6 examines an *n-body pipeline* for direct force summation of n bodies which interact through gravitation only. The parallel complexity is predicted and verified by experiments.

Part III develops a *multiplication paradigm* that includes matrix multiplication and the all-pairs shortest paths problems as special cases.

Chapter 7 presents a generic algorithm for a *multiplication pipeline* and derives pipelines for matrix multiplication and shortest paths computation. The performance of the matrix multiplication pipeline is predicted and measured.

Part IV uses a *divide and conquer paradigm* to develop multicomputer algorithms for quicksort and the fast Fourier transform.

Chapter 8 explains the *fast Fourier transform*, which has numerous applications in signal and image processing. The FFT is illustrated by examples and defined by SuperPascal algorithms.

Chapter 9 develops a generic algorithm for *parallel divide and conquer*. The generic algorithm is turned into balanced parallel versions of quicksort and the fast Fourier transform. The performance of these algorithms is predicted and measured on a Computing Surface configured as a binary tree machine with distributed memory.

Chapter 10 on *hypercubes and tree machines* presents a balanced parallel quicksort for a hypercube and compares it with the similar algorithm for a tree machine.

Part V uses simulated annealing and primality testing as examples of a *Monte Carlo paradigm* for probabilistic algorithms.

Chapter 11 describes *simulated annealing*, an optimization method based on the principles of statistical mechanics. The method is illustrated by a Pascal algorithm for the traveling salesperson problem. The performance is measured on a Computing Surface.

Chapter 12 explains the Miller-Rabin algorithm for *primality testing* of large integers and determines its performance.

Chapter 13 defines *multiple-length division* of natural numbers, which is used for primality testing. It includes a complete SuperPascal algorithm and performance measurements.

Chapter 14 shows how to obtain the best results of a Monte Carlo method by repeating the same computation many times with different random numbers. A generic algorithm for *parallel Monte Carlo trials* is applied to simulated annealing and primality testing on a multicomputer.

Part VI uses a *cellular automata paradigm* to solve Laplace's equation and simulate a forest fire.

Chapter 15 discusses *Laplace's equation* for steady-state heat flow in a two-dimensional region with fixed temperatures on the boundaries. The numerical method is illustrated by a Pascal algorithm.

Chapter 16 develops a multicomputer algorithm for *parallel cellular automata*. The generic algorithm is modified for simulation of a forest fire and numerical solution of Laplace's equation. The performance of the parallel algorithm is analyzed and measured on a Computing Surface configured as a matrix of processors with distributed memory.

Part VII presents the *parallel model programs*, discussed in the earlier chapters, as *complete SuperPascal programs* in Chapter 17.

Acknowledgements

I owe a debt of gratitude to Syracuse University and Miles Chesney, Meiko Ltd, who made it possible for me to work on the Computing Surface.

While writing earlier drafts of this text, I have benefited from the perceptive comments of

Suad Alagić	Paul Dubois	Harlan Mills
James Allwright	Geoffrey Fox	Peter O'Hearn
Thomas Brinch Hansen	Christian Gram	Hans Riesel
Coen Bron	Jonathan Greenfield	Fred Schlereth
Mani Chandi	Erik Hemmingsen	Les Valiant
Nawal Copty	Tony Hey	Peter Villemoes
Peter Denning	Konrad Jahn	Virgil Wallentine
Jack Dongarra	Skip Mattson	

The book includes revised versions of the following papers written by me:

- Householder reduction of linear equations. *ACM Computing Surveys*, **24**, pp. 185–194, June 1992. Copyright ©1992 Association for Computing Machinery, Inc. Reprinted by permission.

- Model programs for computational science: a programming methodology for multicomputers. *Concurrency—Practice and Experience*, **5**, pp. 407–423, August 1993. Copyright ©1993 John Wiley & Sons, Ltd. Reprinted by permission.

- Parallel cellular automata: a model program for computational science. *Concurrency–Practice and Experience*, **5**, pp. 425–448, August 1993. Copyright ©1993 John Wiley & Sons, Ltd. Reprinted by permission.

- Do hypercubes sort faster than tree machines? *Concurrency—Practice and Experience*, **6**, pp. 143–151, April 1994. Copyright ©1994 John Wiley & Sons, Ltd. Reprinted by permission.

- Multiple-length division revisited: a tour of the minefield. *Software—Practice and Experience*, **24**, pp. 579–601, June 1994. Copyright ©1994 John Wiley & Sons, Ltd. Reprinted by permission.

- SuperPascal—a publication language for parallel scientific computing. *Concurrency–Practice and Experience*, **6**, pp. 461–483, August 1994. Copyright ©1994 John Wiley & Sons, Ltd. Reprinted by permission.

PER BRINCH HANSEN
Syracuse University

Contents

I PROGRAMMING CONCEPTS   1

1 Parallel Programming Paradigms   3
   1.1   Introduction   3
   1.2   The Computing Surface   5
   1.3   The All-Pairs Pipeline   6
   1.4   The Multiplication Pipeline   8
   1.5   The Divide and Conquer Tree   9
   1.6   The Divide and Conquer Cube   11
   1.7   Parallel Monte Carlo Trials   12
   1.8   Parallel Cellular Automata   14
   1.9   Program Characteristics 16
   1.10 Programming Languages   18
   1.11 Research Method 21
   1.12 Final Remarks 22

2 The SuperPascal Language   24
   2.1   Introduction 24
   2.2   A Programming Example   27
   2.3   Message Communication   28
   2.4   Parallel Processes 34
   2.5   Interference Control 42
   2.6   SuperPascal Versus Occam   50
   2.7   Final Remarks 51

II   THE ALL-PAIRS PARADIGM   **53**

3   Householder Reduction   **55**
   3.1   Introduction   55
   3.2   Gaussian Elimination   55
   3.3   Scalar Products   58
   3.4   Reflection   59
   3.5   Householder Reduction   62
   3.6   Numerical Stability   64
   3.7   Computational Rules   65
   3.8   A Numerical Example   65
   3.9   Pascal Procedure   68
   3.10   Final Remarks   70
   3.11   Appendix: Matrix Algebra   71

4   The All-Pairs Pipeline   **73**
   4.1   Introduction   73
   4.2   The All-Pairs Problem   74
   4.3   Sequential Algorithms   75
   4.4   A Coarse-Grain Pipeline   77
   4.5   A Medium-Grain Pipeline   82
   4.6   Variation on a Theme   82
   4.7   An Example: Householder Reduction   86
   4.8   Final Remarks   88

5   Balancing a Pipeline   **90**
   5.1   Introduction   90
   5.2   Pipeline Nodes   91
   5.3   A Simple Pipeline   92
   5.4   A Folded Pipeline   93
   5.5   The Effect of Communication   94
   5.6   Performance Measurements   96
   5.7   Final Remarks   97
   5.8   Appendix: Performance Analysis   98

6   The N-Body Pipeline   **101**
   6.1   Introduction   101
   6.2   Force Summation   102

6.3   Time Integration 103
6.4   Sequential Algorithm 104
6.5   Pipeline Algorithm 105
6.6   Load Balancing 108
6.7   Performance 112
6.8   Final Remarks 113
6.9   Appendix: Vector Arithmetic 113

III   THE MULTIPLICATION PARADIGM   115

7   The Multiplication Pipeline   117
7.1   Introduction 117
7.2   Tuple Multiplication 117
7.3   Pipeline Algorithm 118
7.4   Matrix Multiplication 122
7.5   All-Pairs Shortest Paths 124
7.6   Performance 132
7.7   Final Remarks 134

IV   THE DIVIDE AND CONQUER PARADIGM   135

8   The Fast Fourier Transform   137
8.1   Introduction 137
8.2   Mathematical Background 137
8.3   The Discrete Fourier Transform 140
8.4   The Fast Fourier Transform 146
8.5   Final Remarks 159
8.6   Appendix: Complete Algorithm 159

9   Parallel Divide and Conquer   163
9.1   Introduction 163
9.2   Sequential Paradigm 164
9.3   Parallel Paradigm 165
9.4   Parallel Quicksort 167
9.5   Parallel FFT 172
9.6   Complexity 174

9.7   Performance 177
9.8   Final Remarks 178

10 Hypercubes and Tree Machines   **180**
10.1 Introduction 180
10.2 Hypercube Sorting 180
10.3 Complexity 184
10.4 Performance 187
10.5 Hypercubes Versus Tree Machines 188
10.6 Final Remarks 189

V   THE MONTE CARLO PARADIGM   **191**

11 Simulated Annealing   **193**
11.1 Introduction 193
11.2 Naivete 194
11.3 Annealing 194
11.4 Configurations 195
11.5 Cooling 196
11.6 Searching 196
11.7 Rearrangement 198
11.8 Parameters 200
11.9 Complexity 202
11.10 Experiments 203
11.11 Final Remarks 204

12 Primality Testing   **205**
12.1 Introduction 205
12.2 Fermat's Theorem 206
12.3 The Fermat Test 207
12.4 Quadratic Remainders 208
12.5 The Miller-Rabin Test 209
12.6 A Probabilistic Algorithm 209
12.7 Complexity 211
12.8 Experiments 212
12.9 Final Remarks 213

13 Multiple-Length Division Revisited **214**
  13.1 Introduction 214
  13.2 Long Division 217
  13.3 The Essence of the Problem 221
  13.4 Trial Iteration 223
  13.5 SuperPascal Algorithm 227
  13.6 Final Remarks 237
  13.7 Appendix: Proof of Theorems 238

14 Parallel Monte Carlo Trials **242**
  14.1 Introduction 242
  14.2 Sequential Paradigm 243
  14.3 Parallel Paradigm 243
  14.4 Simulated Annealing 247
  14.5 Primality Testing 248
  14.6 Final Remarks 250

VI THE CELLULAR AUTOMATA PARADIGM **251**

15 Laplace's Equation **253**
  15.1 Introduction 253
  15.2 The Heat Equation 253
  15.3 Difference Equations 256
  15.4 Numerical Solution 258
  15.5 Relaxation Methods 260
  15.6 Pascal Algorithm 264
  15.7 Final Remarks 267

16 Parallel Cellular Automata **268**
  16.1 Introduction 268
  16.2 Cellular Automata 268
  16.3 Initial States 270
  16.4 Data Parallelism 271
  16.5 Processor Nodes 273
  16.6 Parallel Relaxation 274
  16.7 Local Communication 277
  16.8 Global Output 279

16.9   Processor Network 282
16.10 Example: Forest Fire 283
16.11 Example: Laplace's Equation 285
16.12 Complexity 288
16.13 Performance 290
16.14 Final Remarks 290

VII   PARALLEL MODEL PROGRAMS   291

17 Complete SuperPascal Programs   293
17.1   Introduction 293
17.2   The Householder Pipeline 293
17.3   The N-Body Pipeline 299
17.4   The Multiplication Pipeline 306
17.5   The Shortest Paths Pipeline 310
17.6   The Quicksort Tree 315
17.7   The FFT Tree 320
17.8   The Annealing Pipeline 326
17.9   The Primality Testing Pipeline 333
17.10 The Forest Fire Matrix 345
17.11 The Laplace Matrix 353

Bibliography   360

Part I

PROGRAMMING CONCEPTS

Chapter 1

Parallel Programming Paradigms

1.1 Introduction

For three years I have studied *computational science* from the point of view of a computer scientist [Brinch Hansen 1990c–1992f]. I have followed the advice of Geoffrey Fox [1990] to "use real hardware to solve real problems with real software." But, where the Caltech group concentrated on scientific applications for their own sake, I have used them as realistic case studies to illustrate the use of *structured programming* in computational science.

My research explores the role of *programming paradigms* in parallel computing. In programming, the word *paradigm* is often used with a general (but vague) connotation, such as "the high level methodologies that we recognize as common to many of our effective algorithms" [Nelson 1987]. I will use the term in a more narrow (but precise) sense: A *programming paradigm is a class of algorithms that solve different problems but have the same control structure.*

I have studied paradigms for all-pairs computations, tuple multiplication, divide-and-conquer, Monte Carlo trials and cellular automata [Brinch Hansen 1990d, 1991b, 1991d, 1992d, 1992f]. For each paradigm I have written a general program that defines the common control structure. Such a program is sometimes called an *algorithmic skeleton*, a *generic program*, or a *program template* [Cole 1989; Brinch Hansen 1991b].

From a general parallel program I derive two or more *model programs* that illustrate the use of the paradigm to solve specific problems. A general program includes a few unspecified data types and procedures that vary from one application to another. A model program is obtained by replacing these data types and procedures with the corresponding data types and procedures from a sequential program that solves a specific problem. The essence of the programming methodology is that a model program has a parallel component that implements a paradigm and a sequential component for a specific application. The clear separation of the issues of parallelism and the details of application is essential for writing model programs that are easy to understand.

My own model programs solve typical problems in science and engineering: linear equations, n-body simulation, matrix multiplication, shortest paths in graphs, sorting, fast Fourier transforms, simulated annealing, primality testing, Laplace's equation, and forest fire simulation.

I have run these parallel programs on a *Computing Surface* configured as a pipeline, a tree, a cube, or a matrix of *transputers*.

It has been fun to enter an interdisciplinary field, refresh my memory of mathematics and physics I learned as an undergraduate, study numerical analysis, and teach myself the art of *multicomputer programming*.

My one serious criticism of computational science is that it largely has ignored the issue of *precision* and *clarity* in parallel programming that is essential for the education of future scientists. A written explanation is not an algorithm. A graph of computational steps is not an algorithm. A picture of a systolic array is not an algorithm. A mathematical formula is not an algorithm. A program outline written in non-executable "pseudocode" is not an algorithm. And, a complicated "code" that is difficult to understand will not do either.

Subtle algorithms must be presented in their entirety as well-structured programs written in readable, executable programming languages [Forsythe 1966; Ignizio 1973; Wirth 1976; Brinch Hansen 1977; Dunham 1982; Press 1989]. This has been my main reason for publishing model programs for computational science.

In the following, I will describe parallel programming paradigms and explain why I use different programming languages and computers for publication and implementation of model programs. I will also outline the steps involved in developing model programs based on paradigms. Finally, I will argue that the study of programming paradigms provides an architectural vision of parallel scientific computing.

1.2   The Computing Surface

When I started this research, I knew that my programs would soon become obsolete unless I wrote them for parallel architectures of the future. So, I had to make an educated guess about the direction in which hardware and software technology would move parallel architectures during the 1990s.

By 1989, I had tentatively formulated the following requirements for a general purpose parallel computer of the future [May 1988, 1990; Valiant 1989; Brinch Hansen 1990b]:

1. A parallel architecture must be expandable from tens to thousands of processors.

2. A parallel computer must consist of general-purpose processors.

3. A parallel computer must support different process structures (pipelines, trees, matrices, and so on) in a transparent manner.

4. Process creation, communication, and termination must be hardware operations that are only an order of magnitude slower than memory references.

5. A parallel computer should automatically distribute the computational load and route messages between the processors.

The first three requirements eliminated multiprocessors, SIMD machines, and hypercubes, respectively. The only architecture that satisfied the first four requirements was the *Computing Surface* [Meiko 1987; McDonald 1991]. No parallel computer satisfied the fifth condition.

In the summer of 1989, a Computing Surface was installed at Syracuse University. It is a *multicomputer* with 48 processors that can be extended to 1000 processors. Every processor is a T800 *transputer* with one or more megabytes of memory. The transputers are connected by a communication network that can be reconfigured before program execution. Direct communication is possible only among connected transputers, but is very fast (a few microseconds). Process creation and termination are also hardware operations.

The programming tool is the parallel programming language *occam 2* [Inmos 1988; Cok 1991]. This language makes it possible to define parallel processes that communicate by messages.

1.3   The All-Pairs Pipeline

Although I knew nothing about numerical analysis, I thought that parallel solution of *linear equations* would be a useful programming exercise for a beginner. I chose the problem for the following reason: When a pipeline with p processors solves n linear equations, the numerical computation requires $O(n^3/p)$ time, while the input/output takes $O(n^2)$ time. If the problem size n is large compared to the machine size p, the overhead of processor communication is negligible. The high ratio of computation to communication makes the problem ideal for efficient parallel computing.

A colleague recommended *Householder reduction* as an attractive method for solving linear equations on a parallel computer. The main strength of the method is its unconditional numerical stability [Householder 1958]. The familiar Gaussian elimination is faster but requires a dynamic rearrangement of the equations, known as *pivoting*, which complicates a parallel program somewhat [Fox 1988].

Unfortunately, I could not find a well-written, understandable explanation of Householder's method. Most textbooks on numerical analysis produce Householder's matrix like a rabbit from a magician's top hat without explaining why it is defined the way it is. At this point, I stopped writing parallel programs and concentrated on sequential Householder reduction. After several frustrating weeks I was able to write a *tutorial* on Householder reduction [Chap. 3 and Brinch Hansen 1990c]. Two pages were sufficient to explain the purpose and derive the equation of Householder's matrix. I then explained the computational rules for Householder reduction and illustrated the method by a numerical example and a Pascal program.

I was beginning to think that others might have the same difficulty understanding this fundamental computation. So I submitted the tutorial to a journal that published it. One of the reviewers wrote that he "found the presentation far superior to the several descriptions I have seen in numerical analysis books." I quote this review not just because I like it, but because it was my first lesson about computational science. In order to understand a computation, I must first explain it to myself by writing a tutorial that includes a complete sequential program.

After studying parallel programming for 25 years it was not too difficult for me to program a *Householder pipeline* [Chap. 4 and Brinch Hansen 1990d]. The parallel program was written in occam for the Computing Surface. I used a coarse-grain pipeline to reduce communication overhead. To achieve approximate *load-balancing*, the pipeline was folded three times across an array of p transputers [Chap. 5 and Brinch Hansen 1990e]. Figure 1.1 shows the *folded pipeline*. The squares and lines represent pipeline nodes and communication channels, respectively. Each column represents a single transputer that executes four parallel nodes.

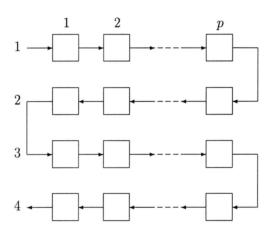

Figure 1.1: A folded pipeline.

My next exercise was to compute the trajectories of n particles that interact by gravitation only. I considered the *n-body problem* to be particularly challenging on a parallel computer since it involves interactions among all the particles in each computational step. This means that every processor must communicate, directly or indirectly, with every other processor. My description of an *n-body pipeline* included a brief summary of Newton's laws of gravitation and a Pascal program for sequential n-body simulation [Chap. 6 and Brinch Hansen 1991a]. Others have solved the same problem using a ring of processors [Ellingworth 1988; Fox 1988].

It was a complete surprise for me to discover that the sequential Pascal programs for Householder reduction and n-body simulation had practically identical control structures. I suddenly understood that both of them are instances of the same *programming paradigm*: Each algorithm solves an *all-pairs problem*—a computation on every possible subset consisting of two elements chosen from a set of n elements. I have not found this insight mentioned in any textbook on numerical analysis or computational physics.

I now discarded both parallel algorithms and started all over. This time I programmed a general pipeline algorithm for all-pairs computations [Brinch Hansen 1990d]. This program is a parallel implementation of the common control structure. It provides a mechanism for performing the same operation on every pair of elements chosen from an array of n elements without specifying what the elements represent and how they "interact" pairwise.

I then turned the *all-pairs pipeline* into a Householder pipeline by using a few data types and procedures from the sequential Householder program. This transformation of the parallel program was completely mechanical and required no understanding of Householder's method. A similar transformation turned the all-pairs pipeline into an n-body pipeline.

Later I discovered that all-pairs pipelines were described informally by Shih [1987] and Cosnard [1988], but without concise algorithms.

I had now found my *research theme*: the use of parallel programming paradigms in computational science.

1.4   The Multiplication Pipeline

After programming a subtle parallel program, I looked for the simplest problem that would illustrate the benefits of developing generic algorithms for parallel programming paradigms that can be adapted to different applications.

This time I chose *matrix multiplication*, which can be pipelined in a straightforward way as shown in Fig. 1.2 [Kung 1989]. The pipeline inputs the rows of a matrix a followed by the columns of a matrix b and outputs the rows of the product matrix $a \times b$.

For sequential algorithms it is well-known that matrix multiplication is similar to the problem of finding the *shortest paths* between every pair of nodes in a directed graph with n nodes [Cormen 1990].

After studying both algorithms, the unifying concept seemed to me to be an operation that I called *tuple multiplication*: the product of two n-tuples a and b is an $n \times n$ matrix c. The matrix elements are obtained by applying

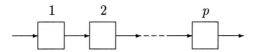

Figure 1.2: A simple pipeline.

the same function f to every ordered pair consisting of an element of a and an element of b, that is $c_{ij} = f(a_i, b_j)$.

In the case of matrix multiplication, the tuple elements are rows and columns, respectively, and every function value is the dot product of a row and a column. The input to the shortest paths problem is the adjacency matrix of a graph. The output is a distance matrix computed by a sequence of tuple multiplications. In every multiplication, tuple a consists of the n rows of the adjacency matrix, while tuple b consists of the n columns of the distance matrix. The function value $f(a_i, b_j)$ defines the shortest path length found so far between nodes i and j of the graph.

The task was now obvious. I wrote a paper that defined a pipeline algorithm for tuple multiplication. I briefly explained matrix multiplication and the all-pairs shortest-path problem by means of Pascal algorithms. I then transformed the parallel program into pipeline algorithms for the two applications by defining the data types of the tuples and the corresponding variants of the function f. After rewriting the parallel programs in occam, I analyzed and measured their performance on the Computing Surface [Chap. 7 and Brinch Hansen 1991b].

1.5   The Divide and Conquer Tree

My third paradigm was a parallel *divide-and-conquer* algorithm for a binary tree of processor nodes [Browning 1980; Brinch Hansen 1991d and Chap. 9]. Figure 1.3 shows the *tree machine*.

The root node of the tree inputs a problem, divides it into two smaller problems, and outputs one problem to each of its child nodes. The division of problems is repeated higher up in the tree until every leaf node has received a problem. Every leaf returns the solution of its problem to its own parent. Every parent combines the solutions from its children into a single solution,

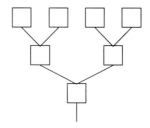

Figure 1.3: A tree machine.

which is returned to its own parent. Eventually, the root outputs the solution to the original problem.

A problem and its solution are both defined by an array of n elements of the same type. The element type and the procedures for splitting problems and combining solutions are the only parts of the parallel algorithm that depend on the nature of a specific problem. Consequently, it was easy to transform the general algorithm into parallel versions of *quicksort* [Hoare 1961] and the *fast Fourier transform* [Cooley 1965; Brigham 1974; Brinch Hansen 1991c and Chaps. 8–9].

The emphasis on the common paradigm enabled me to discover an unexpected similarity between these well-known algorithms. After programming an iterative version of the fast Fourier transform, I suddenly realized that it must also be possible to write a *quicksort without a stack!* In standard quicksort, the *partition* procedure divides an array into two slices of unpredictable sizes. Why not replace this algorithm with the *find* procedure [Hoare 1971b] and use it to split an array into two halves? Then you don't need a stack to remember where you split the array.

On the average, *find* is twice as slow as *partition*. That is probably the reason why a balanced quicksort is seldom used for sequential computers. However, on a multicomputer, the unpredictable nature of standard quicksort causes severe *load imbalance* [Fox 1988]. If the two halves of a tree machine sort sequences of very different lengths, half of the processors are doing most of the work, while the other half are idle most of the time. As a compromise, I used *find* in the parent nodes and *partition* in the leaf nodes. Measurements show that the *balanced parallel quicksort* consistently runs faster than the unbalanced algorithm.

I selected the divide-and-conquer paradigm to demonstrate that some parallel computations are inherently *inefficient*. The average sorting time of n elements is $O(n \log n)$ on a sequential computer. A tree machine cannot reduce the sorting time below the $O(n)$ time required to input and output the n elements through the root node. So, for problems of size n, the *parallel speed-up* cannot exceed $O(\log n)$. No matter how many processors you use to sort, say, a million numbers, they can do it only an order of magnitude faster than a single processor. This modest speed-up makes divide-and-conquer algorithms unsatisfactory for multicomputers with hundreds or thousands of processors.

1.6   The Divide and Conquer Cube

I have never been enamored of *hypercube* architectures [Seitz 1985]. I felt that hypercube algorithms would be dominated by the problem of mapping problem-oriented process configurations onto a hypercube. This prediction turned out to be true, I think [Fox 1988]. Hypercubes can probably be made reasonably easy to use if they are supported by a library of programming paradigms that hide the mapping problem from scientific users. But I pity the professional programmers who will have to cope with the awkward details of paradigm implementation.

In the future, most parallel architectures will almost certainly support automatic routing of messages between any pair of nodes. Although the hardware architecture may be a hypercube, this structure will be transparent to the programmer, who will define abstract configurations of nodes connected by virtual channels [May 1988; Valiant 1989]. In the meantime, reconfigurable multicomputers are a reasonable compromise.

On a general-purpose multicomputer, a programmer may, of course, choose the hypercube as a programming paradigm in its own right. So, I was curious to find out if a hypercube sorts faster than a tree machine. Figure 1.4 shows a *cube* with eight processor nodes.

First, node 0 inputs n numbers, splits them into two halves, sends one half to node 1, and keeps the other half. Then nodes 0 and 1 each split their halves into quarters. Finally, nodes 0, 1, 2, and 3 each keep an eighth of the numbers and sends the other eighths to nodes 4, 5, 6, and 7. All the nodes now work in parallel while each of them sorts one eighth of the numbers. Afterwards, nodes 0, 1, 2, and 3 each input a sorted sequence of size $n/8$

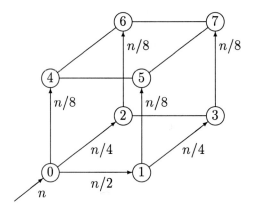

Figure 1.4: Data distribution in a cube.

from their "children" and combine them with their own numbers to form sorted sequences of size $n/4$. Nodes 0 and 1 repeat the combination process and form sorted sequences of size $n/2$. At the end, node 0 outputs n sorted numbers to its environment.

A larger hypercube follows the same general divide and conquer method. Needless to say, the sorting algorithm can easily be replaced by a fast Fourier transform.

On a hypercube, every node sorts a portion of the numbers. However, on a tree machine, sorting is done by the leaf nodes only. In spite of this, I found that a hypercube with 32 or more nodes sorts only marginally faster than a tree machine of the same size. This conclusion was based on a performance model verified by experiments [Chap. 10 and Brinch Hansen 1991e]. The reason is simple. On a large tree machine, the sorting time of the leaf nodes is small compared to the data distribution time of the remaining nodes. So, there is not much gained by reducing the sorting time further.

1.7   Parallel Monte Carlo Trials

Monte Carlo methods are algorithms that use random number generators to simulate stochastic processes. Probabilistic algorithms have been applied successfully to combinatorial problems, which cannot be solved exactly because they have a vast number of possible solutions.

The most famous example is the problem of the *traveling salesperson* who must visit n cities [Lawler 1985]. No computer will ever be able to find the shortest possible tour through 100 cities by examining all the 5×10^{150} possible tours. For practical purposes, the problem can be effectively solved by *simulated annealing* [Kirkpatrick 1983; Aarts 1989]. This Monte Carlo method has a high probability of finding a near-optimal tour of 100 cities after examining a random sample of one million tours.

Fox *et al.* [1988] have shown that a hypercube can solve the traveling salesperson problem by simulated annealing. Allwright and Carpenter [1989] have solved the same problem on an array of transputers. These algorithms use parallelism to speed up the annealing process.

After a while I noticed that papers on simulated annealing often included remarks such as the following: "Our results [are] averaged over 20 initial random tours" [Moscato 1989]. When you think about it, it makes sense: Due to the probabilistic nature of Monte Carlo methods, the best results are obtained by performing the same computation many times with different random numbers.

The advantage of using a multicomputer for *parallel Monte Carlo trials* is obvious. When the same problem has been broadcast to every processor, the trials can be performed simultaneously without any communication between the processors. Consequently, the processor efficiency is very close to 1 for non-trivial problems.

A straightforward implementation of the Monte Carlo paradigm requires a *master* processor that communicates directly with p *servers*. Each processor performs m/p trials. The master then collects the m solutions from the servers. Unfortunately, most multicomputers permit each processor to communicate with only a few neighboring processors. For p larger than, say, 4, the data must be transmitted through a chain of processors. The simplest way to do this is to use a *pipeline* with p processors controlled by a master processor [Chap. 14 and Brinch Hansen 1992d].

I used this paradigm to compute ten different tours of 2500 cities simultaneously and select the shortest tour obtained [Chap. 11 and Brinch Hansen 1992a].

My second application of the paradigm was *primality testing* of a large integer, which is of considerable interest in *cryptography* [Rivest 1978]. It is not feasible to determine whether or not a 150-digit integer is a prime by examining all the 10^{75} possible divisors. The *Miller–Rabin algorithm* tests the same integer many times using different random numbers [Rabin 1980]. If any one of the trials shows that a number is composite, then this is the correct answer. However, if all trials fail to prove that a number is composite, then it is almost certainly prime. The probability that the algorithm gives the wrong answer after, say, 40 trials is less than 10^{-24}.

I programmed the Miller–Rabin algorithm in occam and used the Monte Carlo paradigm to perform 40 tests of a 160-digit random number simultaneously on 40 transputers [Chap. 12 and Brinch Hansen 1992b].

For primality testing, I had to program multiple-length arithmetic. These serial operations imitate the familiar paper-and-pencil methods. I thought it would be easy to find a textbook that includes a simple algorithm for *multiple-length division* with a complete explanation. Much to my surprise, I was unable to find such a book. I ended up spending weeks on this "well-known" problem and finally wrote a tutorial that includes a complete Pascal algorithm [Chap. 13 and Brinch Hansen 1992c]. I mention this unexpected difficulty to illustrate what happens when a standard algorithm is not published as a well-structured program in an executable language.

1.8   Parallel Cellular Automata

A *cellular automaton* is a discrete model of a system that varies in time and space. The discrete space is an array of identical cells, each representing a local state. As time advances in discrete steps, the system evolves according to universal laws. Every time the clock ticks, the cells update their states simultaneously. The next state of a cell depends only on the current states of the cell and its nearest neighbors.

John von Neumann [1966] and Stan Ulam [1986] introduced cellular automata to study self-reproducing systems. John Conway's game, *Life*, is undoubtedly the most widely known cellular automaton [Gardner 1970, 1971; Berlekamp 1982]. Another well-known automaton simulates the life cycles of sharks and fish on the imaginary planet *Wa-Tor* [Dewdney 1984].

Cellular automata can simulate continuous physical systems described by *partial differential equations*. The numerical solution of, say, Laplace's equation by grid iteration is really a discrete simulation of heat flow performed by a cellular automaton.

Fox *et al.* [1988] described a Wa-Tor simulator for a hypercube. Numer-

ical solution of Laplace's equation on multicomputers has been discussed by
Barlow and Evans [1982], Evans [1984], Pritchard *et al.* [1987], Saltz *et al.*
[1987], and Fox *et al.* [1988].

I developed and published a model program for parallel execution of a
cellular automaton on a multicomputer configured as a *matrix* of processors
(Fig. 1.5).

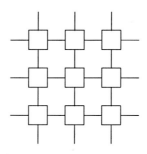

Figure 1.5: Processor matrix.

The combined state of a cellular automaton is represented by an $n \times n$
grid. The $q \times q$ processors hold *subgrids* of size $n/q \times n/q$. In each step,
every node exchanges boundary values with its four nearest neighbors (if
any). The nodes then update their subgrids simultaneously. At the end of
a simulation, the nodes output their final values to a master processor that
assembles a complete grid (Chap. 16).

The only parts of the parallel program that vary from one application to
another are the possible *states* of the cells and the state *transition function*.

I have used a 6×6 matrix of transputers to simulate a *forest fire* on a
480×480 grid. Every element represents a tree that is either alive, burning,
or dead. In each step, the next state of every tree is defined by probabilistic
rules [Bak 1990].

I used the same paradigm to solve *Laplace's equation* for equilibrium temperatures in a square region with fixed temperatures at the boundaries. In
each step, the temperature of every interior element is replaced by a weighted
sum of the previous temperature and the average of the surrounding temperatures [Chap. 15 and Brinch Hansen 1992e]. In numerical analysis, this
method is known as *successive overrelaxation* with *parity ordering* [Young
1971; Press 1989]. The parallel program used 6×6 transputers to solve the

heat equation on a 1500×1500 grid.

1.9   Program Characteristics

After studying the paradigms separately, it is instructive to consider what they have in common.

I was surprised by the *specialized* nature of some of the paradigms (Table 1.1). It may well be that some of them apply to only a small number of problems. To me that is a minor concern. The essence of the programming method is that you attempt to write two or more programs simultaneously. The intellectual discipline required to do this seems almost inevitably to produce well structured programs that are easy to understand.

Table 1.1: Paradigms.

Program	Paradigm
Annealing	Monte Carlo trials
Primality	Monte Carlo trials
Multiply	Multiplication
Paths	Multiplication
Householder	All-pairs
N-body	All-pairs
FFT tree	Divide-and-conquer
Sorting tree	Divide-and-conquer
Sorting cube	Divide-and-conquer
Laplace	Cellular automata
Forest fire	Cellular automata

The model programs illustrate programming methods for a variety of multicomputer *architectures* (Table 1.2). The reconfigurable Computing Surface was ideal for this purpose.

If a parallel architecture is not reconfigurable, it may be necessary to reprogram some of the paradigms. However, since all instances of a paradigm have the same sequential control structure, you know that if you can implement any one of them on a parallel architecture, the rest will turn out to be variations of the same theme.

Every program has a parallel component that implements a *paradigm* and a sequential component for a specific *application* (Table 1.3). The paradigm

Table 1.2: Architectures.

Program	Architecture
Annealing	Pipeline
Primality	Pipeline
Multiply	Pipeline
Paths	Pipeline
Householder	Pipeline
N-body	Pipeline
FFT tree	Tree
Sorting tree	Tree
Sorting cube	Cube
Laplace	Matrix
Forest fire	Matrix

typically accounts for 60% of a program and is the most difficult part to write.

Table 1.3: Program lengths.

Program	Paradigm (lines)	Application (lines)
Annealing	150	200
Primality	150	520
Multiply	150	30
Paths	150	90
Householder	190	120
N-body	190	130
FFT tree	140	100
Sorting tree	140	80
Sorting cube	170	80
Laplace	280	30
Forest fire	280	60

To make the programs *readable*, I divided them into short procedures of 10–20 lines each. No procedure exceeds one page of text (Table 1.4).

I have always found that a good *description* of a program is considerably longer than the program text (Table 1.5). Fifteen years ago, I put it this

Table 1.4: Procedure lengths.

Program	Lines/procedure		
	Min	Aver	Max
Annealing	1	12	34
Primality	3	15	43
Multiply	6	12	28
Paths	6	14	28
Householder	8	18	50
N-body	2	12	26
FFT tree	6	14	24
Sorting tree	6	13	24
Sorting cube	6	13	29
Laplace	3	12	31
Forest fire	3	13	31

way: "Programming is the art of writing essays in crystal clear prose and making them executable" [Brinch Hansen 1977].

Table 1.5: Program descriptions.

Program	Program (pages)	Report (pages)
Annealing	8	20
Multiply	5	10
Householder	7	40
FFT tree	6	30
Laplace	7	40

Table 1.6 illustrates the *performance* of the model programs on a Computing Surface in terms of the size of the problems solved and the speedup S_p achieved by p processors running in parallel.

1.10   Programming Languages

As I was describing my first parallel paradigm, I became disenchanted with occam as a *publication language*. To my taste, occam looks clumsy compared

Table 1.6: Program performance.

Program	Problem size	p	S_p
Annealing	400	10	10
Primality	160	40	40
Multiply	1400×1400	35	31
Householder	1250×1250	25	20
N-body	9000	45	36
FFT tree	32768	31	4
Sorting tree	131072	31	3
Sorting cube	131072	8	2
Laplace	1500×1500	36	34

to Pascal. (I hasten to add that I prefer occam to its competitors: Fortran, C, and Ada.)

At the time, no programming language was suitable for writing elegant, portable programs for multicomputers. As a compromise, I used *Pascal* extended with *parallel statements* and *communication channels* as a publication language.

To avoid dealing with the obscure behavior of incorrect programs on a multicomputer, I tested the parallel programs on a sequential computer. Since my publication language was not executable, I rewrote the model programs in an executable Pascal dialect that includes parallel statements and conditional critical regions. I used conditional critical regions to implement message passing and tested the programs on an *IBM-PC* with 64 Kbytes of memory.

When the parallel programs worked, I rewrote them in occam, changed a few constants, and used them to solve much larger problems on a *Computing Surface* with 48 transputers and 48 Mbytes of distributed memory. Sometimes I used *Joyce* to run the same computation on an *Encore Multimax*, a multiprocessor with 16 processors and 128 Mbytes of shared memory [Brinch Hansen 1987, 1989]. The manual translation of correct readable programs into occam or Joyce was a trivial task.

The ease with which I could express the model programs in three different programming languages and run them on three different computer architectures proves that they are eminently *portable*.

The development of an executable publication language was a long-term goal of my research. One of my reasons for writing the model programs was to identify language features that are indispensable and some that are unnecessary for parallel scientific computing.

The published paradigm for the tree machine includes a recursive procedure that defines a tree of processes as a root process running in parallel with two subtrees. A notation for *recursive parallel processes* is essential for expressing this idea concisely [Brinch Hansen 1990b]. After using Joyce, I found the lack of recursion in occam unacceptable.

So far I have not found it necessary to use a statement that enables a process to poll several channels until a communication takes place on one of them. I have tentatively adopted the position that *non-deterministic communication* is necessary at the hardware level in a routing network, but is probably superfluous for scientific programming. It would be encouraging if this turns out to be true, since polling can be inefficient [Brinch Hansen 1989].

In practice, programmers will often be obligated to implement programs in complicated languages. However, wise programmers will prefer to develop and publish their ideas in the simplest possible languages, even if they are expected to use archaic or abstruse *implementation languages* for their final software products. Since it is no problem to rewrite a model program in another language, it is not particularly important to be able to use publication and implementation languages on the same machine.

Nevertheless, I must confess that the relentless efforts to adapt the world's oldest programming language for parallel computing strike me as futile. A quarter of a century ago, Alan Perlis boldly selected *Algol 60* as the publication language for algorithms in *Communications of the ACM*. In response to his critics, he said: "It is argued that more programmers now know Fortran than Algol. While this is true, it is not necessarily relevant since this does not increase the readability of algorithms in Fortran" [Perlis 1966].

Present multicomputers are difficult to program, because every program must be tailored to a particular architecture. It makes no sense to me to complicate hard intellectual work by poor notation. Nor am I swayed by the huge investment in existing Fortran programs. Every generation of scientists must reprogram these programs if they wish to understand them in depth and verify that they are correct. And the discovery of new architectures will continue to require reprogramming in unfamiliar notations that have not been invented yet.

1.11   Research Method

It took me a year to study numerical analysis, learn multicomputer programming, select a research theme, understand the development steps involved and complete the first paradigm. From then on, every paradigm took about one semester of research.

I followed the same steps for every paradigm:

1. Identify two computational problems with the same sequential control structure.

2. For each problem, write a tutorial that explains the theory of the computation and includes a complete Pascal program.

3. Write a parallel program for the programming paradigm in a readable publication language.

4. Test the parallel program on a sequential computer.

5. Derive a parallel program for each problem by trivial substitutions of a few data types, variables and procedures, and analyze the complexity of these programs.

6. Rewrite the parallel programs in an implementation language and measure their performance on a multicomputer.

7. Write clear descriptions of the parallel programs.

8. Rewrite the programs using the same terminology as in the descriptions.

9. Publish the programs and descriptions in their entirety with no hidden mysteries and every program line open to scrutiny.

The most difficult step is the *discovery* of paradigms and the *selection* of interesting instances of these paradigms. This creative process cannot be reduced to a simplistic recipe. Now that I know what I am looking for, I find it helpful to browse through books and journals on the computational aspects of biology, engineering, geology, mathematics and physics. When I see an interesting problem I ask myself: "Is there any way this computation can be regarded as similar to another one?" *Luck* clearly plays a role in the search for paradigms. However, as the French philosopher Bernard de Fontenelle (1657–1757) once observed: "These strokes of fortune are only for those that play well!" So I keep on trying.

1.12 Final Remarks

I have described a collection of model programs for computational science. Every program is a realistic case study that illustrates the use of a paradigm for parallel programming. A programming paradigm is a class of algorithms that solve different problems but have the same control structure. The individual algorithms may be regarded as refinements of a general algorithm that defines the common control structure.

Parallel programming paradigms are elegant solutions to non-trivial problems:

1. Paradigms are *beautiful programs* that challenge your intellectual abilities and programming skills.

2. A programming paradigm is a *unifying concept* that reveals unexpected similarities between algorithms and raises new questions about familiar algorithms.

3. Viewing a parallel algorithm as an instance of a paradigm enables you to *separate issues* of parallelism from details of application. This sharp distinction contributes to program clarity.

4. Every paradigm defines an effective *programming style* that becomes part of your mental toolkit and enables you to apply previous insight to new problems [Nelson 1987].

5. Paradigms serve as case studies that illustrate the use of *structured programming* in scientific computing [Dijkstra 1972].

6. A commitment to *publish paradigms* as complete, executable programs imposes an intellectual discipline that leaves little room for vague statements and missing details. Such programs may serve as *models* for other scientists who wish to study them with the assurance that every detail has been considered, explained, and tested.

7. Model programs may also teach students the neglected art of *program reading* [Wirth 1976; Mills 1988].

8. Parallel paradigms capture the essence of *parallel architectures* such as pipelines, trees, hypercubes, and matrices.

9. Parallel programs based on the same paradigm can be *moved* to different architectures with a reasonable effort by rewriting the general program that defines the common control structure. The individual programs can then be moved by making minor changes to the paradigm [Dongarra 1989].

10. Since a paradigm defines a whole class of useful algorithms, it is an excellent choice as a *benchmark* for parallel architectures.

11. A collection of paradigms can provide valuable guidance for *programming language design* [Floyd 1987]. If the paradigms are written in a proposed notation, the readability of the programs will reveal whether or not the language concepts are essential and concise.

After using this programming methodology for three years, the evidence strikes me as overwhelming: *The study of programming paradigms provides an architectural vision of parallel scientific computing!*

Chapter 2

The SuperPascal Language

2.1 Introduction

One of the major challenges in computer science today is to develop effective programming tools for the next generation of parallel computers. It is equally important to design educational programming tools for the future users of parallel computers. Since the 1960s, computer scientists have recognized the distinction between *publication languages* that emphasize clarity of concepts, and *implementation languages* that reflect pragmatic concerns and historical traditions [Forsythe 1966; Perlis 1966]. I believe that parallel computers will not become widely used until scientists and engineers adopt a common programming language for publication of parallel scientific algorithms.

It is instructive to consider the historical role of Pascal as a publication language for sequential computing. The first paper on Pascal appeared in 1971 [Wirth 1971]. At that time, there were not very many textbooks on computer science. A few years later, universities began to use Pascal as the standard programming language for computer science courses. The spreading of Pascal motivated authors to use the language in textbooks for a wide variety of computer science courses: introductory programming [Wirth 1973], operating systems [Brinch Hansen 1973], program verification [Alagić 1978], compilers [Welsh 1980], programming languages [Tennent 1981], and algorithms [Aho 1983]. In 1983, IEEE acknowledged the status of Pascal as the *lingua franca* of computer science by publishing a Pascal standard [IEEE 1983]. Pascal was no longer just another programming tool for computer users. It had become a thinking tool for researchers exploring new fields in computer science.

We now face a similar need for a common programming language for students and researchers in computational science. To understand the requirements of such a language, I spent three years developing a collection of *model programs* that illustrate the use of structured programming in parallel scientific computing [Chap. 1 and Brinch Hansen 1993a]. These programs solve a variety of problems in science and engineering: linear equations, *n*-body simulation, matrix multiplication, shortest paths in graphs, sorting, fast Fourier transforms, simulated annealing, primality testing, Laplace's equation, and forest fire simulation. I wrote these programs in *occam* and tested their performance on a *Computing Surface* configured as a pipeline, a tree, a cube, or a matrix of *transputers* [Inmos 1988; McDonald 1991].

This practical experience led me to the following conclusions about the future of parallel scientific computing [Forsythe 1966; Dunham 1982; May 1989; Brinch Hansen 1993a]:

1. A *general-purpose parallel computer* of the near future will probably be a multicomputer with tens to thousands of processors with local memories only. The computer will support automatic routing of messages between any pair of processors. The hardware architecture will be transparent to programmers, who will be able to connect processors arbitrarily by virtual communication channels. Such a parallel computer will enable programmers to think in terms of problem-oriented process configurations. There will be no need to map these configurations onto a fixed architecture, such as a hypercube.

2. The regular problems in computational science can be solved efficiently by *deterministic parallel computations.* Nondeterministic communication is necessary at the hardware level in a routing network, but appears to be of minor importance in parallel programs for computational science.

3. Parallel scientific algorithms can be developed in an *elegant publication language* and tested on a sequential computer. When an algorithm works, it can easily be moved to a particular multicomputer by rewriting the algorithm in another programming language chosen for pragmatic rather than intellectual reasons.

A publication language for computational science should, in my opinion, have the following properties:

1. The language should extend a widely used standard language with *deterministic parallelism* and *message communication.* The extensions should be defined in the spirit of the standard language.

2. The language should make it possible to program *arbitrary configurations* of parallel processes connected by communication channels. These configurations may be defined iteratively or recursively and created dynamically.

3. The language should enable a single-pass compiler to check that parallel processes do not interfere in a time-dependent manner. This check is known as *syntactic interference control.*

    The following describes *SuperPascal*—a publication language for parallel scientific computing. *SuperPascal* extends Pascal with deterministic statements for parallel processes and synchronous communication. The language permits unrestricted combinations of recursive procedures and parallel statements. *SuperPascal* omits ambiguous and insecure features of Pascal. Restrictions on the use of variables permit a single-pass compiler to check that parallel processes are disjoint, even if the processes use procedures with global variables.

    Since the model programs cover a broad spectrum of algorithms for scientific computing, I have used them as a guideline for language design. The language features of *SuperPascal* are well-known [Dijkstra 1968; Hoare 1971a, 1972b, 1985; Ambler 1977; Lampson 1977; IEEE 1983; Brinch Hansen 1987; Inmos 1988]. My only contribution has been to select the smallest number of concepts that enable me to express the model programs elegantly. This paper illustrates the parallel features of *SuperPascal* by examples. The *SuperPascal* language report defines the syntax and semantics concisely and explains the differences between *SuperPascal* and Pascal [Brinch Hansen 1993b]. The interference control is further discussed in [Brinch Hansen 1993d].

    A *portable implementation* of *SuperPascal* has been developed on a Sun workstation under Unix. The *SuperPascal* compiler is based on the Pascal compiler described and listed in [Brinch Hansen 1985]. The *SuperPascal* software is in the public domain (see the Preface). The software has been used to rewrite the model programs for computational science in *SuperPascal* (Chap. 17).

2.2   A Programming Example

I will use pieces of a model program to illustrate the features of *SuperPascal*. The Miller-Rabin algorithm is used for *primality testing* of a large integer [Rabin 1980]. The model program performs p probabilistic tests of the same integer simultaneously on p processors. Each test either proves that the integer is composite, or it fails to prove anything. However, if, say, 40 trials of a 160-digit decimal number all fail, the number is prime with virtual certainty [Chap. 12 and Brinch Hansen 1992b, 1992d].

The program performs multiple-length arithmetic on natural numbers represented by arrays of w digits (plus an overflow digit):

type number = **array** [0..w] **of** integer;

A single trial is defined by a procedure with the heading

procedure test(a: number; seed: real;
var composite: boolean)

Each trial initializes a random number generator with a distinct seed.

The parallel computation is organized as a ring network consisting of a master process and a pipeline connected by two communication channels (Fig. 2.1).

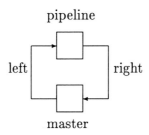

Figure 2.1: A ring network.

The pipeline consists of p identical, parallel nodes connected by $p + 1$ communication channels (Fig. 2.2).

The master sends a number through the pipeline and receives p boolean values from the pipeline. The booleans are the results of p independent trials performed in parallel by the nodes.

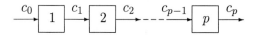

Figure 2.2: A pipeline.

2.3 Message Communication

Communication Channels

The communication channels of *SuperPascal* are *deterministic synchronous channels:*

1. A channel can transmit one message at a time in either direction between two parallel processes.

2. Before a communication, a process makes a deterministic selection of a communication channel, a communication direction, and a message type.

3. A communication takes place when one process is ready to send a message of some type through a channel and another process is ready to receive a message of the same type through the same channel.

Channel and Message Types

A channel is not a variable, but a communication medium shared by two parallel processes. Each channel is created dynamically and identified by a distinct value known as a *channel reference.* A variable that holds a channel reference is called a *channel variable.* An expression that denotes a channel reference is called a *channel expression.* These concepts are borrowed from *Joyce* [Brinch Hansen 1987].

As an example, the declarations

> **type** channel = *(boolean, number);
> **var** left: channel;

define a new type named *channel* and a variable of this type named *left.* The value of the variable is a reference to a channel that can transmit messages of types *boolean* and *number* only.

In general, a type definition of the form

$$\textbf{type } T = *(T_1, T_2, \ldots, T_n);$$

introduces a new *channel type* T. The values of type T are an unordered set of channel references created dynamically. Each channel reference of type T denotes a distinct channel that can transmit messages of types $T_1, T_2, \ldots, T_n$ only (the *message types*).

Channel Creation

The effect of an *open* statement

$$\text{open}(v)$$

is to create a new channel and assign the corresponding channel reference to a channel variable v. The channel reference is of the same type as the channel variable.

The abbreviation

$$\text{open}(v_1, v_2, \ldots, v_n)$$

is equivalent to

$$\textbf{begin } \text{open}(v_1); \text{open}(v_2, \ldots, v_n) \textbf{ end}$$

As an example, two channels, *left* and *right*, can be opened as follows

$$\text{open}(\text{left, right})$$

or as shown below

$$\textbf{begin } \text{open}(\text{left}); \text{open}(\text{right}) \textbf{ end}$$

A channel exists until the program execution ends.

Communication Procedures

Consider a process that receives a number a through a channel *left* and sends it through another channel *right:*

> **var** left, right: channel; a: number;
> receive(left, a); send(right, a)

The message communication is handled by two required procedures, *send* and *receive.*

In general, a *send* statement

$$\text{send(b, e)}$$

denotes *output* of the value of an expression e through the channel denoted by an expression b. The expression b must be of a channel type T, and the type of the expression e must be a message type of T.

A *receive* statement

$$\text{receive(c, v)}$$

denotes *input* of the value of a variable v through the channel denoted by an expression c. The expression c must be of a channel type T, and the type of the variable v must be a message type of T.

The send and receive operations defined by the above statements are said to *match* if they satisfy the following conditions:

1. The channel expressions b and c are of the same type T and denote the same channel.

2. The output expression e and the input variable v are of the same type, which is a message type of T.

The execution of a send operation delays a process until another process is ready to execute a matching receive operation (and vice versa). If and when this happens, a *communication* takes place as follows:

1. The sending process obtains a value by evaluating the output expression e.

2. The receiving process assigns the value to the input variable v.

After the communication, the sending and receiving processes proceed independently.

The abbreviation

$$\text{send}(b, e_1, e_2, \ldots, e_n)$$

is equivalent to

$$\textbf{begin } \text{send}(b, e_1); \text{send}(b, e_2, \ldots, e_n) \textbf{ end}$$

Similarly,

$$\text{receive}(c, v_1, v_2, \ldots, v_n)$$

is equivalent to

$$\textbf{begin } \text{receive}(c, v_1); \text{receive}(c, v_2, \ldots, v_n) \textbf{ end}$$

The following *communication errors* are detected at run-time:

1. *Undefined channel reference:* A channel expression does not denote a channel.

2. *Channel contention:* Two parallel processes both attempt to send (or receive) through the same channel at the same time.

3. *Message type error:* Two parallel processes attempt to communicate through the same channel, but the output expression and the input variable are of different message types.

Message communication is illustrated by two procedures in the primality testing program. The *master* process, shown in Fig. 2.1, sends a number a through its left channel and receives p booleans through its right channel. If at least one of the booleans is true, the number is composite; otherwise, it is considered to be prime (Fig. 2.3).

The pipeline *nodes*, shown in Fig. 2.2, are numbered 1 through p. Each node receives a number a through its left channel and sends a through its right channel (unless the node is the last one in the pipeline). The node then tests the number for primality using the node index i as the seed of its random number generator. Finally, the node outputs the boolean result of its own trial and copies the results obtained by its $i-1$ predecessors (if any) in the pipeline (Fig. 2.4).

```
procedure master(
  a: number; var prime: boolean;
  left, right: channel);
var i: integer; composite: boolean;
begin
  send(left, a); prime := true;
  for i := 1 to p do
    begin
      receive(right, composite);
      if composite then
        prime := false
    end
end;
```

Figure 2.3: Master algorithm.

```
procedure node(i: integer;
  left, right: channel);
var a: number; j: integer;
  composite: boolean;
begin
  receive(left, a);
  if i < p then send(right, a);
  test(a, i, composite);
  send(right, composite);
  for j := 1 to i − 1 do
    begin
      receive(left, composite);
      send(right, composite)
    end
end;
```

Figure 2.4: Node algorithm.

Channel Arrays

Since channel references are typed values, it is possible to define an array of channel references. A variable of such a type represents an array of channels.

The pipeline nodes in Fig. 2.2 are connected by a row of channels created as follows:

```
type channel = *(boolean, number);
   row = array [0..p] of channel;
var c: row; i: integer;
for i := 0 to p do open(c[i])
```

Later, I will program a matrix of processes connected by a horizontal and a vertical matrix of channels. The channel matrices h and v are defined and initialized as follows:

```
type
   row = array [0..q] of channel;
   net = array [0..q] of row;
var h, v: net; i, j: integer;
for i := 0 to q do
   for j := 0 to q do
      open(h[i,j], v[i,j])
```

Channel Variables

The value of a channel variable v of a type T is undefined, unless a channel reference of type T has been assigned to v by executing an open statement

$$open(v)$$

or an assignment statement

$$v := e$$

If the value of the expression e is a channel reference of type T, the effect of the assignment statement is to make the values of v and e denote the same channel.

If e and f are channel expressions of the same type, the boolean expression

$$e = f$$

is true, if e and f denote the same channel, and is false otherwise. The boolean expression

$$e <> f$$

is equivalent to

$$\textbf{not } (e = f)$$

In the following example, the references to two channels, *left* and *right*, are assigned to the first and last elements of a channel array *c*:

$$c[0] := \text{left}; \ c[p] := \text{right}$$

After the first assignment, the value of the boolean expression

$$c[0] = \text{left}$$

is *true*.

2.4   Parallel Processes

Parallel Statements

The effect of a *parallel statement*

$$\textbf{parallel } S_1|S_2|\ldots|S_n \textbf{ end}$$

is to execute the *process statements* $S_1, S_2, \ldots, S_n$ as parallel processes until all of them have terminated.

Figure 2.5 defines a *ring net* that determines if a given integer a is prime. The ring, shown in Fig. 2.1, consists of two parallel processes, a master and a pipeline, which share two channels. The master and the pipeline run in parallel until both of them have terminated.

A parallel statement enables you to run different kinds of algorithms in parallel. This idea is useful only for a small number of processes. It is impractical to write thousands of process statements, even if they are identical.

```
          procedure ring(a: number;
            var prime: boolean);
        var left, right: channel;
        begin
          open(left, right);
          parallel
            pipeline(left, right)|
            master(a, prime, left, right)
          end
        end;
```

Figure 2.5: Ring algorithm.

Forall Statements

To exploit parallel computing with many processors, you need the ability to run multiple instances of the same algorithm in parallel.

As an example, consider the *pipeline* for primality testing. From the abstract point of view, shown in Fig. 2.1, the pipeline is a single process with two external channels. At the more detailed level, shown in Fig. 2.2, the pipeline consists of an array of identical, parallel nodes connected by a row of channels.

Figure 2.6 defines the pipeline.

The first and last elements of the channel array c

$$c[0] = \text{left} \qquad c[p] = \text{right}$$

refer to the external channels of the pipeline. The remaining elements

$$c[1], c[2], \ldots, c[p-1]$$

denote the internal channels.

For $p \geq 1$, the statement

```
        forall i := 1 to p do
          node(i, c[i–1], c[i])
```

is equivalent to the following statement (which is too tedious to write out in full for a pipeline with more than, say, ten nodes):

```
procedure pipeline(left, right: channel);
type row = array [0..p] of channel;
var c: row; i: integer;
begin
  c[0] := left; c[p] := right;
  for i := 1 to p − 1 do
    open(c[i]);
  forall i := 1 to p do
    node(i, c[i−1], c[i])
end;
```

Figure 2.6: Iterative pipeline algorithm.

```
parallel
    node(1, c[0], c[1])|
    node(2, c[1], c[2])|
          . . .
    node(p, c[p–1], c[p])
end
```

The variable i used in the *forall* statement is not the same variable as the variable i declared at the beginning of the pipeline procedure.

In the *forall* statement, the clause

$$i := 1 \text{ to } p$$

is a *declaration* of an *index variable* i that is local to the procedure statement

$$node(i, c[i–1], c[i])$$

Each node process has its own instance of this variable, which holds a distinct index in the range from 1 to p.

It is a coincidence that the control variable of the *for* statement and the index variable of the *forall* statement have the same identifier in this example. However, the scopes of these variables are different.

In general, a *forall* statement

$$\text{forall } i := e_1 \text{ to } e_2 \text{ do } S$$

denotes a (possibly empty) array of parallel processes, called *element processes*, and a corresponding range of values, called *process indices*. The lower and upper bounds of the index range are denoted by two expressions e_1 and e_2 of the same simple type. Every index value corresponds to a separate element process defined by an *index variable i* and an *element statement S*.

The *index variable declaration*

$$i := e_1 \textbf{ to } e_2$$

introduces the variable i that is local to S.

A *forall* statement is executed as follows:

1. The expressions e_1 and e_2 are evaluated. If $e_1 > e_2$, the execution of the *forall* statement terminates; otherwise, step 2 takes place.

2. $e_2 - e_1 + 1$ element processes run in parallel until all of them have terminated. Every element process creates a local instance of the index variable i, assigns the corresponding process index to the variable, and executes the element statement S. When an element process terminates, its local instance of the index variable ceases to exist.

A model program that solves *Laplace's equation* uses a *process matrix* [Chap. 16 and Brinch Hansen 1992f]. Figure 2.7 shows a $q{\times}q$ matrix of parallel nodes connected by two channel matrices h and v.

Each node process is defined by a procedure with the heading:

$$\textbf{procedure } node(i, j: integer;$$
$$up, down, left, right: channel)$$

A node has a pair of indices (i, j) and is connected to its four nearest neighbors by channels, *up, down, left*, and *right*.

The process matrix is defined by nested *forall* statements:

```
forall i := 1 to q do
   forall j := 1 to q do
      node(i, j, v[i–1,j], v[i,j], h[i,j–1], h[i,j])
```

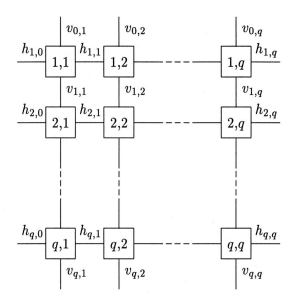

Figure 2.7: A process matrix.

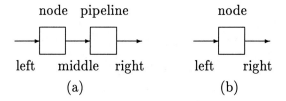

Figure 2.8: A recursive pipeline.

Recursive Parallel Processes

SuperPascal supports the beautiful concept of recursive parallel processes. Figure 2.8 illustrates a recursive definition of a *pipeline* with p nodes.

1. If $p > 1$, the pipeline consists of a single node followed by a shorter pipeline of $p - 1$ nodes (Fig. 2.8a).

2. If $p = 1$, the pipeline consists of a single node only (Fig. 2.8b).

The pipeline is defined by combining a recursive procedure with a parallel statement (Fig. 2.9).

```
procedure pipeline(min, max: integer;
    left, right: channel);
var middle: channel;
begin
  if min < max then
    begin
      open(middle);
      parallel
        node(min, left, middle)|
        pipeline(min + 1, max,
          middle, right)
      end
    end
  else node(min, left, right)
end;
```

Figure 2.9: Recursive pipeline algorithm.

The pipeline nodes have indices in the range from *min* to *max* (where $min \leq max$). The pipeline has a left and a right channel. If $min < max$, the pipeline opens a middle channel and splits into a single node and a smaller pipeline running in parallel; otherwise, the pipeline behaves as a single node.

The effect of the procedure statement

$$pipeline(1, p, left, right)$$

is to activate a pipeline that is equivalent to the one shown in Fig. 2.2.

The recursive pipeline has a *dynamic length* defined by parameters. The nodes and channels are created by recursive parallel activations of the pipeline procedure. The iterative pipeline programmed earlier has a fixed length because it uses a channel array of fixed length (Fig. 2.6).

A model program for *divide and conquer* algorithms uses a binary *process tree* [Chap. 9 and Brinch Hansen 1991d]. Figure 2.10 shows a tree of seven parallel processes connected by seven channels.

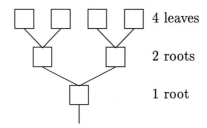

Figure 2.10: A specific process tree.

The bottom process of the tree inputs data from the bottom channel and sends half of the data to its left child process and the other half to its right child process. The splitting of data continues in parallel higher up in the tree until the data are evenly distributed among the leaf processes at the top. Each leaf transforms its own portion of the data and outputs the results to its parent process. Each parent combines the partial results of its children and outputs them to its own parent. The parallel combination of results continues at lower levels in the tree until the final results are output through the bottom channel.

A process tree can be defined recursively as illustrated by Fig. 2.11. A binary tree is connected to its environment by a single bottom channel. A closer look reveals that the tree takes one of two forms:

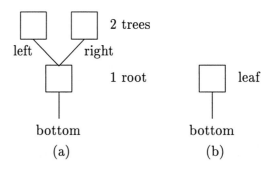

Figure 2.11: A recursive tree.

1. A tree with more than one node consists of a root process and two smaller trees running in parallel (Fig. 2.11a).

2. A tree with one node only is a leaf process (Fig. 2.11b).

The process *tree* is defined by a recursive procedure (Fig. 2.12). The *depth* of the tree is the number of process layers above the bottom process. Figure 2.10 shows a tree of depth 2.

```
procedure tree(depth: integer;
    bottom: channel);
var left, right: channel;
begin
  if depth > 0 then
    begin
      open(left, right);
      parallel
        tree(depth − 1, left)|
        tree(depth − 1, right)|
        root(bottom, left, right)
      end
    end
  else leaf(bottom)
end;
```

Figure 2.12: Recursive tree algorithm.

The behavior of *roots* and *leaves* is defined by two procedures of the form:

procedure root(bottom, left, right: channel)

procedure leaf(bottom: channel)

These procedures vary from one application of the tree to another.
  The effect of the procedure statement

tree(2, bottom)

is to activate a binary tree of depth 2.

A notation for recursive processes is essential in a parallel programming language. The reason is simple. It is impractical to formulate thousands of processes with different behaviors. We must instead rely on repeated use of a small number of behaviors. The simplest problems that satisfy this requirement are those that can be reduced to smaller problems of the same kind and solved by combining the partial results. Recursion is the natural programming tool for these *divide and conquer* algorithms.

2.5   Interference Control

Disjoint Processes

The relative speeds of asynchronous, parallel processes are generally unknown. If parallel processes update the same variables at unpredictable times, the combined effect of the processes is time-dependent. Similarly, if two parallel processes both attempt to send (or receive) messages through the same channel at unpredictable times, the net effect is time-dependent. Processes with *time-dependent errors* are said to *interfere* with one another due to *variable* or *channel conflicts*.

When a program with a time-dependent error is executed repeatedly with the same input, the output usually varies in an unpredictable manner from one run to another. The irreproducible behavior makes it difficult to locate interference by systematic program testing. The most effective remedy is to introduce additional restrictions, which make process interference impossible. These restrictions must be checked by a compiler before a parallel program is executed.

In the following, I concentrate on syntactic detection of variable conflicts. The basic requirement is simple: Parallel processes can only update disjoint sets of variables. A variable that is updated by a process may only be used by that process. Parallel processes may, however, share variables that are not updated by any of them. Parallel processes that satisfy this requirement are called *disjoint processes*.

Variable Contexts

I will illustrate the issues of interference control by small examples only. The problem is discussed concisely in [Brinch Hansen 1993d].

In theory, syntactic detection of variable conflicts is a straightforward process. A single-pass compiler scans a program text once. For every statement S, the compiler determines the set of variables that may be updated and the set of variables that may be used as expression operands during the execution of S. These sets are called the *target* and *expression variables* of S. Together they define the *variable context* of S. If you know the variable context of every statement, it is easy to check if parallel statements define disjoint processes.

As an example, the *open* statement

$$\text{open(h[i,j])}$$

denotes creation of a component $h_{i,j}$ of a channel array h. Since the index values i and j are known during execution only, a compiler is unable to distinguish between different elements of the same array. Consequently, the entire array h is regarded as a target variable (the only one) of the open statement. The expression variables of the statement are i and j.

An *entire variable* is a variable denoted by an identifier only, such as h, i, or j above. During compilation any operation on a component of a *structured variable* is regarded as an operation on the entire variable. The target and expression variables of a statement are therefore sets of entire variables.

A compiler cannot predict if a component of a conditional statement will be executed or skipped. To be on the safe side, the variable context of a *structured statement* is defined as the union of the variable contexts of its components.

Consider the conditional statement

$$\textbf{if } i < p \textbf{ then } \text{send(right, a)}$$

It has no target variables, but uses three expression variables, i, *right* and a (assuming that p is a constant).

Parallel Statements

The choice of a notation for parallel processes is profoundly influenced by the requirement that a compiler must be able to detect process interference. The syntax of a parallel statement

$$\textbf{parallel } S_1|S_2|\dots|S_n \textbf{ end}$$

clearly shows that the process statements $S_1, S_2, \dots, S_n$ are executed in parallel.

The following restriction ensures that a parallel statement denotes disjoint processes: *A target variable of one process statement cannot be a target or an expression variable of another process statement.* This rule is enforced by a compiler.

Let me illustrate this restriction with three examples. The parallel statement

$$\textbf{parallel } \text{open(h[i,j])|open(v[i,j])} \textbf{ end}$$

defines two *open* statements executed simultaneously. The target variable h of the first process statement does not occur in the second process statement. Similarly, the target variable v of the second process statement is not used in the first process statement. Consequently, the parallel statement defines disjoint processes.

However, the parallel statement

> **parallel**
>   receive(left, a)|
>   **if** i < p **then** send(right, a)
> **end**

is incorrect, because the target variable a of the first process statement is also an expression variable of the second process statement.

Finally, the parallel statement

$$\textbf{parallel } \text{c[0] := left|c[p] := right} \textbf{ end}$$

is incorrect, since the process statements use the same target variable c.

Occasionally, a programmer may wish to override the interference control of parallel statements. This is useful when it is obvious that parallel processes update distinct elements of the same array. The previous restriction does not apply to a parallel statement prefixed by the clause *[sic]*. This is called an *unrestricted statement*. The programmer must prove that such a statement denotes disjoint processes.

The following example is taken from a model program that uses the process matrix shown in Fig. 2.7:

[**sic**] { 1 <= k <= m }
parallel
    receive(up, u[0,k])|
    send(down, u[m,k])|
    receive(left, u[k,0])|
    send(right, u[k,m])
end

This statement enables a node process to simultaneously exchange four elements of a local array u with its nearest neighbors. The initial comment implies that the two input elements are distinct and are not used as output elements.

The programmer should realize that the slightest mistake in an unrestricted statement may introduce a subtle time-dependent error. The incorrect statement

[**sic**] { 1 <= k <= m }
parallel
    receive(up, u[1,k])|
    send(down, u[m,k])|
    receive(left, u[k,1])|
    send(right, u[k,m])
end

is time-dependent, but only if $k = 1$.

Forall Statements

The following restriction ensures that the statement

$$\textbf{forall } i := e_1 \textbf{ to } e_2 \textbf{ do } S$$

denotes disjoint processes: *In a forall statement, the element statement S cannot use target variables.* This is checked by a compiler.

This restriction implies that a process array must output its final results to another process or a file. Otherwise, the results will be lost when the element processes terminate and their local variables disappear. For technological reasons, the same restriction is necessary if the element processes run on separate processors in a parallel computer with distributed memory.

In the primality testing program, a pipeline is defined by the statement

$$\textbf{forall } i := 1 \textbf{ to } p \textbf{ do } node(i, c[i{-}1], c[i])$$

Since the node procedure has value parameters only, the procedure statement

$$node(i, c[i{-}1], c[i])$$

uses expression variables only (*i* and *c*).

The incorrect statement

$$\textbf{forall } i := 1 \textbf{ to } p - 1 \textbf{ do } open(c[i])$$

denotes element processes that attempt to update the same variable *c* in parallel.

If it is desirable to use the above statement, it must be turned into an *unrestricted statement*:

> [**sic**] { distinct elements c[i] }
> **forall** i := 1 **to** p − 1 **do** open(c[i])

The initial comment shows that the node processes are disjoint, since they update distinct elements of the channel array *c*.

Again, it needs to be said that a programming error in an unrestricted statement may cause time-dependent behavior. The incorrect statement

> [**sic**] **forall** i := 1 **to** p − 1 **do** open(c[1])

denotes parallel assignments of channel references to the same array element c_1.

Needless to say, syntactic interference control is of limited value if it is frequently overridden. A programmer should make a conscientious effort to limit the use of unrestricted statements as much as possible. The thirteen model programs that I wrote include five unrestricted statements only; all of them denote operations on distinct array elements.

Variable Parameters

To enable a compiler to recognize distinct variables, a language should have the property that distinct variable identifiers occurring in the same statement denote distinct entire variables. Due to the scope rules of Pascal, this assumption is satisfied by all entire variables except variable parameters.

The following procedure denotes parallel creation of a pair of channels:

> **procedure** pair(**var** c, d: channel);
> **begin**
>   **parallel** open(c)|open(d) **end**
> **end**;

The parallel processes are disjoint only if the formal parameters, c and d, denote distinct actual parameters.

The procedure statement

$$\text{pair(h[i,j], v[i,j])}$$

is valid, since the actual parameters are elements of different arrays, h and v.

However, the procedure statement

$$\text{pair(left, left)}$$

is incorrect, because it makes the identifiers c and d *aliases* of the same variable *left*.

Aliasing of variable parameters is prevented by the following restriction: *The actual variable parameters of a procedure statement must be distinct entire variables (or components of such variables).*

An *unrestricted statement* is not subject to this restriction. A model program for *n-body simulation* computes the gravitational forces between a pair of bodies p_i and p_j and adds each force to the total force acting on the corresponding body [Chap. 6 and Brinch Hansen 1991a]. This operation is denoted by a procedure statement

$$\{ \text{ i } <> \text{ j } \} \text{ [\textbf{sic}] addforces(p[j], p[i])}$$

with two actual variable parameters. The initial comment shows that the parameters p_i and p_j are distinct elements of the same array variable p.

Global Variables

Global variables used in procedures are another source of aliasing. Consider a procedure that updates a global seed and returns a random number (Fig. 2.13).

The procedure statement

```
var seed: real;

procedure random(var number: real);
var temp: real;
begin
   temp := a*seed;
   seed := temp − m*trunc(temp/m);
   number := seed/m
end;
```

Figure 2.13: Random number generator.

$$random(x)$$

denotes an operation that updates two distinct variables, x and *seed*.

On the other hand, the procedure statement

$$random(seed)$$

turns the identifier *number* into an alias for *seed*.

To prevent aliasing, it is necessary to regard the global variable as an *implicit parameter* of both procedure statements. Since the procedure uses the global variable as a target *and* an expression variable, it is both an *implicit variable parameter* and an *implicit value parameter* of the procedure statements.

The rule that actual variable parameters cannot be aliases applies to all variable parameters of a procedure statement, explicit as well as implicit parameters. However, since implicit value parameters can also cause trouble, we need a stronger restriction, defined as follows [Brinch Hansen 1993d]: The *restricted actual parameters* of a procedure statement are the explicit variable parameters that occur in the statement and the implicit parameters of the corresponding procedure block. *The restricted actual parameters of a procedure statement must be distinct entire variables (or components of such variables).*

In the primality testing program, the pipeline nodes use a random number generator. If the seed variable is global to the node procedure, then the seed is also an implicit variable parameter of the procedure statement

$$\text{node(i, c[i-1], c[i])}$$

Consequently, the statement

$$\textbf{forall } i := 1 \textbf{ to } p \textbf{ do } \text{node(i, c[i-1], c[i])}$$

denotes parallel processes that (indirectly) update the same global variable at unpredictable times. The concept of implicit parameters enables a compiler to detect this variable conflict. The problem is avoided by making the procedure *random* and its global variable *seed* local to the node procedure. The node processes will then be updating different instances of this variable.

The parallel statement

$$\textbf{parallel } \text{write(x)|writeln } \textbf{end}$$

is invalid because the required textfile *output* is an implicit variable parameter of both *write* statements.

Similarly, the parallel statement

$$\begin{array}{l} \textbf{parallel} \\ \quad \text{read(x)|} \\ \quad \text{if eof } \textbf{then } \text{writeln} \\ \textbf{end} \end{array}$$

is incorrect because the required textfile *input* is an implicit variable parameter of the *read* statement and an implicit value parameter of the *eof* function designator.

Functions

Functions may use global variables as implicit value parameters only. The following rules ensure that functions have no side-effects:

1. Functions cannot use implicit or explicit variable parameters.

2. Procedure statements cannot occur in the statement part of a function block.

The latter restriction implies that functions cannot use the required procedures for message communication and file input/output. This rule may seem startling at first. I introduced it after noticing that my model programs include over 40 functions, none of which violate this restriction.

Since functions have no side-effects, expressions cannot cause process interference.

Further Restrictions

Syntactic detection of variable conflicts during single-pass compilation requires additional language restrictions:

1. *Pointer types* are omitted.

2. *Goto statements* and *labels* are omitted.

3. *Procedural* and *functional parameters* are omitted.

4. *Forward declarations* are omitted.

5. *Recursive functions* and *procedures* cannot use implicit parameters.

These design decisions are discussed in [Brinch Hansen 1993d].

Channel Conflicts

Due to the use of channel references, a compiler is unable to detect process
interference caused by channel conflicts. From a theoretical point of view,
I have serious misgivings about this flaw. In practice, I have found it to be
a minor problem only. Some channel conflicts are detected by the run-time
checking of communication errors mentioned earlier. For regular process
configurations, such as pipelines, trees, and matrices, the remaining channel
conflicts are easy to locate by proofreading the few procedures that define
how parallel processes are connected by channels.

2.6   SuperPascal Versus Occam

occam2 is an admirable implementation language for transputer systems [In-
mos 1988]. It achieves high efficiency by relying on static allocation of
processors and memory. The occam notation is somewhat bulky and not
sufficiently general for a publication language:

1. Key words are capitalized.

2. A real constant requires eight additional characters to define the length
   of its binary representation.

3. Simple statements must be written on separate lines.

4. An *if* statement requires two additional lines to describe an empty *else* statement.

5. Array types cannot be named.

6. Record types cannot be used.

7. Process arrays must have constant lengths.

8. Functions and procedures cannot be recursive.

occam3 includes type definitions, but is considerably more complicated than occam2 [Kerridge 1993].

occam was an invaluable source of inspiration for *SuperPascal*. Years ahead of its time, occam set a standard of simplicity and security against which future parallel languages will be measured. The parallel features of *SuperPascal* are a subset of occam2 with the added generality of dynamic process arrays and recursive parallel processes. This generality enables you to write parallel algorithms that cannot be expressed in occam.

2.7   Final Remarks

Present multicomputers are quite difficult to program. To achieve high performance, each program must be tailored to the configuration of a particular computer. Scientific users, who are primarily interested in getting numerical results, constantly have to reprogram new parallel architectures and are getting increasingly frustrated at having to do this [Sanz 1989].

As educators we should ignore this short-term problem and teach our students to write programs for the next generation of parallel computers. These will probably be general-purpose multicomputers that can run portable scientific programs written in parallel programming languages.

In this chapter, I have suggested that universities should adopt a common programming language for publication of papers and textbooks on parallel scientific algorithms. The language Pascal has played a major role as a publication language for sequential computing. Building on that tradition, I have developed *SuperPascal* as a publication language for computational science. *SuperPascal* extends Pascal with deterministic statements for parallel processes and message communication. The language enables you to define arbitrary configurations of parallel processes, both iteratively and re-cursively. The number of processes may vary dynamically.

I have used the *SuperPascal* notation to write portable programs for regular problems in computational science. I found it easy to express these programs in three different programming languages (*SuperPascal*, Joyce, and occam2) and run them on three different architectures (a Unix workstation, an Encore Multimax, and a Meiko Computing Surface).

Part II

THE ALL-PAIRS
PARADIGM

Chapter 3

Householder Reduction

3.1 Introduction

The solution of *linear equations* is important in many areas of science and engineering [Kreyszig 1988]. This chapter discusses *Householder reduction* of n linear equations to a triangular form that can be solved by back substitution [Householder 1958; Press 1989]. I will explain how Householder reduction can be derived from elementary matrix algebra. The method is illustrated by a numerical example and a Pascal procedure.

I assume that you have a general knowledge of vector and matrix algebra, but are less familiar with linear transformation of a vector space.

I begin by looking at Gaussian elimination.

3.2 Gaussian Elimination

The classical method for solving a system of linear equations is *Gaussian elimination*. Suppose you have three linear equations with three unknowns x_1, x_2, x_3:

$$
\begin{array}{rcrcrcl}
2x_1 & + & 2x_2 & + & 4x_3 & = & 18 \\
x_1 & + & 3x_2 & - & 2x_3 & = & 1 \\
3x_1 & + & x_2 & + & 3x_3 & = & 14
\end{array}
$$

First, you eliminate x_1 from the second equation by subtracting 1/2 of the first equation from the second one. Then you eliminate x_1 from the third equation by subtracting 3/2 of the first equation from the third one. Now, you have three equations in which x_1 occurs in the first equation only:

$$
\begin{array}{rcrcrcr}
2x_1 & + & 2x_2 & + & 4x_3 & = & 18 \\
     &   & 2x_2 & - & 4x_3 & = & -8 \\
     & - & 2x_2 & - & 3x_3 & = & -13
\end{array}
$$

Finally, you eliminate x_2 from the third equation by adding the second equation to the third one. The equations have been reduced now to a triangular form that has the same solution as the original equations but is easier to solve:

$$
\begin{array}{rcrcrcr}
2x_1 & + & 2x_2 & + & 4x_3 & = & 18 \\
     &   & 2x_2 & - & 4x_3 & = & -8 \\
     &   &   & - & 7x_3 & = & -21
\end{array}
$$

The triangular equations are solved by *back substitution*. From the third equation, you immediately have $x_3 = 3$. By substituting this value in the second equation, you find $x_2 = 2$. Substituting these two values in the first equation you obtain $x_1 = 1$.

In general, you have n linear equations with n unknowns:

$$
\begin{array}{l}
a_{11}x_1 + a_{12}x_2 + \quad \cdots \quad + a_{1n}x_n = b_1 \\
a_{21}x_1 + a_{22}x_2 + \quad \cdots \quad + a_{2n}x_n = b_2 \\
\qquad\qquad\qquad \cdots \\
a_{n1}x_1 + a_{n2}x_2 + \quad \cdots \quad + a_{nn}x_n = b_n
\end{array}
\tag{3.1}
$$

The a's and b's are known real numbers. The x's are the unknowns you must find.

The equation system (3.1) can be expressed as a vector equation

$$
Ax = b \tag{3.2}
$$

where A is the $n \times n$ matrix

$$
A = \begin{bmatrix}
a_{11} & a_{12} & \cdots & a_{1n} \\
a_{21} & a_{22} & \cdots & a_{2n} \\
\cdot & \cdot & \cdots & \cdot \\
a_{n1} & a_{n2} & \cdots & a_{nn}
\end{bmatrix}
$$

while x and b are n-dimensional column vectors

$$x = \begin{bmatrix} x_1 \\ x_2 \\ \vdots \\ x_n \end{bmatrix}$$

$$b = \begin{bmatrix} b_1 \\ b_2 \\ \vdots \\ b_n \end{bmatrix}$$

The equation system has a unique solution only if the matrix A is *non-singular* as defined in the Appendix.

Gaussian elimination reduces (3.2) to an equivalent form

$$U x = c$$

where U is an $n \times n$ upper triangular matrix

$$U = \begin{bmatrix} u_{11} & u_{12} & \cdots & u_{1n} \\ 0 & u_{22} & \cdots & u_{2n} \\ \cdot & \cdot & \cdots & \cdot \\ 0 & 0 & \cdots & u_{nn} \end{bmatrix}$$

with all zeros below the main diagonal. The elimination process replaces the original right-hand side b by another n-dimensional column vector c.

The scaling of equations is a source of numerical errors in Gaussian elimination. To eliminate the first unknown x_1 from, say, the second equation, you subtract the first equation multiplied by a_{21}/a_{11} from the second equation. However, if the *pivot element* a_{11} is very small, the scaling factor a_{21}/a_{11} becomes very large, and you may end up subtracting very large reals from very small ones. This makes the results highly inaccurate.

The numerical instability of Gaussian elimination can be reduced by a process called *pivoting*: By changing the order in which the equations are written, you can make the pivot element as large as possible. You examine the first coefficient of every equation, that is

$$a_{11}, a_{21}, \cdots, a_{n1}$$

If the largest of these coefficients is, say, a_{51}, then you exchange equations 1 and 5. After this rearrangement, you subtract multiples of the (new) first equation from the remaining ones. The pivoting process is repeated for each submatrix during the Gaussian elimination.

Pivoting rearranges both the rows of the matrix and the elements of the right-hand side. The algorithm must keep track of this permutation in an additional vector. Although pivoting does not guarantee numerical stability, numerical analysts believe that it works in practice [Golub 1989; Press 1989].

In the following, I describe an alternative method that is numerically stable and does not require pivoting. This method has been used in a parallel algorithm [Chaps. 4–5 and Brinch Hansen 1990d, 1990e].

3.3   Scalar Products

Householder's method requires the computation of scalar products and vector reflections. The following is a brief explanation of these basic operations. The Appendix defines the elementary laws of vector and matrix algebra, which I will take for granted.

Let a and b be two n-dimensional column vectors:

$$a = \begin{bmatrix} a_1 \\ a_2 \\ \vdots \\ a_n \end{bmatrix}$$

$$b = \begin{bmatrix} b_1 \\ b_2 \\ \vdots \\ b_n \end{bmatrix}$$

The *transpose* of a and b are the row vectors

$$a^T = [\, a_1 \; a_2 \; \cdots \; a_n \,]$$

$$b^T = [\, b_1 \;\; b_2 \;\; \cdots \;\; b_n \,]$$

The *scalar product* of a and b is

$$a^T b = a_1 b_1 + a_2 b_2 + \cdots + a_n b_n \tag{3.3}$$

A scalar product is obviously symmetric:

$$a^T b = b^T a \tag{3.4}$$

The Euclidean *norm*

$$\|a\| = \sqrt{a_1^2 + a_2^2 + \cdots + a_n^2} \tag{3.5}$$

is the length of the n-dimensional vector a.

From (3.3) and (3.5) you obtain an equivalent definition of the norm:

$$\|a\|^2 = a^T a \tag{3.6}$$

3.4   Reflection

Householder reduction of an $n \times n$ real matrix has a simple geometric interpretation: The matrix columns are regarded as vectors in an n-dimensional space. Each vector is replaced by its mirror image on the other side of a particular plane. This plane reflects the first column onto the first axis of the coordinate system to produce a new column with all zeros after the first element.

First, I will look at reflection in three-dimensional space. The reflection plane P includes the origin O and is perpendicular to a given vector v. For an arbitrary vector a, I wish to find another vector b, which is the reflection of a on the other side of the plane P. Figure 3.1 shows a plane that includes the vectors v, a, and b. The dotted line represents the reflection plane P, which is perpendicular to v.

The concept of *reflection* is defined by three equations. The reflection plane P is determined by the vector v. To simplify the algebra, I assume that v is of length 1:

$$\|v\| = 1 \tag{3.7}$$

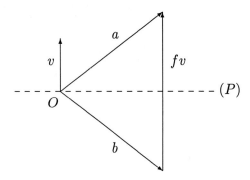

Figure 3.1: Reflection.

Reflection preserves the norm of a vector:

$$\|a\| = \|b\| \tag{3.8}$$

The difference between a vector a and its reflection b is a vector fv, which is a multiple of v:

$$fv = a - b \tag{3.9}$$

The (unknown) scalar f is the distance between a vector and its reflection.

I must find the reflection of an arbitrary vector a through a plane P defined by a given unit vector v. Now,

$$
\begin{aligned}
\|a\|^2 &= \|b\|^2 && \text{by (3.8)} \\
&= (a - fv)^T(a - fv) && \text{by (3.6), (3.9)} \\
&= a^T a - f a^T v - f v^T a + f^2 v^T v \\
&= \|a\|^2 - 2f v^T a + f^2 && \text{by (3.4), (3.6), (3.7)}
\end{aligned}
$$

This equality determines the distance f between vector a and its image b:

$$f = 2v^T a \tag{3.10}$$

The reflection of b into a displaces b by the same distance f in the opposite direction. So, you can also express the distance as

$$f = -2v^T b \qquad (3.11)$$

Finally I define b in terms of a and v

$$
\begin{aligned}
b \quad &= \quad a - vf & \text{by (3.9)} \\
&= \quad Ia - v(2v^T a) & \text{by (3.10)} \\
&= \quad (I - 2vv^T)a &
\end{aligned}
$$

where I is the $n{\times}n$ *identity matrix* defined in the appendix.

In other words, the reflection of a vector a is the vector

$$b = Ha \qquad (3.12)$$

obtained by multiplying a by the $n{\times}n$ reflection matrix

$$H = I - 2vv^T \qquad (3.13)$$

H is also called a *Householder matrix*. This is the "rabbit" that is often pulled out of the hat without any explanation of why it has this particular form (Sec. 1.3).

Figure 3.1 is a geometric definition of reflection in three-dimensional space. However, the algebraic equations derived from this figure make no assumptions about the dimension of space. In the following, I will simply assume that (3.12) and (3.13) define a transformation of an n-dimensional vector. By analogy, I will call this transformation a "reflection" through an $(n-1)$-dimensional plane. The essential property is that reflection of an n-dimensional vector preserves the norm:

$$\|Ha\| = \|a\|$$

This follows from (3.8) and (3.12).

If you reflect a vector twice through the same plane, you get the same vector again:

$$H(Ha) = a$$

In other words, two reflections are equivalent to an identity transformation:

$$HH = I$$

Consequently, H is a nonsingular matrix that is its own inverse:

$$H^{-1} = H$$

(see the Appendix).

3.5 Householder Reduction

I am looking for an algorithm that reduces an $n \times n$ real matrix A to triangular form without increasing the magnitude of the elements significantly.

An element of a column can never exceed the total length of the column vector. That is,

$$|a_{ij}| \leq \|a_i\| \qquad \text{for } i, j = 1, 2, \ldots, n$$

In other words, the norm of a column vector is an upper bound on the magnitude of its elements.

A method that changes the elements of a matrix A without changing the norms of its columns will obviously limit the magnitude of the matrix elements. This can be achieved by multiplying A by a Householder matrix H.

If you multiply a system of linear equations

$$Ax = b$$

by a nonsingular matrix H, you obtain an equation

$$(HA)x = Hb$$

that has the same solution as the original system.

The first step in Householder reduction produces a matrix HA that has all zeros below the first element of the first column.

The reflection must transform column

$$a_1 = [\, a_{11} \ a_{21} \ \cdots \ a_{n1} \,]^T \qquad (3.14)$$

into a column of the form

$$Ha_1 = [\, d_{11} \; 0 \; \cdots \; 0 \,]^T \qquad (3.15)$$

where the diagonal element is

$$\overset{'}{d}_{11} = \pm\|a_1\| \qquad (3.16)$$

The choice of sign will be made later.

Equations (3.14)–(3.16) define the computation of the first column of the matrix HA.

The difference between column a_1 and its reflection Ha_1 is the column vector

$$f_1 v \; = a_1 - b_1 \qquad \text{by (3.9)}$$

$$= a_1 - Ha_1 \quad \text{by (3.12)}$$

Combining this with (3.14) and (3.15) you find

$$f_1 v = [\, w_{11} \; a_{21} \; \cdots \; a_{n1} \,]^T \qquad (3.17)$$

where the first element is

$$w_{11} = a_{11} - d_{11} \qquad (3.18)$$

The distance between a_1 and its image Ha_1 is f_1 where

$$f_1^2 \; = f_1(-2v^T Ha_1) \quad \text{by (3.11), (3.12)}$$

$$= -2(f_1 v)^T Ha_1$$

$$= -2w_{11}d_{11} \qquad \text{by (3.3), (3.15), (3.17)}$$

In short,

$$f_1 = \sqrt{-2w_{11}d_{11}} \qquad (3.19)$$

The unit vector v that determines the appropriate Householder matrix is

$$v = f_1 v / f_1$$

or by (3.17):

$$v = [\, w_{11}\ a_{21}\ \cdots\ a_{n1}\,]^T / f_1 \tag{3.20}$$

After the transformation of the first column a_1, each remaining column a_i is also replaced by its reflection through the same plane defined by (3.9), (3.10), and (3.12):

$$H a_i = a_i - f_i v \tag{3.21}$$

$$f_i = 2 v^T a_i \tag{3.22}$$

The reflection of a column is obtained by subtracting a multiple of the unit vector v.

3.6   Numerical Stability

I still need to decide which sign to use for the diagonal element d_{11} in (3.16).

If $d_{11} = a_{11}$, the scalars w_{11} and f_1 are zero by (3.18) and (3.19), and the division by f_1 in (3.20) causes overflow. You can avoid this problem by selecting the sign that makes $d_{11} \neq a_{11}$.

The overflow occurs when a_1 is a multiple of the unit vector

$$e_1 = [\, 1\ 0\ \cdots\ 0\,]^T$$

For $a_1 = a_{11} e_1$ there are four cases to consider:

$$a_{11} > 0:$$
$$
\begin{aligned}
d_{11} &= +\|a_1\| &= \ \ a_{11} &\quad \text{(overflow)} \\
d_{11} &= -\|a_1\| &= -a_{11} &\quad \text{(no overflow)}
\end{aligned}
$$
$$a_{11} < 0:$$
$$
\begin{aligned}
d_{11} &= +\|a_1\| &= -a_{11} &\quad \text{(no overflow)} \\
d_{11} &= -\|a_1\| &= \ \ a_{11} &\quad \text{(overflow)}
\end{aligned}
$$

If a_1 is close to a multiple of e_1, serious rounding errors may occur if f_1 is very small.

This insight leads to the following rule:

$$d_{11} = \text{ if } a_{11} > 0 \text{ then } -\|a_1\| \text{ else } \|a_1\| \tag{3.23}$$

3.7 Computational Rules

I am now ready to summarize the rules for computing the matrix HA as defined by (3.3), (3.6), (3.15), and (3.18)–(3.23):

$$
\begin{aligned}
\|a_1\| &= \sqrt{a_1^T a_1} \\
d_{11} &= \text{ if } a_{11} > 0 \text{ then } -\|a_1\| \text{ else } \|a_1\| \\
w_{11} &= a_{11} - d_{11} \\
f_1 &= \sqrt{-2 w_{11} d_{11}} \\
H a_1 &= [\, d_{11} \; 0 \; \cdots \; 0 \,]^T \\
v &= [\, w_{11} \; a_{21} \; \cdots \; a_{n1} \,]^T / f_1 \\
f_i &= 2 v^T a_i \quad \text{ for } 1 < i \leq n \\
H a_i &= a_i - f_i v
\end{aligned}
\tag{3.24}
$$

Householder's algorithm reduces a system of linear equations to upper triangular form in $n - 1$ steps.

The first step reduces A to a matrix HA with all zeros below the diagonal element in the first column. At the same time, b is transformed into a vector Hb. This computation, defined by (3.24), is called a *Householder transformation* (Fig. 3.2).

The second step reduces the $(n - 1) \times (n - 1)$ submatrix of HA, shown in Fig. 3.2, by Householder transformation. Now, you obtain a matrix with zeros below the diagonal elements in the first two columns. The same transformation is applied to the $(n - 1) \times 1$ subvector of Hb shown in Fig. 3.2.

By a series of Householder transformations, applied to smaller and smaller submatrices and subvectors, the equation system is reduced, one column at a time, to upper triangular form.

3.8 A Numerical Example

I now return to the previous example of three equations with three unknowns. For convenience, I combine the matrix A and the vector b into a single 3×4

$$
\begin{bmatrix} * & \begin{array}{c} \\ 0 \\ \vdots \\ 0 \end{array} & \begin{bmatrix} * & * & \cdots & * \\ * & \cdots & * \\ \vdots & \vdots & \vdots \\ * & \cdots & * \end{bmatrix} \end{bmatrix}
\qquad
\begin{bmatrix} * \\ * \\ \vdots \\ * \end{bmatrix}
$$

$$HA \qquad\qquad Hb$$

Figure 3.2: Householder transformation.

matrix:

$$
A0 = \begin{bmatrix} 2 & 2 & 4 & 18 \\ 1 & 3 & -2 & 1 \\ 3 & 1 & 3 & 14 \end{bmatrix}
$$

First, you reduce $A0$ to a matrix $A1$ with all zeros below the diagonal element in the first column. This is done column by column using (3.24). The numbers shown below were produced by a computer using 64-bit real arithmetic and rounded to four decimal places in the printing.

First column:

$$
\begin{aligned}
a_1 &= [\,2\ 1\ 3\,]^T \\
v &= [\,0.8759\ 0.1526\ 0.4577\,]^T \\
f_1 &= 6.5549 \\
Ha_1 &= [\,-3.7417\ 0\ 0\,]^T
\end{aligned}
$$

Second column:

$$
\begin{aligned}
a_2 &= [\,2\ 3\ 1\,]^T \\
f_2 &= 5.3344 \\
Ha_2 &= [\,-2.6726\ 2.1862\ -1.4414\,]^T
\end{aligned}
$$

Third column:

$$
a_3 = [\,4\ -2\ 3\,]^T
$$

$$f_3 = 9.1433$$
$$Ha_3 = [\,-4.0089\ -3.3949\ -1.1846\,]^T$$

Fourth column:

$$a_4 = [\,18\ 1\ 14\,]^T$$
$$f_4 = 44.6536$$
$$Ha_4 = [\,-21.1136\ -5.8123\ -6.4368\,]^T$$

You now have the matrix

$$A1 = \begin{bmatrix} -3.7417 & -2.6726 & -4.0089 & -21.1136 \\ 0 & 2.1862 & -3.3949 & -5.8123 \\ 0 & -1.4414 & -1.1846 & -6.4368 \end{bmatrix}$$

The next step of the algorithm reduces the 2×3 submatrix

$$A1' = \begin{bmatrix} 2.1862 & -3.3949 & -5.8123 \\ -1.4414 & -1.1846 & -6.4368 \end{bmatrix}$$

to

$$A2' = \begin{bmatrix} -2.6186 & 2.1822 & 1.3093 \\ 0 & -2.8577 & -8.5732 \end{bmatrix}$$

The final triangular matrix

$$A2 = \begin{bmatrix} -3.7417 & -2.6726 & -4.0089 & -21.1136 \\ 0 & -2.6186 & 2.1822 & 1.3093 \\ 0 & 0 & -2.8577 & -8.5732 \end{bmatrix}$$

consists of the first row and column of $A1$ and the submatrix $A2'$.

The triangular equation system is solved by back substitution to obtain

$$x = [\,1.0000\ 2.0000\ 3.0000\,]^T$$

3.9   Pascal Procedure

The following Pascal procedure assumes that the matrix A is stored by columns, that is, $a[i]$ denotes the ith column of A. For each submatrix of A, the *eliminate* operation is applied to the first column, and the *transform* operation is applied to each remaining column (including b).

```
type
   column = array [1..n] of real;
   matrix = array [1..n] of column;

procedure reduce(var a: matrix;
   var b: column);
var vi: column; i, j: integer;

   function product(i: integer;
      a, b: column): real;
   { the scalar product of
      elements i..n of a and b }
   var ab: real; k: integer;
   begin
      ab := 0.0;
      for k := i to n do
         ab := ab + a[k]*b[k];
      product := ab
   end;

   procedure eliminate(i: integer;
      var ai, vi: column);
   var anorm, dii, fi, wii: real;
      k: integer;
   begin
      anorm := sqrt(
         product(i, ai, ai));
      if ai[i] > 0.0
         then dii := −anorm
         else dii := anorm;
      wii := ai[i] − dii;
```

```
      fi := sqrt(−2.0*wii*dii);
      vi[i] := wii/fi;
      ai[i] := dii;
      for k := i + 1 to n do
        begin
          vi[k] := ai[k]/fi;
          ai[k] := 0.0
        end
  end;

  procedure transform(i: integer;
      var aj, vi: column);
  var fi: real; k: integer;
  begin
    fi := 2.0*product(i, vi, aj);
    for k := i to n do
      aj[k] := aj[k] − fi*vi[k]
  end;

begin
  for i := 1 to n − 1 do
    begin
      eliminate(i, a[i], vi);
      for j := i + 1 to n do
        transform(i, a[j], vi);
      transform(i, b, vi)
    end
end { reduce };
```

For $n \gg 1$, the *execution time* of the algorithm is dominated by the *transform* procedure, which uses one addition, one subtraction, and two multiplications per array element. The ith submatrix requires $n - i + 1$ *transform* operations, each involving $4(n - i + 1)$ arithmetic operations. So the total number of numerical operations is approximately

$$\sum_{i=1}^{n-1} 4(n - i + 1)^2 = \sum_{k=2}^{n} 4k^2 \approx 4n^3/3$$

A similar analysis shows that Gaussian elimination requires $2n^3/3$ arithmetic operations only.

3.10   Final Remarks

I have explained Householder's method for reducing a matrix to triangular
form. The main advantage of the method is its unconditional stability. I have
illustrated the computation by a numerical example and a Pascal procedure.

   Gaussian elimination and Householder reduction of an $n \times n$ matrix both
have $O(n^3)$ complexity. However, Householder reduction requires twice as
many numerical operations. For that reason, Householder reduction is seldom used to solve linear equations on a sequential computer.

   Why then should you be interested in Householder reduction?

1. For some matrices, Gaussian elimination with pivoting is highly inac-
    curate. Numerical analysts believe that such matrices are so rare that
    pivoting is stable "in practice." However, I have not found a theoretical
    or statistical justification of this claim in the literature. Householder's
    method is unconditionally stable, both in theory and in practice. An
    engineer usually prefers a stable method with reasonable speed to a
    faster, but potentially unstable, technique.

2. When a *multicomputer* with p processors solves n linear equations in
    parallel, the solution time has the form

    $$T_p = an^3/p + bn^2$$

    where a and b are system-dependent constants of matrix transforma-
    tion and processor communication. The transformation time is reduced
    by the number of processors. The communication time is proportional
    to the number of matrix elements. Parallelism reduces the transforma-
    tion time, but not the communication time. Since Gaussian elimination
    and Householder reduction require the same amount of communication,
    a multicomputer reduces the timé difference between these methods.
    On a Computing Surface with 45 transputers, I used both methods
    to solve 1000 equations. The parallel solution times differed by only
    50% [Chap. 5 and Brinch Hansen 1990e, 1992g]. For parallel solution
    of linear equations, Householder reduction is an attractive compromise
    between unconditional numerical stability and computing speed.

3. Finally, it should be mentioned that Householder reduction is used for *least squares* and *eigenvalue* computations in the *Linpack* procedures developed at Argonne National Laboratory [Dongarra 1979].

Householder reduction is an interesting example of a fundamental computation with a subtle theory and a short algorithm. If you are interested in further details and alternative methods, you will find them in the books by Golub [1989] and Press [1989].

3.11   Appendix: Matrix Algebra

In the algebraic laws, A, B, and C denote matrices, while k is a scalar.

The *identity matrix* is

$$I = \begin{bmatrix} 1 & 0 & \cdots & 0 & 0 \\ 0 & 1 & \cdots & 0 & 0 \\ & & \cdots & & \\ 0 & 0 & \cdots & 0 & 1 \end{bmatrix}$$

The *transpose* A^T is the matrix obtained by exchanging the rows and columns of the matrix A.

The *inverse* of a matrix A is a matrix A^{-1} such that

$$AA^{-1} = I$$

If A^{-1} exists then A is called a *nonsingular* matrix.

The laws apply also to vectors since they are $n \times 1$ (or $1 \times n$) matrices.

Identity Law:

$$IA = AI = A$$

Symmetry Law:

$$A + B = B + A$$

Associative Laws:

$$A \pm (B \pm C) = (A \pm B) \pm C$$
$$A(BC) = (AB)C$$

Distributive Laws:

$$A(B \pm C) = AB \pm AC$$
$$(A \pm B)C = AC \pm BC$$

Transposition Laws:

$$I^T = I$$
$$(A^T)^T = A$$
$$(A \pm B)^T = A^T \pm B^T$$
$$(AB)^T = B^T A^T$$

Scaling Laws:

$$kA = Ak$$

$$k(AB) = (kA)B = A(kB)$$
$$kA^T = (kA)^T$$

Chapter 4

The All-Pairs Pipeline

4.1 Introduction

Successful exploitation of parallel computers depends to a large extent on the development of useful concepts which enable programmers to view different applications as variations of a common theme. Our most fundamental concepts, such as parallel processes and message communication, are embedded in programming languages. In other cases, we discover programming paradigms which can be used to solve a class of applications.

An *all-pairs problem* is a computation on every possible subset consisting of two elements chosen from a set of n elements. N-body simulation is an all-pairs problem [Fox 1988; and Chap. 6]. Householder reduction of a matrix to triangular form is a less obvious example [Press 1989; Brinch Hansen 1990c and Chap. 3]. This paper develops the all-pairs paradigm discussed by Shih [1987] and Cosnard [1988]. I define the problem concisely by means of precedence matrices and derive a parallel algorithm. The algorithm is presented in both coarse-grain and medium-grain form. The all-pairs paradigm is illustrated by a pipeline for Householder reduction.

Pipeline algorithms for matrix reduction have already been developed based on a detailed understanding of various reduction methods, such as Gaussian elimination, Givens rotations, and Householder reduction [Ortega 1988].

I will take a different approach. I am convinced that the emphasis on paradigms is the appropriate way to study parallel algorithms. I will illustrate the benefits of this approach by developing a parallel algorithm for Householder reduction from a sequential algorithm. The program transformation is completely mechanical.

4.2   The All-Pairs Problem

Let A be a set of n elements:

$$A = \{a_1, a_2, \ldots, a_n\}$$

There are $(n-1)n/2$ ways to select a subset of A consisting of two elements:

$$
\begin{array}{llll}
\{a_2, a_1\} & & & \\
\{a_3, a_1\} & \{a_3, a_2\} & & \\
\{a_4, a_1\} & \{a_4, a_2\} & \{a_4, a_3\} & \\
\cdots & \cdots & \cdots & \cdots \\
\{a_n, a_1\} & \{a_n, a_2\} & \{a_n, a_3\} & \cdots & \{a_n, a_{n-1}\}
\end{array}
$$

Each subset $\{a_i, a_j\}$ can be represented by an ordered pair (a_i, a_j), where a_i and a_j are elements of A, and $1 \le j < i \le n$.

An all-pairs computation performs an operation $Q(a_i, a_j)$ on every pair (a_i, a_j). This operation transforms a_i and a_j without involving any other elements of A. Inspired by the n-body problem, I will say that the operation defines an "interaction" between a pair of elements.

I will consider the all-pairs computation defined by Fig. 4.1. In this *precedence graph*, an arrow from one operation to another indicates that the former operation must be performed before the latter in any solution to the problem. The figure shows that control flows from top to bottom and left to right.

Element a_1 interacts with $a_2, a_3, \ldots, a_n$ in that order. Element a_2 interacts with $a_1, a_3, \ldots, a_n$, and so on. Finally, element a_n interacts with $a_1, a_2, \ldots, a_{n-1}$. All operations on a particular element a_i take place strictly one at a time. There is no possibility of race conditions when the all-pairs computation is performed in parallel.

Figure 4.2 is a more compact representation of the precedence graph in the form of a triangular *precedence matrix*. The elements of the precedence matrix are operations. Each operation is preceded by the operations (if any) immediately above and to the left of it, and is followed by the operations (if any) immediately below and to the right of it. In other words, $Q(a_i, a_j)$ is

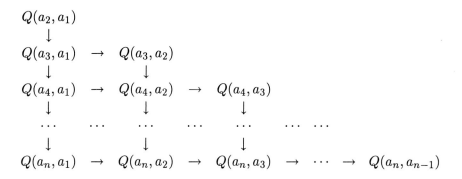

$$Q(a_2, a_1)$$
$$\downarrow$$
$$Q(a_3, a_1) \quad \rightarrow \quad Q(a_3, a_2)$$
$$\downarrow \qquad\qquad\qquad \downarrow$$
$$Q(a_4, a_1) \quad \rightarrow \quad Q(a_4, a_2) \quad \rightarrow \quad Q(a_4, a_3)$$
$$\downarrow \qquad\qquad\qquad \downarrow \qquad\qquad\qquad \downarrow$$
$$\cdots \qquad \cdots \qquad \cdots \qquad \cdots \qquad \cdots \qquad \cdots \quad \cdots$$
$$\downarrow \qquad\qquad\qquad \downarrow \qquad\qquad\qquad \downarrow$$
$$Q(a_n, a_1) \quad \rightarrow \quad Q(a_n, a_2) \quad \rightarrow \quad Q(a_n, a_3) \quad \rightarrow \quad \cdots \quad \rightarrow \quad Q(a_n, a_{n-1})$$

Figure 4.1: All-pairs precedence graph.

preceded by $Q(a_{i-1}, a_j)$ and $Q(a_i, a_{j-1})$ and is followed by $Q(a_{i+1}, a_j)$ and $Q(a_i, a_{j+1})$.

$$Q(a_2, a_1)$$
$$Q(a_3, a_1) \quad Q(a_3, a_2)$$
$$Q(a_4, a_1) \quad Q(a_4, a_2) \quad Q(a_4, a_3)$$
$$\cdots \qquad\qquad \cdots \qquad\qquad \cdots \qquad \cdots$$
$$Q(a_n, a_1) \quad Q(a_n, a_2) \quad Q(a_n, a_3) \quad \cdots \quad Q(a_n, a_{n-1})$$

Figure 4.2: All-pairs precedence matrix.

4.3 Sequential Algorithms

Figure 4.3 defines a sequential solution of the all-pairs problem for n elements of type T. The correctness of the algorithm is obvious when you compare it with Fig. 4.2. It defines the same sequence of operations as the precedence matrix, column by column, from left to right.

Example 1:

An *n-body simulation* computes the trajectories of n particles which interact through gravitational forces only. For each time step, the algorithm

```
type table = array [1..n] of T;
var a: table; i, j: integer;
for i := 1 to n − 1 do
    for j := i + 1 to n do Q(a[j], a[i])
```

Figure 4.3: All-pairs algorithm.

computes the forces between each pair of particles (a_i, a_j) and adds them to the total forces acting on these particles. The main loop of the force summation is programmed as follows:

```
type system = array [1..n] of body;
var a: system; i, j: integer;
for i := 1 to n − 1 do
    for j := i + 1 to n do
        [sic] addforces(a[j], a[i])
```

Force interactions are symmetric, since addforces(a_j, a_i) is equivalent to addforces(a_i, a_j). The example shows that an interaction between a pair of elements may transform both elements. For large n, the $O(n\log n)$ force calculation of Barnes and Hut [1986] is much faster than the all-pairs algorithm.

Example 2:

Gaussian elimination reduces an $n{\times}n$ real matrix to upper triangular form in $n-1$ steps. In the ith step, the algorithm subtracts row a_i multiplied by a_{ji}/a_{ii} from row a_j. If you ignore the (serious) rounding problems which occur when the pivot element a_{ii} is very small, you have the following loop:

```
type matrix = array [1..n] of row;
var a: matrix; i, j: integer;
for i := 1 to n − 1 do
    for j := i + 1 to n do
        subtract(i, a[j], a[i])
```

The row interactions are asymmetric: subtract(i, a_j, a_i) is not the same as subtract(j, a_i, a_j). Gaussian elimination without pivoting is numerically unstable [Press 1989]. I use it only as a simple example of the all-pairs problem.

Householder reduction, which will be discussed later, is numerically stable and well-suited for parallel execution.

Another sequential algorithm for the all-pairs problem is obtained by implementing the precedence matrix, row by row, from top to bottom (Fig. 4.4). For $i = 1$, the inner *for* statement defines an empty operation, so it makes no difference whether the initial value of i is 1 or 2.

```
var a: table; i, j: integer;
for i := 1 to n do
    for j := 1 to i − 1 do Q(a[i], a[j])
```

Figure 4.4: Equivalent all-pairs algorithm.

4.4 A Coarse-Grain Pipeline

I will solve the all-pairs problem on a pipeline with p nodes, where $1 \leq p \leq n - 1$ (Fig. 4.5). The nodes communicate by messages only. The first node inputs the original elements of A. The last node outputs the final elements of A. Without loss of generality, I assume that $n - 1$ is divisible by p. Each node implements $(n - 1)/p$ columns of the precedence matrix (Fig. 4.2).

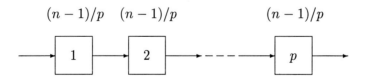

Figure 4.5: The all-pairs pipeline.

The pipeline can be designed to output the elements in either natural order $a_1, a_2, \ldots, a_n$, or reverse order $a_n, a_{n-1}, \ldots, a_1$. I will use *reverse output* to facilitate back substitution after matrix reduction.

I will program the pipeline nodes in *SuperPascal*. Each node has an input channel, named *left*, and an output channel, named *right*. In program assertions, a channel name denotes the sequence of messages transmitted through the channel up to that point. As an example, the assertion

$$\text{left} = <\,a_r..a_n\,>\mathbf{rev}<\,a_1..a_{r-1}\,>$$

shows that a node has input the elements a_r through a_n, in that order, followed by the elements a_1 through a_{r-1} in reverse order. In other words,

$$\text{left} = <\,a_r, a_{r+1}, \ldots, a_n, a_{r-1}, a_{r-2}, \ldots, a_1\,>$$

Some sequences are, per definition, empty:

$$<\,a_i..a_j\,> = <>,\quad \mathbf{rev}<\,a_i..a_j\,> = <>\quad \text{for } i > j$$

Figure 4.6 shows how the precedence matrix in Fig. 4.2 is partitioned for an all-pairs pipeline with 2 nodes and 5 elements. An arrow in row i denotes either input of element a_i by the first node, communication of a_i from the first to the second node, or output of a_i by the second node. At the end of the computation, node 1 holds elements a_1 and a_2, node 2 stores a_3 and a_4, while a_5 has been output. The final task of the nodes is to output the stored elements in reverse order a_4, a_3, a_2, a_1.

Node 1   Node 2

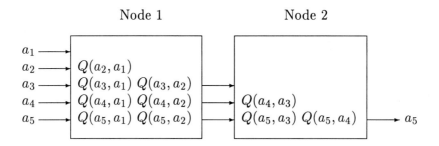

Figure 4.6: Precedence matrix of a pipeline.

Figure 4.7 shows the precedence matrix of a pipeline node that implements columns r through s of Fig. 4.2, where $1 \le r \le s \le n-1$. This matrix enables you to develop an algorithm for a pipeline node.

A pipeline node goes through four phases:

$$
\begin{array}{llllll}
a_r & \rightarrow & & & & \\
a_{r+1} & \rightarrow & Q(a_{r+1}, a_r) & & & \\
\cdots & \cdots & \cdots & \cdots & & \\
a_s & \rightarrow & Q(a_s, a_r) & \cdots & Q(a_s, a_{s-1}) & \\
a_{s+1} & \rightarrow & Q(a_{s+1}, a_r) & \cdots & Q(a_{s+1}, a_{s-1}) & Q(a_{s+1}, a_s) & \rightarrow & a_{s+1} \\
\cdots & \cdots & \cdots & \cdots & \cdots & \cdots & \cdots & \cdots \\
a_n & \rightarrow & Q(a_n, a_r) & \cdots & Q(a_n, a_{s-1}) & Q(a_n, a_s) & \rightarrow & a_n
\end{array}
$$

Figure 4.7: Precedence matrix of a pipeline node.

1. *Input phase:* The node inputs elements a_r through a_s and stores them in a local array a. Every input element a_i interacts with each of the previously stored elements a_r through a_{i-1}.

> { left = <>, right = <> }
>   **for** i := r **to** s **do**
>   **begin**
>   receive(left, a[i]);
>   **for** j := r **to** i − 1 **do** Q(a[i], a[j])
>   **end**
> { left = < $a_r..a_s$ >, right = <> }

2. *Transfer phase:* The node inputs elements a_{s+1} through a_n. Every transfer element a_j interacts with every local element and is then immediately output to the next node. There is no room for transfer elements in the local array. They are stored temporarily in a local variable a_j. (The last node transfers element a_n only, since $s = n - 1$.) This phase completes the local computation defined by Fig. 4.7.

> { left = < $a_r..a_s$ >, right = <> }
>   **for** j := s + 1 **to** n **do**
>   **begin**
>   receive(left, aj);
>   **for** i := r **to** s **do** Q(aj, a[i]);
>   send(right, aj)
>   **end**
> { left = < $a_r..a_n$ >, right = < $a_{s+1}..a_n$ > }

3. *Output phase:* The node outputs the local elements in reverse order.

$$\{ \text{ left } = < a_r..a_n >, \text{ right } = < a_{s+1}..a_n > \}$$
    for i := s **downto** r **do**
        send(right, a[i])
$$\{ \text{ left } = < a_r..a_n >,$$
$$\text{ right } = < a_{s+1}..a_n > \textbf{rev} < a_r..a_s > \}$$

4. *Copy phase:* The node copies all elements output in reverse order by the previous nodes. (The first node copies no elements since $r = 1$.)

$$\{ \text{ left } = < a_r..a_n >,$$
$$\text{ right } = < a_{s+1}..a_n > \textbf{rev} < a_r..a_s > \}$$
    for j := r − 1 **downto** 1 **do**
      begin
        receive(left, aj);
        send(right, aj)
      end
$$\{ \text{ left } = < a_r..a_n > \textbf{rev} < a_1..a_{r-1} >,$$
$$\text{ right } = < a_{s+1}..a_n > \textbf{rev} < a_1..a_s > \}$$

Putting these program pieces together, I obtain the complete algorithm for a pipeline node (Fig. 4.8). To suppress irrelevant detail, I use an array type with dynamic bounds $r..s$ (which does not exist in *SuperPascal*).

The algorithm does not duplicate the whole set A within each node. The first $n - 1$ elements of the set are distributed evenly among the nodes of the pipeline. The last element is transferred through the pipeline without being stored.

The postcondition of the last phase shows that the input sequence of a node is a function of its lower bound r, while the output sequence is determined by the upper bound s:

$$\text{left}(r) = < a_r..a_n > \textbf{rev} < a_1..a_{r-1} >$$
$$\text{right}(s) = < a_{s+1}..a_n > \textbf{rev} < a_1..a_s >$$

This assertion implies that the first node inputs the numbers in natural order:

$$\text{left}(1) = < a_1..a_n > \textbf{rev} < a_1..a_0 > = < a_1..a_n >$$

```
procedure node(r, s: integer;
  left, right: channel);
type block = array [r..s] of T;
var a: block; aj: T; i, j: integer;
begin
  { 1 <= r <= s <= n − 1 }
  for i := r to s do
    begin
      receive(left, a[i]);
      for j := r to i − 1 do Q(a[i], a[j])
    end;
  for j := s + 1 to n do
    begin
      receive(left, aj);
      for i := r to s do Q(aj, a[i]);
      send(right, aj)
    end;
  for i := s downto r do
    send(right, a[i]);
  for j := r − 1 downto 1 do
    begin
      receive(left, aj);
      send(right, aj)
    end
end;
```

Figure 4.8: Node algorithm.

while the last node outputs them in reverse order:

$$\text{right}(n-1) = <a_n..a_n>\text{rev}<a_1..a_{n-1}> = \text{rev}<a_1..a_n>$$

I leave it as an exercise for you to write a modified algorithm which accepts input and produces output in natural order. The key idea is to use the input/output sequences

$$\text{left}(r) = <a_r..a_{n-1}><a_1..a_{r-1}><a_n>$$

$$\text{right}(s) = < a_{s+1}..a_{n-1} >< a_1..a_s >< a_n >$$

The all-pairs paradigm enables a programmer to formulate parallel versions of similar sequential algorithms by trivial substitution.

Example 3:

You can derive a pipelined algorithm for the force summation in *n-body simulation* by performing the following substitutions in Fig. 4.8:

type body	replaces	type T
addforces(a[i], a[j])	replaces	Q(a[i], a[j])
addforces(aj, a[i])	replaces	Q(aj, a[i])

By setting $r = 1$ and $s = n - 1$ in Fig. 4.8, you obtain a single-processor version of the all-pairs pipeline which is equivalent to Fig. 4.4.

4.5   A Medium-Grain Pipeline

A medium-grain pipeline consists of $n - 1$ nodes, each of which holds only one element of the set A. The medium-grain algorithm is derived from the coarse-grain version by setting $i = r = s$ in Fig. 4.8. Figure 4.9 defines a node that implements the ith column of the precedence matrix (Fig. 4.2).

Example 4:

From a sequential algorithm for *Gaussian elimination* without pivoting, you can design a pipeline algorithm by making the following substitutions in Fig. 4.9:

type row	replaces	type T
subtract(i, aj, ai)	replaces	Q(aj, ai)

4.6   Variation on a Theme

In the all-pairs computation discussed so far, each operation is an interaction between two elements of the same set

$$A = \{a_1, a_2, \ldots, a_n\}$$

In some applications, it is more convenient to use A to compute another set

```
procedure node(i: integer;
  left, right: channel);
var ai, aj: T; j: integer;
begin
  { 1 <= i <= n − 1 }
  receive(left, ai);
  for j := i + 1 to n do
    begin
      receive(left, aj);
      Q(aj, ai);
      send(right, aj)
    end;
  send(right, ai);
  for j := i − 1 downto 1 do
    begin
      receive(left, aj);
      send(right, aj)
    end
end;
```

Figure 4.9: Medium-grain node algorithm.

$$B = \{b_1, b_2, \ldots, b_{n-1}\}$$

and let the elements of A interact with the elements of B. The set B is a temporary data structure which exists during the computation only.

Figure 4.10 shows the precedence matrix for this variant of the all-pairs computation.

The all-pairs variant is a computation on every set $\{a_i, b_j\}$, where a_i is a member of A, b_j is a member of B, and $j \leq i$. For each of these sets, one of two operations is performed:

1. The operation $P(a_i, b_i)$ transforms element a_i and computes the corresponding element b_i, where $1 \leq i \leq n - 1$.

$P(a_1, b_1)$

$Q(a_2, b_1)$ $P(a_2, b_2)$

$Q(a_3, b_1)$ $Q(a_3, b_2)$ $P(a_3, b_3)$

$Q(a_4, b_1)$ $Q(a_4, b_2)$ $Q(a_4, b_3)$

$\cdots$ $\cdots$ $\cdots$ $\cdots$

$Q(a_{n-1}, b_1)$ $Q(a_{n-1}, b_2)$ $Q(a_{n-1}, b_3)$ $\cdots$ $P(a_{n-1}, b_{n-1})$

$Q(a_n, b_1)$ $Q(a_n, b_2)$ $Q(a_n, b_3)$ $\cdots$ $Q(a_n, b_{n-1})$

Figure 4.10: Variant precedence matrix.

2. The operation $Q(a_i, b_j)$ transforms elements a_i and b_j, where $1 \leq j < i \leq n$.

From the precedence matrix, I derive a sequential algorithm (Fig. 4.11). In this case, each element of B exists only during a single step of the computation. So, the set B is represented by a variable b_i, which holds a single element only. This is a variant of Fig. 4.3.

```
var a: table; bi: T; i, j: integer;
for i := 1 to n − 1 do
  begin
    P(a[i], bi);
    for j := i + 1 to n do Q(a[j], bi)
  end
```

Figure 4.11: All-pairs variant.

Example 5:

Householder's method reduces an $n \times n$ real matrix to upper triangular form in $n - 1$ steps. The main loop of a sequential Householder reduction is shown below [Chap. 3 and Brinch Hansen 1990c]:

```
type matrix = array [1..n] of column;
var a: matrix; vi: column; i, j: integer;
for i := 1 to n − 1 do
    begin
        eliminate(i, a[i], vi);
        for j := i + 1 to n do
            transform(i, a[j], vi)
    end
```

The matrix is stored by columns, that is, a[i] denotes the ith column of A. In the ith step, the algorithm uses column a[i] to compute a column vector v_i. This vector is then used to transform each remaining column a[j], where $i + 1 \leq j \leq n$. The *eliminate* and *transform* operations are defined in Chap. 3. The elements of the set A are matrix columns a_1 through a_n. The elements of the set B are column vectors v_1 through v_{n-1}. For each element a_i of A (except a_n), the algorithm computes the corresponding element v_i of B.

Figure 4.12 is a variant of Fig. 4.4 obtained from Fig. 4.10.

Figure 4.13 defines a pipeline node for the all-pairs variant. All elements of A and B (except a_n) are distributed evenly among the nodes. The elements of B are temporary local entities which are not transmitted between the nodes.

```
var a, b: table; i, j: integer;
for i := 1 to n − 1 do
    begin
        for j := 1 to i − 1 do Q(a[i], b[j]);
        P(a[i], b[i])
    end;
for i := 1 to n − 1 do Q(a[n], b[i])
```

Figure 4.12: Equivalent all-pairs variant.

For $a = b$ and $P = empty$, the algorithm reduces to the algorithm in Fig. 4.8. A medium-grain version of this pipeline is similar to Fig. 4.9.

```
procedure node(r, s: integer;
  left, right: channel);
type block = array [r..s] of T;
var a, b: block; aj: T; i, j: integer;
begin
  { 1 <= r <= s <= n − 1 }
  for i := r to s do
    begin
      receive(left, a[i]);
      for j := r to i − 1 do Q(a[i], b[j]);
      P(a[i], b[i])
    end;
  for j := s + 1 to n do
    begin
      receive(left, aj);
      for i := r to s do Q(aj, b[i]);
      send(right, aj)
    end;
  for i := s downto r do
    send(right, a[i]);
  for j := r − 1 downto 1 do
    begin
      receive(left, aj);
      send(right, aj)
    end
end;
```

Figure 4.13: The all-pairs variant.

4.7 An Example: Householder Reduction

Many problems in science and engineering involve a system of n linear equations. The equations can be solved in two steps: First, the equations are reduced to triangular form by systematic elimination of unknowns. The triangular equations are then solved by back substitution.

The most time-consuming part of the computation is the reduction of the coefficient matrix to triangular form. The standard Gaussian and Gauss-Jordan eliminations are straightforward reduction algorithms. They do, however, require pivoting, a rearrangement of the rows and columns, which in most cases, prevents numerical instability [Press 1989]. On a parallel computer, pivoting complicates these algorithms [Fox 1988].

For a parallel computer, Householder reduction is an attractive method that is numerically stable and does not require pivoting [Press 1989; Brinch Hansen 1990c]. In the following, I derive a pipeline algorithm for Householder reduction directly from the all-pairs paradigm.

Example 5 defines the main loop of sequential Householder reduction. The theory behind Householder reduction is explained in Chap. 3 and Brinch Hansen [1990c] and will not be repeated here.

A comparison of Fig. 4.11 and Example 5 shows that Householder reduction is an all-pairs variant. So, you can derive a pipeline for Householder reduction by making the following substitutions in Fig. 4.13:

type column	replaces	type T
variable v	replaces	variable b
eliminate(i, a[i], v[i])	replaces	P(a[i], b[i])
transform(j, a[i], v[j])	replaces	Q(a[i], b[j])
transform(i, aj, v[i])	replaces	Q(aj, b[i])

Figure 4.14 defines a node of the Householder pipeline which holds columns r through s, where $1 \leq r \leq s \leq n-1$. The pipeline inputs the columns in natural order, reduces the matrix to triangular form, and outputs the final columns in reverse order. The performance of the parallel algorithm has been analyzed and measured on a Computing Surface [Chap. 5 and Brinch Hansen 1990e].

The parallel Householder algorithm is an ideal algorithm for experimenting with a parallel computer:

1. It is a fundamental algorithm of considerable practical value.

2. It demonstrates the use of a general paradigm to transform a sequential algorithm into a parallel one.

3. It illustrates the subtleties of distributing a large computation evenly among parallel processors.

```
procedure node(r, s: integer;
   left, right: channel);
type block = array [r..s] of column;
var a, v: block; aj: column;
   i, j: integer;
begin
  { 1 <= r <= s <= n − 1 }
  for i := r to s do
    begin
      receive(left, a[i]);
      for j := r to i − 1 do
        transform(j, a[i], v[j]);
      eliminate(i, a[i], v[i])
    end;
  for j := s + 1 to n do
    begin
      receive(left, aj);
      for i := r to s do
        transform(i, aj, v[i]);
      send(right, aj)
    end;
  for i := s downto r do
    send(right, a[i]);
  for j := r − 1 downto 1 do
    begin
      receive(left, aj);
      send(right, aj)
    end
end;
```

Figure 4.14: Householder node algorithm.

4.8 Final Remarks

After programming n-body simulation and Householder reduction in occam
for the Computing Surface, I was delighted to discover that these seem-

ingly unrelated problems can be solved by refinements of the same abstract program.

I have presented pipeline algorithms for two variants of the all-pairs paradigm. As a non-trivial example, I have used the paradigm to derive a pipeline algorithm for Householder reduction of a real matrix to triangular form. The parallel algorithm was derived from a sequential one by trivial substitution of data types, variables, and procedure statements.

Chapter 5

Balancing a Pipeline

5.1 Introduction

Reduction of a matrix to triangular form plays a crucial role in the solution of linear equations. In this chapter, I analyze a pipeline algorithm for Householder reduction [Chap. 4 and Brinch Hansen 1990d]. The pipeline is folded several times across an array of processors to achieve approximate load balancing.

The pipeline inputs, transforms, and outputs a matrix, column by column. During the computation, the columns are distributed evenly among the processors. The computing time per column decreases rapidly from the first to the last column. So, the performance of the algorithm is limited mainly by the order in which the columns are distributed among the processors.

The simplest idea is to store a block of columns with consecutive indices in each processor [Ortega 1988]. *Block storage* performs poorly because it assigns the most time-consuming columns to a single processor and leaves much less work for other processors.

It is much better to distribute the columns cyclically among the processors, so that each processor holds a similar mixture of columns. This storage pattern is called *wrapped mapping* or *scattered decomposition* [Ortega 1988; Fox 1988].

A third method is *reflection storage* where the columns are distributed one at a time by going back and forth across the processors several times [Ortega 1988].

The *folded pipeline* combines block and reflection storage. On a Computing Surface with 25 transputers, the Householder pipeline achieves an efficiency of 81% for a 1250×1250 real matrix.

The performance analysis applies not only to Householder reduction, but also to Gaussian elimination and Givens reduction.

5.2 Pipeline Nodes

Figure 5.1 shows a pipeline which transforms an $n \times n$ matrix in $n - 1$ steps. Each node of the pipeline holds q columns of the matrix and performs q of the $n - 1$ steps. The number of nodes is $(n - 1)/q$, assuming that $n - 1$ is divisible by q. I am not yet making any assumptions about how the pipeline nodes are distributed among the available processors.

Figure 5.1: A simple pipeline.

Initially I will concentrate on the computing time of the parallel algorithm and ignore communication between the nodes. It is convenient to number the steps and nodes in reverse order as follows:

$$
\begin{aligned}
\text{step numbers} \quad &(n-1), \ldots, 2, 1 \\
\text{node numbers} \quad &(n-1)/q, \ldots, 2, 1
\end{aligned}
$$

For Householder reduction, the computing time of the ith step is approximately

$$c(i + 1)^2$$

where c is a system-dependent constant [Chap. 3 and Brinch Hansen 1990c].

The computing time $T(k)$ of the kth node is the sum of the computing times of steps $(k - 1)q + 1$ through kq. For $q \gg 2$, the sum is approximately equal to the integral

$$\int_{(k-1)q}^{kq} cx^2 dx = \frac{1}{3}cq^3(3k^2 - 3k + 1)$$

The formula can be rewritten as follows

$$T(k) = aq^3(3k^2 - 3k + 1) \tag{5.1}$$

where $a = c/3$. The performance analysis is valid for any pipeline algorithm which satisfies (5.1).

When a matrix is reduced by a pipeline of 50 nodes, the computing times of the first and last nodes differ by a factor of 7350. This enormous variation creates a load-balancing problem when you attempt to distribute the computation evenly among the processors.

5.3   A Simple Pipeline

My goal is to predict the parallel computing time T_p when the pipeline is executed by p processors. I am still ignoring communication.

First I will consider *block storage* with each node running on a separate processor. For $n \gg 1$, the block length $(n - 1)/q$ is approximately n/p. Due to the computational imbalance, the first processor has more work to do than any other processor. So, it determines the parallel computing time. Using (5.1), you find for $q \approx n/p$

$$
\begin{aligned}
T_p &= T(p) \\[2mm]
&= a(n/p)^3(3p^2 - 3p + 1) \\[2mm]
&= a(n/p)^3(p^2 + (p - 1)(2p - 1))
\end{aligned}
$$

which can be rewritten as

$$T_p = a(1 + f)n^3/p \tag{5.2}$$

where

$$f = (1 - 1/p)(2 - 1/p) \tag{5.3}$$

Notice that $0 \le f \le 2$.

If the pipeline runs on a single processor (where $p = 1$ and $f = 0$), the computing time is

$$T_1 = an^3 \tag{5.4}$$

The *speedup*

$$S_p = T_1/T_p \tag{5.5}$$

shows how much faster the computation runs on p processors compared to a single processor.

The *efficiency* of the parallel computation is

$$E_p = S_p/p \tag{5.6}$$

For the *simple pipeline*, I use (5.2) and (5.4) to obtain

$$E_p = 1/(1+f) \tag{5.7}$$

where f is a measure of the *load imbalance* which reduces the processor efficiency below 100%.

Table 5.1 shows how E_p approaches 0.33 for $p \gg 1$. The load imbalance wastes two thirds of the processing capacity!

Table 5.1: Load imbalance.

p	f	E_p
1	0.00	1.00
5	1.44	0.41
10	1.71	0.37
20	1.85	0.35
30	1.90	0.34

5.4   A Folded Pipeline

To reduce the load imbalance, I fold the pipeline an odd number of times m as shown in Fig. 5.2.

The pipeline now consists of $(m+1)p$ nodes. Every processor executes $m+1$ nodes, each holding q columns, where $q = (n-1)/(m+1)p$. For $n \gg 1$, the block length is approximately

$$q \approx \frac{n}{(m+1)p} \tag{5.8}$$

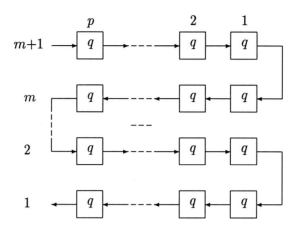

Figure 5.2: A folded pipeline.

The idea is to reduce the computing time of the first node by reducing the block length q by a factor of $(m + 1)$.

In the Appendix, I show that the *parallel computing time* T_p is

$$T_p = a(1 + f)n^3/p \qquad (5.9)$$

where (5.3) is replaced by

$$f = \frac{(1 - 1/p)(2 - 1/p)}{(m + 1)^2} \qquad (5.10)$$

Notice how folding reduces the load imbalance f.

The processor efficiency is

$$E_p = 1/(1 + f) \qquad (5.11)$$

Table 5.2 shows f and E_p for various values of m, assuming that $p \gg 1$.

5.5 The Effect of Communication

The remaining task is to consider how communication affects the performance of the folded pipeline.

Table 5.2: Folding.

m	f	E_p
0	2.00	0.33
1	0.50	0.67
3	0.13	0.89
5	0.06	0.95
7	0.03	0.97
9	0.02	0.98

In the single-processor case, the $n \times n$ matrix passes through $m+1$ pipeline nodes. The *sequential run time* is the sum of the computing and communication times

$$T_1 = an^3 + b(m+1)n^2 \qquad (5.12)$$

where a and b are system-dependent constants. This replaces (5.4).

For a sufficiently large matrix, the communication time is negligible compared to the computing time and you have approximately

$$T_1 = an^3 \qquad \text{for } n \gg (b/a)(m+1) \qquad (5.13)$$

If you use several processors, each of them must still transmit the matrix through $m+1$ nodes of the pipeline. The *parallel run time* determined by the first processor is

$$T_p = a(1+f)n^3/p + b(m+1)n^2 \qquad (5.14)$$

This is a refinement of (5.9).

The *grain-size* of a parallel computation is the ratio of the computing time to the communication time. In the Appendix, I show that

$$g = (a/b)(1+f)q \qquad (5.15)$$

According to (5.10), f becomes constant when $p \gg 1$. This makes the grain size proportional to the block length q.

The *processor efficiency* is

$$E_p = \frac{1}{(1+f)(1+1/g)} \qquad (5.16)$$

(see the Appendix).

Since communication decreases the efficiency, I would like to make it negligible in the parallel case as well. Equation (5.16) shows that this can be done by making the algorithm *coarse-grained* ($g \gg 1$). This, in turn, means that the blocks must be large.

The efficiency approaches

$$E_p \approx 1/(1+f) \qquad \text{for } g \gg 1 \tag{5.17}$$

From (5.8) and (5.15), I conclude that if

$$\frac{n}{(m+1)p} \gg \frac{b}{a}$$

then $g \gg 1 + f$. Since $f \geq 0$, this implies that $g \gg 1$. In other words, the problem size n must be large compared to the pipelength $(m+1)p$. This is an example of the necessity of *scaling* both the problem and the parallel computer to maintain constant efficiency [Gustafson 1988].

5.6   Performance Measurements

The Householder pipeline was programmed in occam for a Computing Surface with 45 transputers. Each transputer is connected to its two neighbors by four bidirectional channels. The channels make it possible to fold the pipeline three times.

For 64-bit real matrices, measurements show that

$$a = 2.8\mu s \qquad b = 4.2\mu s$$

According to Table 5.2 and (5.17), it should be possible to obtain a processor efficiency close to 0.89 for $m = 3$, provided $n/p \gg 6$.

The first experiment is Householder reduction of a 1000×1000 matrix. Table 5.3 shows the values of T_1, T_p, S_p, and E_p predicted by (5.13) and (5.14). The measured run times are shown in parentheses. As the number of processors increases from 20 to 45, communication reduces the efficiency from 0.81 to 0.72.

In the second experiment, I let $n/p = 50$ to maintain an efficiency of 0.81, which is independent of the number of processors. (With the available memory, the computation can be scaled only for $p \leq 25$. See Table 5.4.)

Table 5.3: Fixed problem size.

p	n	$T_1(s)$	T_p (s)		S_p	E_p
20	1000	2800	173	(171)	16	0.81
25	1000	2800	142	(141)	20	0.79
30	1000	2800	121	(120)	23	0.77
35	1000	2800	106	(105)	26	0.75
40	1000	2800	95	(95)	29	0.74
45	1000	2800	87	(87)	32	0.72

Table 5.4: Scaled problem size.

p	n	$T_1(s)$	T_p (s)		S_p	E_p
10	500	350	43	(42)	8	0.81
15	750	1181	97	(96)	12	0.81
20	1000	2800	173	(171)	16	0.81
25	1250	5469	271	(268)	20	0.81

5.7 Final Remarks

I have analyzed a pipeline for Householder reduction. The algorithm illustrates the subtleties of distributing a large computation evenly among parallel processors. Load balancing is achieved by folding the pipeline several times across the array of processors. The predicted efficiency has been confirmed by experiments on a Computing Surface.

5.8   Appendix: Performance Analysis

When the Householder pipeline is folded, as shown in Fig. 5.2, the ith processor from the right executes the $m + 1$ nodes with indices

$$
\begin{aligned}
&mp + i \\
&mp - i + 1 \\
&\cdots \\
&3p + i \\
&3p - i + 1 \\
&p + i \\
&p - i + 1
\end{aligned}
$$

The processor executes $(m + 1)/2$ pairs of nodes. The kth pair has the indices

$$(2k - 1)p + i \qquad (2k - 1)p - i + 1$$

$$\text{for } 1 \le i \le p \quad \text{and} \quad 1 \le k \le (m + 1)/2$$

From (5.1), you have

$$T((2k - 1)p + i)$$

$$= aq^3(3((2k - 1)p + i)^2 - 3((2k - 1)p + i) + 1)$$

$$= aq^3(3(2k - 1)^2 p^2 + 3(2k - 1)(2i - 1)p + 3i^2 - 3i + 1)$$

and

$$T((2k - 1)p - i + 1)$$

$$= aq^3(3((2k - 1)p - i + 1)^2 - 3((2k - 1)p - i + 1) + 1)$$

$$= aq^3(3(2k - 1)^2 p^2 - 3(2k - 1)(2i - 1)p + 3i^2 - 3i + 1)$$

The combined computing time of the kth pair of nodes is

$$T_{pair}(i, k) \;=\; T((2k - 1)p + i) + T((2k - 1)p - i + 1)$$

$$= \quad 2aq^3(3(2k-1)^2p^2 + 3i^2 - 3i + 1)$$

$$= \quad aq^3(24p^2k^2 - 24p^2k + 6p^2 + 6i^2 - 6i + 2)$$

The total computing time of processor i is

$$T_i = \sum_{k=1}^{(m+1)/2} T_{pair}(i, k)$$

I use the standard formulas

$$\sum_{k=1}^n k = n(n+1)/2 \qquad \sum_{k=1}^n k^2 = n(n+1/2)(n+1)/3$$

to find the previous sum

$$\begin{aligned} T_i = \quad & aq^3(p^2(m+1)(m+2)(m+3) - 3p^2(m+1)(m+3) \\ & + (3p^2 + 3i^2 - 3i + 1)(m+1)) \end{aligned}$$

which can be reduced to

$$T_i = aq^3(m+1)(p^2(m^2+2m) + 3i^2 - 3i + 1)$$

T_i is an increasing function of the processor index i. It reaches its maximum value for $i = p$:

$$\begin{aligned} T_p \quad &= \quad aq^3(m+1)(p^2(m^2+2m) + 3p^2 - 3p + 1) \\[4pt] &= \quad aq^3(m+1)(p^2(m+1)^2 + 2p^2 - 3p + 1) \\[4pt] &= \quad aq^3(m+1)^3(p^2 + (p-1)(2p-1)/(m+1)^2) \\[4pt] &= \quad an^3/p(1 + (1-1/p)(2-1/p)/(m+1)^2) \qquad \text{by (5.8)} \\[4pt] &= \quad an^3/p(1+f) \qquad\qquad\qquad\qquad\qquad \text{by (5.10)} \end{aligned}$$

T_p is the computing time of the whole pipeline.

The time grain g is the ratio of the computing time and the communication time:

$$
\begin{aligned}
g &= \frac{a(1+f)n^3/p}{b(m+1)n^2} \qquad \text{by (5.14)} \\[2mm]
&= \frac{a(1+f)n}{b(m+1)p} \\[2mm]
&= (a/b)(1+f)q \qquad \text{by (5.8)}
\end{aligned}
$$

The efficiency E_p is derived as follows:

$$
\begin{aligned}
1/E_p &= pT_p/T_1 \qquad\qquad\qquad\qquad\qquad\qquad\quad \text{by (5.5), (5.6)} \\[2mm]
&= p(a(1+f)n^3/p + b(m+1)n^2)/(an^3) \quad \text{by (5.13), (5.14)} \\[2mm]
&= a(1+f)n^3\left(1 + \frac{b(m+1)p}{a(1+f)n}\right)/(an^3) \\[2mm]
&= (1+f)(1+1/g)
\end{aligned}
$$

Chapter 6

The N-Body Pipeline

6.1 Introduction

I will describe the use of a programming paradigm to solve the n-body problem on a parallel computer. An n-body simulation computes the trajectories of n bodies which interact through gravitational forces only. At discrete time intervals, the algorithm computes the forces on the bodies and adjusts their velocities and positions [Feynman 1989]. Similar algorithms are used in computational fluid dynamics and molecular dynamics [Hockney 1988].

The parallel algorithm presented here uses a pipeline to compute the forces between all pairs of bodies. For $n \leq 10000$, the direct method of force summation allows very accurate simulations of star clusters [van Albada 1986]. For larger systems, the approximate algorithm of Barnes and Hut is much faster [Barnes 1986; Salmon 1991].

The complexity analysis of the n-body pipeline is based on a simple wavefront model of the computation. The pipeline is as fast as the standard ring algorithms [Ellingworth 1988; Fox 1988; Li 1990]. On a Computing Surface with 45 transputers, the pipeline computes the forces on 9000 bodies in 72 s with an efficiency of 79%.

The pipeline algorithm was *not* developed for n-body simulation. It was derived from a general pipeline for all-pairs computations by trivial substitution of types, variables, and procedure statements. A similar pipeline has been used to solve linear equations by Householder reduction [Chaps. 4–5 and Brinch Hansen 1990d, 1990e].

6.2   Force Summation

I consider each body to be a point in three-dimensional space. The state of
a body is defined by its mass m and three vectors representing its position
r, its velocity v, and the total force f by which the other bodies attract the
given body.

Figure 6.1 shows two bodies, p_i and p_j, with masses, m_i and m_j, and
positions, r_i and r_j, relative to the origin O.

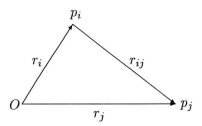

Figure 6.1: Two bodies in space.

The body p_j attracts p_i with a force f_{ij}. The magnitude of the force
is proportional to the mass of each body and inversely proportional to the
square of the distance between the bodies:

$$|f_{ij}| = \frac{G m_i m_j}{|r_{ij}|^2}$$

G is the universal gravitational constant.

The distance $|r_{ij}|$ is the length of the vector

$$r_{ij} = r_j - r_i$$

Newton's law of gravitation can also be stated as a vector equation

$$f_{ij} = |f_{ij}| e_{ij}$$

where e_{ij} is a unit vector in the same direction as r_{ij}

$$e_{ij} = \frac{r_{ij}}{|r_{ij}|}$$

The body p_i attracts p_j with a force f_{ji} of the same magnitude in the opposite direction of f_{ij}:

$$f_{ji} = -f_{ij}$$

This is Newton's third law.

The total force f_i acting on the body p_i is the sum of all forces exerted on p_i by the other $n - 1$ bodies:

$$f_i = \sum_{j \neq i} f_{ij}$$

6.3 Time Integration

Since I am interested in parallel programming rather than astrophysics, I will use a simple integration method.

The acceleration a_i of a body p_i is determined by its mass m_i and the total force f_i acting on it, according to Newton's second law:

$$a_i = \frac{f_i}{m_i}$$

During a small time interval Δt, the acceleration a_i is approximately constant. Consequently, the velocity v_i of the body increases by

$$\Delta v_i = a_i \Delta t$$

At the same time, the position r_i of the body increases by

$$\Delta r_i = \int_0^{\Delta t} (v_i + a_i t) dt = v_i \Delta t + 0.5 a_i \Delta t^2$$

In other words,

$$\Delta r_i = (v_i + 0.5 \Delta v_i) \Delta t$$

Smith [1989] discusses more accurate integration methods. The first-order discrete mechanics method of Greenspan is particularly effective [Marciniak 1985].

In a close encounter between two bodies, the accelerations can become extremely large. To prevent numerical instability, it may be necessary to make the time step so small that a realistic simulation becomes prohibitively time-consuming. Various techniques are used to deal with near-collisions [van Albada 1986; Hockney 1988]. In my performance measurements, I avoid the problem by making the initial mass density of the system sufficiently small.

6.4   Sequential Algorithm

A *SuperPascal* program for *n*-body simulation uses the following data types:

```
type
    vector = record x, y, z: real end;
    body = record m: real; r, v, f: vector end;
    system = array [1..n] of body;
```

SuperPascal extends Pascal with structured function types. The *n*-body program includes the functions listed in Table 6.1 and defined in the Appendix. The function parameters a and b are vectors, while a_x, a_y, a_z, and k are reals. The length function is of type real. The other functions are of type vector.

Table 6.1: Vector functions.

Function	Result
newvector(a_x, a_y, a_z)	(a_x, a_y, a_z)
length(a)	$\sqrt{a_x^2 + a_y^2 + a_z^2}$
sum(a, b)	$a + b$
difference(a, b)	$a - b$
product(a, k)	ka

A *simulation* consists of a fixed number of time steps. Each time step dt involves a force summation followed by a time integration of all bodies (Fig. 6.2). The force on each planet is set to zero during system initialization and is reset to zero during the time integration.

Figure 6.3 defines the sequential force summation.

For each pair of bodies, p_i and p_j, the program computes the gravitational forces between the bodies and adds each force to the total force acting on the corresponding body (Fig. 6.4).

The algorithm shown in Fig. 6.5 defines the forces between two bodies, p_i and p_j. The magnitudes of the distance vector r_{ij} and the force vector f_{ij} are denoted r_m and f_m, respectively.

Figure 6.6 defines the time integration of the n bodies.

Figure 6.7 defines the movement of a single body p_i during the time interval dt. The velocity and position increments are denoted dv_i and dr_i, respectively.

```
procedure simulate(var p: system;
   dt: real; steps: integer);
var i: integer;
begin
  for i := 1 to steps do
    begin
       findforces(p);
       integrate(p, dt)
    end
end;
```

Figure 6.2: Simulation algorithm.

```
procedure findforces(var a: system);
var i, j: integer;
begin
  for i := 1 to n − 1 do
    for j := i + 1 to n do
       [sic] addforces(a[j], a[i])
end;
```

Figure 6.3: Sequential force summation.

6.5 Pipeline Algorithm

Force summation and time integration involve $O(n^2)$ and $O(n)$ operations, respectively. Since summation is the most time-consuming part of the com-

```
procedure addforces(var pi, pj: body);
var fij: vector;
begin
  fij := force(pi, pj);
  pi.f := sum(pi.f, fij);
  pj.f := difference(pj.f, fij)
end;
```

Figure 6.4: Single-pair interaction.

```
function force(pi, pj: body): vector;
var eij, rij: vector; fm, rm: real;
begin
   rij := difference(pj.r, pi.r);
   rm := length(rij);
   fm := G*pi.m*pj.m/sqr(rm);
   eij := product(rij, 1/rm);
   force := product(eij, fm)
end;
```

Figure 6.5: Force calculation.

```
procedure integrate(var p: system; dt: real);
var i: integer;
begin
   for i := 1 to n do movebody(p[i], dt)
end;
```

Figure 6.6: Time integration.

```
procedure movebody(
    var pi: body; dt: real);
var ai, dvi, dri: vector;
begin
    ai := product(pi.f, 1/pi.m);
    dvi := product(ai, dt);
    dri :=
        product(sum(pi.v,
            product(dvi, 0.5)), dt);
    pi.v := sum(pi.v, dvi);
    pi.r := sum(pi.r, dri);
    pi.f := newvector(0, 0, 0)
end;
```

Figure 6.7: Single-body movement.

putation, I will use a pipeline to speed it up. The much faster time integration will remain sequential.

In the parallel program, each force summation activates a new instance of a pipeline controlled by a master process (Fig. 6.8). When the summation is finished, the master and the pipeline nodes terminate and cease to exist.

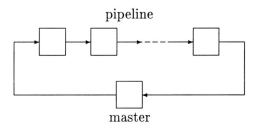

Figure 6.8: Master and pipeline.

The parallel processes are defined in *SuperPascal*.
The master sends the bodies one at a time through the pipeline. The

pipeline sums the forces and returns the bodies to the master (Fig. 6.9). The all-pairs pipeline was designed to output the results in reverse order to facilitate back substitution after matrix reduction [Chap. 4 and Brinch Hansen 1990d].

```
procedure master(var p: system;
    left, right: channel);
var i: integer;
begin
  for i := 1 to n do
    send(left, p[i]);
  for i := n downto 1 do
    receive(right, p[i])
end;
```

Figure 6.9: Pipeline master.

During force summation, the first $n - 1$ bodies are distributed evenly among the nodes of the pipeline. The last body goes through the pipeline without being stored.

Figure 6.10 defines the force summation performed by a node that holds a block of bodies with indices from r to s, where $1 \leq r \leq s \leq n - 1$. To suppress irrelevant detail, I use an array type with dynamic bounds (which does not exist in *SuperPascal*).

First, the node inputs and stores its own bodies. All subsequent bodies then pass through the node. Each body interacts with the previously stored bodies. After the force computation, the node outputs its own bodies. Finally, all bodies stored in previous nodes pass through the node.

I emphasize again that the n-body pipeline was derived from a general pipeline for all-pairs computations (Fig. 4.8) [Brinch Hansen 1990d].

6.6   Load Balancing

The number of force calculations performed by each node drops linearly from the first to the last node. If each node runs on a separate processor, the uneven distribution of the computational load will force the first processor

```
procedure node(r, s: integer;
   left, right: channel);
type block = array [r..s] of body;
var p: block; pj: body;
   i, j: integer;
begin
   { 1 <= r <= s <= n − 1 }
   for i := r to s do
      begin
         receive(left, p[i]);
         for j := r to i − 1 do
         [sic] { i <> j }
            addforces(p[i], p[j])
      end;
   for j := s + 1 to n do
      begin
         receive(left, pj);
         for i := r to s do
            addforces(pj, p[i]);
         send(right, pj)
      end;
   for i := s downto r do
      send(right, p[i]);
   for j := r − 1 downto 1 do
      begin
         receive(left, pj);
         send(right, pj)
      end
end;
```

Figure 6.10: Pipeline node.

to do most of the work. As I will show later, this reduces the speedup of the parallel computation significantly.

To achieve approximate load balancing, I fold the pipeline m times across an array of p processors [Brinch Hansen 1990e]. Figure 6.11 shows the *folded pipeline* with $(m+1)p$ nodes. Each processor runs $m+1$ nodes, each holding q bodies. The effect of the folding is to reduce the computing time of the first (and most time-consuming) node by reducing the block length q.

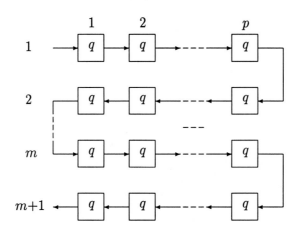

Figure 6.11: A folded pipeline.

In the initial analysis of the force computation, I ignore process communication and assume that the forces between two bodies are computed in unit time.

The force computation travels along the pipeline like a *wavefront,* filling one node at a time with bodies. Since the pipeline is folded, the wave sweeps back and forth across the array of processors $m+1$ times. Each sweep fills another *level* of nodes.

Initially all nodes are empty. I will say that a node is *full* when it holds q local bodies.

First, processor 1 fills node 1. The first body does not yet interact with any other body. The second body interacts with the first one, and so on. If the block length q is large, node 1 accumulates q bodies in time

$$\sum_{k=0}^{q-1} k = 0.5(q-1)q \approx 0.5q^2 \qquad \text{for } q \gg 1$$

While processor 2 fills node 2 with q bodies, the bottleneck is processor 1. Each of these bodies must interact with the q local bodies in node 1 before they can be output to node 2. So, node 2 is filled in time q^2.

Processor 3 then fills node 3 in the same amount of time, and so on. Consequently, the wave sweeps through the first p nodes in time

$$t_1 \approx 0.5q^2 + (p-1)q^2$$

which can be reduced to

$$t_1 \approx (p - 0.5)q^2$$

I now assume that the first $k-1$ levels of nodes are full, and observe the wave sweeping through level k. For each body that enters a node at level k, each of the previous nodes must transfer another body to keep the wave moving.

While level k is being filled with pq bodies, each processor transfers the same number of bodies through each of the previous $k-1$ levels. Each processor must therefore spend $pq(k-1)q$ time units to move the wave through the previous levels. In addition, the wave must sweep through the new level. So, level k is filled in time

$$t_k = pq(k-1)q + t_1$$

Consequently, the kth sweep takes the time

$$t_k \approx (kp - 0.5)q^2$$

The total force calculation time is the time required to complete $m + 1$ sweeps:

$$T_p = \sum_{k=1}^{m+1} t_k$$

This adds up to the following:

$$T_p \approx 0.5(m+1)((m+2)p - 1)q^2 \qquad \text{for } q \gg 1$$

For a large problem, the block length is approximately

$$q \approx \frac{n}{(m+1)p} \qquad \text{for } n \gg 1$$

The parallel computing time can now be expressed as

$$T_p \approx 0.5(1 + f)n^2/p$$

where

$$f = \frac{1 - 1/p}{m+1}$$

is a measure of the computational imbalance.

6.7 Performance

During a force calculation, n messages representing the bodies pass through $m + 1$ nodes in each processor. The communication increases the *parallel run time* of a force calculation to

$$T_p = a(1 + f)n^2/p + b(m + 1)n$$

where a and b are system-dependent constants for force calculation and communication, respectively. You can ignore the time integration, which is a much faster computation.

If the folded pipeline runs on a single processor only (where $p = 1$ and $f = 0$), the run time is

$$T_1 = an^2 + b(m + 1)n$$

The efficiency of the parallel computation is

$$E_p = T_1/(pT_p)$$

I programmed the n-body pipeline in occam and ran it on a Computing Surface with T800 transputers using 64-bit real arithmetic. Measurements show that

$$a = 31.8\mu s \qquad b = 27.5\mu s$$

Table 6.2 shows measured run times for a pipeline with 45 processors which performs a force calculation for 9000 bodies. The predicted run times are shown in parentheses. If the pipeline is not folded ($m = 0$), the efficiency is only 0.50. Folding the pipeline three times increases the efficiency to 0.79.

Table 6.2: Fixed problem size.

p	n	m	T_p (s)		E_p (est)
45	9000	0	110	(113)	0.50
45	9000	1	84	(86)	0.67
45	9000	3	72	(72)	0.79

To reduce the effect of communication, I use a large block $q \gg b/a$. This makes the communication time negligible compared to the computing time.

For $m = 3$, $q \gg 1$, and $p \gg 1$, it should be possible to achieve an efficiency $E_p \geq 0.79$.

Table 6.3 shows measured (and predicted) run times of a force calculation performed by a pipeline that is folded three times. In each experiment, the block size $q = 50$. For $m = 3$, this means that $n/p = 200$. By *scaling* the problem size n in proportion to the computer size p, the parallel computation maintains an almost constant efficiency of 0.79 to 0.81 (see also [Gustafson 1988]).

Table 6.3: Scaled problem size.

p	n	T_p (s)		E_p (est)
1	200	1.3	(1.3)	1.00
10	2000	15.8	(15.8)	0.81
20	4000	31.9	(31.9)	0.80
30	6000	48.0	(48.0)	0.79
40	8000	64.2	(64.2)	0.79

6.8 Final Remarks

I have presented and analyzed a parallel algorithm for direct force summation of n bodies which interact through gravitation only. The algorithm automatically avoids self-interactions and takes advantage of the symmetry of the force calculations.

6.9 Appendix: Vector Arithmetic

The following *SuperPascal* functions implement vector arithmetic:

```
type vector = record x, y, z: real end;

function newvector(ax, ay, az: real): vector;
var a: vector;
begin
    a.x := ax; a.y := ay; a.z := az;
    newvector := a
```

```
  end;

  function length(a: vector): real;
  begin
    length :=
      sqrt(sqr(a.x) + sqr(a.y) + sqr(a.z))
  end;

  function sum(a, b: vector): vector;
  begin
    a.x := a.x + b.x;
    a.y := a.y + b.y;
    a.z := a.z + b.z;
    sum := a
  end;

  function difference(a, b: vector): vector;
  begin
    a.x := a.x − b.x;
    a.y := a.y − b.y;
    a.z := a.z − b.z;
    difference := a
  end;

  function product(a: vector; k: real): vector;
  begin
    a.x := a.x*k;
    a.y := a.y*k;
    a.z := a.z*k;
    product := a
  end;
```

Part III

THE MULTIPLICATION
PARADIGM

Chapter 7

The Multiplication Pipeline

7.1 Introduction

In this chapter, I consider a programming paradigm for a combinatorial problem which I call *tuple multiplication*. The paradigm includes *matrix multiplication* and the *all-pairs shortest paths* problem as special cases.

I develop a generic pipeline algorithm for tuple multiplication. From the generic algorithm, I derive pipelines for matrix multiplication and shortest paths computations by trivial substitution of data types and functions.

Arthur Cayley is generally credited with having invented matrix multiplication [Cayley 1889–97]. The origin of the multiplication algorithm for the all-pairs shortest paths problem is uncertain [Lawler 1976]. The analogy between matrix multiplication and path problems is discussed in Aho [1974] and Cormen [1990]. Pipelined matrix multiplication is described in Kung [1988].

On a Computing Surface with 35 transputers, the multiplication algorithm computes the product of two 1400×1400 real matrices in 345 s with a processor efficiency of 89%.

7.2 Tuple Multiplication

Consider two finite tuples a and b. I will simplify the discussion a bit by assuming that a and b are n-tuples with elements of the same type T:

$$a = (a_1, a_2, \ldots, a_n)$$

117

$$b = (b_1, b_2, \ldots, b_n)$$

A product of two tuples, a and b, is an $n \times n$ matrix c, obtained by applying the same function f to every pair (a_i, b_j), consisting of an element a_i of tuple a and an element b_j of tuple b:

$$c = \begin{bmatrix} f(a_1, b_1) & f(a_1, b_2) & \cdots & f(a_1, b_n) \\ f(a_2, b_1) & f(a_2, b_2) & \cdots & f(a_2, b_n) \\ \cdots & \cdots & \cdots & \cdots \\ f(a_n, b_1) & f(a_n, b_2) & \cdots & f(a_n, b_n) \end{bmatrix}$$

Every matrix element $c_{ij} = f(a_i, b_j)$. Without loss of generality, I assume that the function f maps two elements of type T into a value of type *real*.

Figure 7.1 defines sequential tuple multiplication in Pascal.

```
type tuple = array [1..n] of T;
     vector = array [1..n] of real;
     matrix = array [1..n] of vector;

procedure multiply(var a, b: tuple; var c: matrix);
var i, j: integer;

   function f(ai, bj: T): real;
   begin ... end;

begin
   for i := 1 to n do
     for j := 1 to n do
       c[i,j] := f(a[i], b[j])
end;
```

Figure 7.1: Sequential tuple multiplication.

7.3   Pipeline Algorithm

I will multiply two n-tuples, a and b, on a pipeline controlled by a master process (Fig. 7.2).

$\{$ left $= < a_r..a_n >$, right $= < a_{s+1}..a_n > \}$
for j := 1 **to** n **do**
  begin
    receive(left, bj);
    if s $<$ n **then** send(right, bj);
    for i := r **to** s **do**
      c[i,j] := f(a[i], bj)
  end
$\{$ left $= < a_r..a_n >< b_1..b_n >$,
  right $= < a_{s+1}..a_n >< b_1..b_m > \}$

where

$$m = n \quad \text{for } s < n$$
$$m = 0 \quad \text{for } s = n$$

Since the output sequence $< a_{n+1}..a_n >< b_1..b_0 >$ is empty, the last node does not output any elements of the tuples a and b.

4. *Copy phase:* The node copies all rows of the tuple product output by the previous nodes using a local variable c_i:

$\{$ left $= < a_r..a_n >< b_1..b_n >$,
  right $= < a_{s+1}..a_n >< b_1..b_m > \}$
for i := 1 **to** r $-$ 1 **do**
  begin
    receive(left, ci);
    send(right, ci)
  end
$\{$ left $= < a_r..a_n >< b_1..b_n >< c_1..c_{r-1} >$,
  right $= < a_{s+1}..a_n >< b_1..b_m >< c_1..c_{r-1} > \}$

5. *Output phase:* The node outputs the local portion of the tuple product. This phase completes the output of the product.

$\{$ left $= < a_r..a_n >< b_1..b_n >< c_1..c_{r-1} >$,
  right $= < a_{s+1}..a_n >< b_1..b_m >< c_1..c_{r-1} > \}$
for i := r **to** s **do** send(right, c[i])
$\{$ left $= < a_r..a_n >< b_1..b_n >< c_1..c_{r-1} >$,
  right $= < a_{s+1}..a_n >< b_1..b_m >< c_1..c_s > \}$

Putting these program pieces together, I obtain the complete algorithm for a pipeline node (Fig. 7.4). To suppress irrelevant detail, I use array types with dynamic bounds $r..s$ (which do not exist in *SuperPascal*).

The postcondition of the last phase shows that the input sequence is a function of its lower bound r, while the output sequence is determined by the upper bound s:

$$\text{left}(r) = <a_r..a_n><b_1..b_n><c_1..c_{r-1}>$$
$$\text{right}(s) = <a_{s+1}..a_n><b_1..b_m><c_1..c_s>$$

This assertion implies that the first node inputs the elements of a and b in their natural order

$$\begin{aligned}\text{left}(1) &= <a_1..a_n><b_1..b_n><c_1..c_0>\\ &= <a_1..a_n><b_1..b_n>\end{aligned}$$

while the last node outputs the rows of c in their natural order

$$\begin{aligned}\text{right}(n) &= <a_{n+1}..a_n><b_1..b_0><c_1..c_n>\\ &= <c_1..c_n>\end{aligned}$$

This matches the final assertion in the master algorithm (see Fig. 7.3).

7.4   Matrix Multiplication

Figure 7.5 defines sequential multiplication

$$c := a \times b$$

of two $n \times n$ real matrices a and b. The algorithm assumes that a and c are stored by rows, while b is stored by columns. The function f computes the dot product of a row a_i and a column b_j. The multiplication time is $O(n^3)$.

Matrix multiplication is a tuple multiplication. It can be obtained by making the following type substitutions in Fig. 7.1:

$$\begin{aligned}\text{vector} \quad &\text{replaces} \quad T\\ \text{matrix} \quad &\text{replaces} \quad \text{tuple}\end{aligned}$$

Consequently, you can obtain a pipeline for matrix multiplication by making the same substitutions in Figs. 7.3 and 7.4. This leads to the algorithms shown in Figs. 7.6 and 7.7.

```
procedure node(r, s: integer;
  left, right: channel);
type
  Tblock = array [r..s] of T;
  block = array [r..s] of vector;
var a: Tblock; c: block; i, j: integer;
  ai, bj: T; ci: vector;
begin
  { 1 <= r <= s <= n }
  for i := r to s do
    receive(left, a[i]);
  for i := s + 1 to n do
    begin
      receive(left, ai);
      send(right, ai)
    end;
  for j := 1 to n do
    begin
      receive(left, bj);
      if s < n then
        send(right, bj);
      for i := r to s do
        c[i,j] := f(a[i], bj)
    end;
  for i := 1 to r − 1 do
    begin
      receive(left, ci);
      send(right, ci)
    end;
  for i := r to s do
    send(right, c[i])
end;
```

Figure 7.4: Tuple multiplication node.

```
procedure multiply(var a, b, c: matrix);
var i, j: integer;

    function f(ai, bj: vector): real;
    var cij: real; k: integer;
    begin
      cij := 0.0;
      for k := 1 to n do
        cij := cij + ai[k]*bj[k];
      f := cij
    end;

begin
  for i := 1 to n do
    for j := 1 to n do
      c[i,j] := f(a[i], b[j])
end;
```

Figure 7.5: Sequential matrix multiplication.

A minor refinement has been added to the master procedure: all three matrices are stored by rows. While the pipeline processes a column of b, the master process (which runs on a separate processor) simultaneously unpacks the next column.

7.5   All-Pairs Shortest Paths

As a second example of tuple multiplication, I will compute the shortest paths between every pair of nodes in a *directed graph* with n nodes. I assume that every edge has length 1.

The graph is represented by an $n \times n$ *adjacency matrix* a. A matrix element a_{ij} defines the length of the edge (if any) from node i to node j:

$$
\begin{aligned}
a_{ii} &= 0 && \text{for every node } i \\
a_{ij} &= 1 && \text{if there is an edge from node } i \text{ to node } j \\
a_{ij} &= \infty && \text{if there is no edge from node } i \text{ to node } j
\end{aligned}
$$

```
procedure master(var a, b, c: matrix;
   left, right: channel);
var i, j: integer; bj: vector;
begin
   for i := 1 to n do send(left, a[i]);
   for j := 1 to n do
      begin
         for i := 1 to n do bj[i] := b[i,j];
         send(left, bj)
      end;
   for i := 1 to n do receive(right, c[i])
end;
```

Figure 7.6: Matrix multiplication master.

Figure 7.8 shows a directed graph with four nodes labeled 1, 2, 3, and 4. The adjacency matrix of this graph is

$$a = \begin{bmatrix} 0 & 1 & 1 & \infty \\ \infty & 0 & 1 & \infty \\ \infty & \infty & 0 & 1 \\ 1 & \infty & \infty & 0 \end{bmatrix}$$

The goal is to compute an $n \times n$ *distance matrix d*. A matrix element d_{ij} defines the shortest path from node i to node j. If there is no path, then $d_{ij} = \infty$.

If you follow the shortest path from one node to another, you may have to visit each of the other $n - 1$ nodes, but not more than once. (Otherwise, the path is not the shortest one.) Consequently, the shortest path (if any) always has fewer than n edges.

I will compute a sequence of distance matrices:

$$d^{(1)}, d^{(2)}, \ldots, d^{(n-1)}$$

The first matrix defines all shortest paths of 1 (or 0) edges. I will express this assertion as follows:

$$d_{ij}^{(1)} = \text{shortest}(i, j, 1)$$

```
procedure node(r, s: integer;
  left, right: channel);
type block = array [r..s] of vector;
var a, c: block; i, j: integer;
  ai, bj, ci: vector;
begin
  { 1 <= r <= s <= n }
  for i := r to s do
    receive(left, a[i]);
  for i := s + 1 to n do
    begin
      receive(left, ai);
      send(right, ai)
    end;
  for j := 1 to n do
    begin
      receive(left, bj);
      if s < n then
        send(right, bj);
      for i := r to s do
        c[i,j] := f(a[i], bj)
    end;
  for i := 1 to r − 1 do
    begin
      receive(left, ci);
      send(right, ci)
    end;
  for i := r to s do
    send(right, c[i])
end;
```

Figure 7.7: Matrix multiplication node.

The second matrix defines all shortest paths of 2 (or fewer) edges

$$d_{ij}^{(2)} = \text{shortest}(i, j, 2)$$

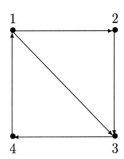

Figure 7.8: A directed graph.

and so on.

The $(n-1)$th matrix defines all shortest paths of $n-1$ (or fewer) edges:

$$d_{ij}^{(n-1)} = \text{shortest}(i, j, n-1)$$

The first distance matrix is the adjacency matrix

$$d^{(1)} = a$$

Since every shortest finite path has fewer than n edges, the $(n-1)$th matrix is the distance matrix we are looking for.

Suppose you already have computed the mth distance matrix

$$d = d^{(m)}$$

where $1 \leq m \leq n-1$. How can you then transform d into the $(m+1)$th matrix in the sequence?

For any two nodes, i and j, you know the shortest path of m (or fewer) edges:

$$d_{ij} = \text{shortest}(i, j, m)$$

However, it might be possible to find a shorter path from i to j of $m+1$ (or fewer) edges by going through a third node k (Fig. 7.9).

For any intermediate node k, you already know the distances

$$
\begin{aligned}
d_{ik} &= \text{shortest}(i, k, m) \\
a_{kj} &= \text{shortest}(k, j, 1)
\end{aligned}
$$

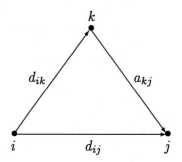

Figure 7.9: Three graph nodes.

If $d_{ij} > d_{ik} + a_{kj}$, the alternative path through k is shorter than the previous shortest distance from i to j. (Since all edges are of length 1, a shorter alternative exists only if $d_{ij} = \infty$. Later, I will consider weighted graphs with edges of arbitrary lengths. In that case, it may be possible to replace a finite distance d_{ij} with a shorter distance from i to j.)

The following loop attempts to reduce d_{ij} by examining an alternative path through every node:

for k := 1 **to** n **do**
    if d[i,j] > d[i,k] + a[k,j] **then**
        d[i,j] := d[i,k] + a[k,j]

At the end of the loop, you have found the shortest path from i to j of $m + 1$ (or fewer) edges:

$$d_{ij} = \text{shortest}(i, j, m + 1)$$

For $k = j$, the "alternative" path computed by the loop is the previous shortest distance since

$$d_{ik} + a_{kj} = d_{ij} + a_{jj} = d_{ij} \qquad \text{for } k = j$$

Consequently, the loop can be replaced by an equivalent computation of the shortest alternative path from i to j:

$$d_{ij} = \min(d_{ik} + a_{kj}) \qquad \text{for all } k = 1..n$$

You must perform the same computation for every pair of nodes to find all shortest paths of $m + 1$ (or fewer) edges. I will show that this can be done by a tuple multiplication of the form

$$d := d * a$$

expressed as follows in *SuperPascal*

<pre>
var a, b, d: matrix;
b := d; multiply(b, a, d)
</pre>

The all-pairs multiplication (Fig. 7.10) is similar to matrix multiplication. The function f computes the shortest alternative path from node i to node j. The algorithm uses two functions to compute the minimum and the sum of two reals. The sum function ensures that addition handles infinity (represented by a large constant) correctly.

The algorithm can be derived from Fig. 7.5 by the following substitutions in function f:

infinity	replaces	0.0
min	replaces	$+$
sum	replaces	$*$

From this analysis, I conclude that the all-pairs shortest path problem is solved by a sequence of all-pairs multiplications:

$$\begin{aligned} d^{(1)} &= a \\ d^{(2)} &= d^{(1)} \times a = a^2 \\ &\cdots \\ d^{(n-1)} &= d^{(n-2)} \times a = a^{n-1} \end{aligned}$$

The computation is defined by Fig. 7.11. The computing time is $O(n^4)$. For the graph in Fig. 7.8, the computation proceeds as follows:

$$d^{(1)} = \begin{bmatrix} 0 & 1 & 1 & \infty \\ \infty & 0 & 1 & \infty \\ \infty & \infty & 0 & 1 \\ 1 & \infty & \infty & 0 \end{bmatrix}$$

$$d^{(2)} = \begin{bmatrix} 0 & 1 & 1 & \infty \\ \infty & 0 & 1 & \infty \\ \infty & \infty & 0 & 1 \\ 1 & \infty & \infty & 0 \end{bmatrix} \times \begin{bmatrix} 0 & 1 & 1 & \infty \\ \infty & 0 & 1 & \infty \\ \infty & \infty & 0 & 1 \\ 1 & \infty & \infty & 0 \end{bmatrix} = \begin{bmatrix} 0 & 1 & 1 & 2 \\ \infty & 0 & 1 & 2 \\ 2 & \infty & 0 & 1 \\ 1 & 2 & 2 & 0 \end{bmatrix}$$

```
procedure multiply(var a, b, c: matrix);
var i, j: integer;

    function min(a, b: real): real;
    begin
      if a <= b then min := a
      else min := b
    end;

    function sum(a, b: real): real;
    begin
      if (a < infinity) and (b < infinity)
        then sum := a + b
        else sum := infinity
    end;

    function f(ai, bj: vector): real;
    var cij: real; k: integer;
    begin
      cij := infinity;
      for k := 1 to n do
        cij := min(cij, sum(ai[k], bj[k]));
      f := cij
    end;

begin
  for i := 1 to n do
    for j := 1 to n do
      c[i,j] := f(a[i], b[j])
end;
```

Figure 7.10: All-pairs multiplication.

```
procedure allpaths(var a, d: matrix);
var b: matrix; m: integer;
begin
    d := a;
    for m := 2 to n − 1 do
        begin
            b := d; multiply(b, a, d)
        end
end;
```

Figure 7.11: Slow all-paths algorithm.

$$
d^{(3)} = \begin{bmatrix} 0 & 1 & 1 & 2 \\ \infty & 0 & 1 & 2 \\ 2 & \infty & 0 & 1 \\ 1 & 2 & 2 & 0 \end{bmatrix} \times \begin{bmatrix} 0 & 1 & 1 & \infty \\ \infty & 0 & 1 & \infty \\ \infty & \infty & 0 & 1 \\ 1 & \infty & \infty & 0 \end{bmatrix} = \begin{bmatrix} 0 & 1 & 1 & 2 \\ 3 & 0 & 1 & 2 \\ 2 & 3 & 0 & 1 \\ 1 & 2 & 2 & 0 \end{bmatrix}
$$

If $n - 1$ is a power of two, you can reduce the run time considerably by *repeatedly squaring d*

$$
\begin{aligned}
d^{(1)} &= a^1 \\
d^{(2)} &= d^{(1)} \times d^{(1)} = a^2 \\
d^{(4)} &= d^{(2)} \times d^{(2)} = a^4
\end{aligned}
$$

and so on. The computing time is now $O(n^3 \log n)$.

Figure 7.12 defines the fast version of the shortest paths computation. The multiplication may be performed sequentially (Fig. 7.10) or in parallel (Figs. 7.6 and 7.7).

It is impossible to find finite shortest paths with more than $n - 1$ edges. They do not exist! Consequently, the distance matrix remains unchanged when the exponent of a exceeds $n - 1$:

$$
a^{n-1} = a^n = a^{n+1} \cdots
$$

This property ensures that the fast algorithm also works when $n - 1$ is not a power of two.

For pedagogical reasons, I have assumed that every edge has length 1. However, the algorithm assumes only that the elements of the adjacency

```
procedure allpaths(var a, d: matrix);
var m: integer;

    procedure square(var a: matrix);
    var b, c: matrix;
    begin
      c := a; b := a;
      multiply(c, b, a)
    end;

begin
  d := a; m := 1;
  while m < n − 1 do
    begin square(d); m := 2∗m end
end;
```

Figure 7.12: Fast all-paths algorithms.

matrix are reals. So, the algorithm also works for a directed, *weighted graph*, where each edge has a weight (or "length") of type real. Weights may even be *negative*, as long as the graph has no cycles of negative lengths. If this constraint is violated, a cyclic path becomes shorter every time it is traversed. Consequently, the shortest paths to all nodes which can be reached from a negative cycle are minus infinity!

7.6   Performance

A multiplication pipeline divides the computational load evenly among the available processors. During a matrix multiplication, n rows and n columns pass through every node except the last one. (The latter inputs n rows and n columns, but outputs n rows only.)

On a pipeline with p processors, the *parallel run time* of a matrix multiplication is

$$T_p = an^3/p + bn^2$$

where a and b are system-dependent constants for computation and communication, respectively.

If the multiplication runs on a single processor (where $p = 1$), the *sequential run time* is

$$T_1 = an^3 + bn^2$$

The *efficiency* of the parallel computation is

$$E_p = T_1/(pT_p)$$

which can be rewritten as follows:

$$E_p = \frac{an + b}{an + bp}$$

Although the computational load is balanced, the communication overhead reduces the efficiency. However, the communication overhead is negligible if

$$n/p \gg b/a$$

that is, if the problem size n is large compared to the pipe length p.

I reprogrammed the pipeline in occam and ran it on a Computing Surface with T800 transputers using 64-bit arithmetic. Measurements show that

$$a = 3.9\mu s \qquad b = 20\mu s$$

Table 7.1 shows measured (and predicted) run times of matrix multiplication. In each experiment, the ratio $n/p = 40$. By *scaling* the problem size n in proportion to the computer size p, the parallel computation maintains an almost constant efficiency of 0.89 to 0.91.

Each node holds $2n/p$ rows of $8n$ bytes each. The *memory requirement* per node M_p is proportional to the pipe length p since

$$M_p = 16n^2/p = 25600p \text{ bytes} \qquad \text{for } n/p = 40$$

The Computing Surface has 1 Mbyte of memory per transputer. This limits the pipeline to a maximum of 35 transputers.

The shortest paths pipeline repeatedly performs multiplication with similar efficiency.

Table 7.1: Scaled problem size.

p	n	T_p (s)		E_p (est)	M_p (bytes)
1	40	0.3	(0.3)	1.00	25600
5	200	6.9	(7.0)	0.91	128000
10	400	27.7	(28.2)	0.90	256000
20	800	112.2	(112.6)	0.89	512000
30	1200	254.6	(253.4)	0.89	768000
35	1400	345.2	(345.0)	0.89	896000

7.7   Final Remarks

I have presented a pipeline algorithm for a programming paradigm known as tuple multiplication. From this algorithm, I have derived pipelines for matrix multiplication and the all-pairs shortest paths problem by substitution of data types and functions.

The predicted efficiency of the parallel matrix multiplication has been confirmed by experiments on a Computing Surface.

Part IV

THE DIVIDE AND CONQUER PARADIGM

Chapter 8

The Fast Fourier Transform

8.1   Introduction

This chapter explains one of the most important algorithms in science and technology: the *discrete Fourier transform* (*DFT*), which has numerous applications in signal and image processing.

After a brief summary of the *continuous Fourier transform*, I define the *DFT*. A straightforward *DFT* computation for n sampled points takes $O(n^2)$ time. The *DFT* is illustrated by examples and a *SuperPascal* algorithm.

The *fast Fourier transform* (*FFT*) computes the *DFT* in $O(n \log n)$ time using the divide-and-conquer paradigm. I explain the *FFT* and develop recursive and iterative *FFT* algorithms in *SuperPascal*.

The *FFT* has a long history [Cooley 1967]. It became widely known when James Cooley and John Tukey rediscovered it in 1965 [Cooley 1965]. The vast literature on the *FFT* and its applications includes Brigham [1974], Macnaghten [1977], and Press [1989].

I assume that you are familiar with elementary calculus.

8.2   Mathematical Background

I begin by summarizing the theory of the *Fourier transform* but will only attempt to make the results plausible. You will find a rigorous analysis in Courant [1989].

The Fourier Series

Consider a physical process that can be described by a continuous (or piece-wise continuous) function of time. I will call this function a *signal.*

A *periodic signal* $a(t)$ repeats itself after a period T

$$a(t + T) = a(t) \qquad \text{for all } t$$

as illustrated by Fig. 8.1.

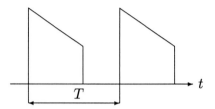

Figure 8.1: A periodic signal.

Any periodic signal $a(t)$ that we ordinarily encounter in physics or engineering can be written as a *Fourier series*—the sum of an infinite number of cosine and sine waves.

Since the algebra of complex exponentials is much simpler than that of cosines and sines, it is convenient to express the Fourier series as the sum of *complex harmonics*

$$a(t) = \sum_{k=-\infty}^{\infty} c_k e^{-i2\pi f_k t} \tag{8.1}$$

where

$$e^{\pm i2\pi f_k t} = \cos(2\pi f_k t) \pm i \sin(2\pi f_k t)$$

Here $e = 2.71828\ldots$ is the base of the natural logarithm, and $i = \sqrt{-1}$ is the imaginary unit.

The discrete *frequencies*

$$f_k = k/T \qquad \text{for } k = 0, \pm 1, \pm 2, \ldots$$

are multiples of the lowest frequency $1/T$.

The *Fourier coefficients* c_k are generally complex numbers. To find a particular coefficient c_j, you multiply both sides of (8.1) by

$$e^{i2\pi f_j t}$$

and average both sides over one period.

The right side is the sum of averages of the form

$$\frac{1}{T} \int_{-T/2}^{T/2} c_k e^{i2\pi(f_j - f_k)t} dt$$

For $k = j$, the exponential is 1 and the corresponding term has the value c_j. For any other k, the average value of a harmonic wave over $j - k$ periods is zero.

Consequently,

$$c_j = \frac{1}{T} \int_{-T/2}^{T/2} a(t) e^{i2\pi f_j t} dt \qquad (8.2)$$

The Fourier Transform

A *pulse* is a signal of finite duration as shown in Fig. 8.2.

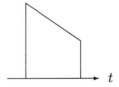

Figure 8.2: A nonperiodic signal.

How do you handle such a *nonperiodic signal?* The trick is to pretend that a pulse is periodic as shown in Fig. 8.1 and then let the period T approach infinity without changing the shape and width of the pulse.

For a periodic signal, the frequency increment is

$$\Delta f = 1/T$$

As $T \to \infty$ and $\Delta f \to 0$, you obtain a *continuous spectrum* of frequencies f.

To help make the transition towards infinity, I will use (8.2) to express a Fourier coefficient c_k as the product of a function value $b(f_k)$ and the frequency increment Δf:

$$c_k = b(f_k)\Delta f$$

Here $b(f_k)$ is the value of a function $b(f)$ for the discrete frequency $f = f_k$. From (8.2), it follows that the appropriate function is

$$b(f) = \int_{-T/2}^{T/2} a(t)a^{i2\pi ft}dt$$

The Fourier series (8.1) can now be expressed as

$$a(t) = \sum_{k=-\infty}^{\infty} b(f_k)e^{-i2\pi f_k t}\Delta f$$

As $T \to \infty$, you obtain the *Fourier transform*

$$b(f) = \int_{-\infty}^{\infty} a(t)e^{i2\pi ft}dt \tag{8.3}$$

which defines the frequency *spectrum* $b(f)$ of the signal $a(t)$.
   The *inverse transform*

$$a(t) = \int_{-\infty}^{\infty} b(f)e^{-i2\pi ft}df \tag{8.4}$$

defines the signal $a(t)$ as a function of its spectrum [Press 1989].

8.3   The Discrete Fourier Transform

The Fourier transform defines the frequency components of a *continuous* signal. When a signal is sampled and analyzed on a computer, you must use the corresponding *discrete Fourier transform* (*DFT*).

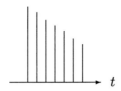

Figure 8.3: A sampled signal.

Definition

Figure 8.3 shows a signal that is *sampled* at n discrete points with intervals of fixed length Δt. I assume that the signal has been sampled *competently*, as explained by Brigham [1974].

The n sampled points are kept in an array

$$a = [\; a_0 \; a_1 \cdots a_{n-1} \;]$$

where

$$a_k = a(t_k) \quad \text{and} \quad t_k = k\Delta t \quad \text{for } k = 0..n{-}1$$

I will use the sampled points to compute an approximation to the Fourier transform $b(f)$ at n discrete points. The discrete Fourier transform will be stored in another array

$$b = [\; b_0 \; b_1 \cdots b_{n-1} \;]$$

where

$$b_j = b(f_j) \quad \text{and} \quad f_j = \frac{j}{n\Delta t} \quad \text{for } j = 0..n{-}1$$

Each discrete frequency f_j is a multiple of f_1, the inverse of the total sampling time $n\Delta t$.

The remaining step is to approximate the integral in (8.3) by a discrete sum:

$$b_j = \sum_{k=0}^{n-1} a(t_k)e^{i2\pi f_j t_k}\Delta t$$

Without loss of generality, I assume that $\Delta t = 1$ and rewrite the sum as

$$b_j = \sum_{k=0}^{n-1} a_k e^{i2\pi jk/n} \tag{8.5}$$

This equation can be simplified by introducing the complex number

$$w(n) = e^{i2\pi/n} = \cos(2\pi/n) + i\sin(2\pi/n) \tag{8.6}$$

$w(n)$ is an nth root of unity in the complex plane, since

$$w(n)^n = e^{i2\pi} = 1$$

When the value of n is obvious from the context, I will write w instead of $w(n)$.

Examples:

$$
\begin{aligned}
w(1) &= e^{i2\pi} &= 1 \\
w(2) &= e^{i\pi} &= -1 \\
w(4) &= e^{i\pi/2} &= i
\end{aligned}
$$

Using $w(n)$, (8.5) can be expressed as follows [Press 1989]:

$$b_j = \sum_{k=0}^{n-1} a_k w(n)^{jk} \qquad \text{for } j = 0..n-1 \tag{8.7}$$

This formula shows that the *DFT* of n points is the product

$$b = F(n)a^T$$

of a matrix $F(n)$ and a transposed vector a^T.

The elements of the *Fourier matrix $F(n)$* are powers of $w(n)$:

$$
F(n) = \begin{bmatrix}
1 & 1 & 1 & \cdots & 1 \\
1 & w & w^2 & \cdots & w^{n-1} \\
1 & w^2 & w^4 & \cdots & w^{2(n-1)} \\
\cdots & \cdots & \cdots & \cdots & \cdots \\
1 & w^{n-1} & w^{2(n-1)} & \cdots & w^{(n-1)^2}
\end{bmatrix}
$$

The elements of the *signal vector* a^T are the signal points

$$a^T = \begin{bmatrix} a_0 \\ a_1 \\ a_2 \\ \ldots \\ a_{n-1} \end{bmatrix}$$

Example:

The following example shows that a single point a_0 is its own *DFT*.

$$F(1) = \begin{bmatrix} 1 \end{bmatrix}$$

$$a^T = \begin{bmatrix} a_0 \end{bmatrix}$$

$$b^T = \begin{bmatrix} a_0 \end{bmatrix}$$

Example:

$$F(2) = \begin{bmatrix} 1 & 1 \\ 1 & -1 \end{bmatrix}$$

$$a^T = \begin{bmatrix} a_0 \\ a_1 \end{bmatrix}$$

$$b^T = \begin{bmatrix} a_0 + a_1 \\ a_0 - a_1 \end{bmatrix}$$

Example:

$$F(4) = \begin{bmatrix} 1 & 1 & 1 & 1 \\ 1 & i & -1 & -i \\ 1 & -1 & 1 & -1 \\ 1 & -i & -1 & i \end{bmatrix}$$

$$a^T = \begin{bmatrix} a_0 \\ a_1 \\ a_2 \\ a_3 \end{bmatrix}$$

$$b^T = \begin{bmatrix} a_0 + a_2 + (a_1 + a_3) \\ a_0 - a_2 + i(a_1 - a_3) \\ a_0 + a_2 - (a_1 + a_3) \\ a_0 - a_2 - i(a_1 - a_3) \end{bmatrix}$$

The pairwise similarity of *DFT* points is no coincidence. It is the main idea behind the fast Fourier transform, which will be discussed later.

A numerical example may be helpful. The *DFT* of the four points

$$a^T = \begin{bmatrix} 0.07 \\ 0.91 \\ 0.32 \\ 0.29 \end{bmatrix}$$

is

$$b^T = \begin{bmatrix} 1.59 \\ -0.25 + i0.62 \\ -0.81 \\ -0.25 - i0.62 \end{bmatrix}$$

The Iterative DFT

Figure 8.4 defines an *iterative DFT* algorithm based on (8.7). The local variables include

$$v \quad \text{denoting} \quad 2\pi j/n$$
$$wj \quad \text{denoting} \quad w^j = \cos(v) + i\sin(v)$$
$$wjk \quad \text{denoting} \quad w^{jk} = (w^j)^k$$

In the mathematical definition of the *DFT*, the complex numbers have subscripts from 0 to $n-1$. However, in algorithms it is more convenient to use array indices from 1 to n (as in Fig. 8.4).

```
type
    complex = record re, im: real end;
    table = array [1..n] of complex;

procedure dft(var a: table);
const pi = 3.1415926536;
var b: table; j, k: integer;
    v: real; wj, wjk: complex;
begin
    for j := 1 to n do
        begin
            v := 2.0*pi*(j − 1)/n;
            wj := pair(cos(v), sin(v));
            wjk := pair(1, 0);
            b[j] := pair(0, 0);
            for k := 1 to n do
                begin
                    b[j] := sum(b[j], product(a[k], wjk));
                    wjk := product(wjk, wj)
                end
        end;
    a := b
end;
```

Figure 8.4: Discrete Fourier transform.

The computation of powers of *wj* by complex multiplication may accumulate rounding errors. So, it is a good idea to use double-precision arithmetic for the *DFT*.

The *DFT* algorithm is written in *SuperPascal*, which extends Pascal with structured function types. The algorithm uses some of the functions listed in Table 8.1 and defined in the Appendix. The parameters a and b are complex numbers, while a_{re} and a_{im} are reals. The functions are of type *complex*.

The run time of the iterative *DFT* is $O(n^2)$.

Table 8.1: Complex functions.

Function	Result
pair(a_{re}, a_{im})	$a_{re} + ia_{im}$
sum(a, b)	$a + b$
difference(a, b)	$a - b$
product(a, b)	$a * b$

8.4 The Fast Fourier Transform

If n is a power of two, the *DFT* can be computed by a much faster algorithm called the *fast Fourier transform* (*FFT*). The *FFT* runs in $O(n\log n)$ time.

Definition

You split the n sampled points into *even* and *odd* numbered points:

$$a'' = [\ a_0\ a_2 \ldots a_{n-2}\ ]$$

$$a' = [\ a_1\ a_3 \ldots a_{n-1}\ ]$$

The *DFT*s of a' and a'' can be computed separately using the $(n/2)$th root of unity

$$w(n/2) = e^{i4\pi/n} = (e^{i2\pi/n})^2 = w(n)^2$$

The equations will look less cluttered if I use the abbreviations

$$m = n/2 \qquad u = w(n/2) \qquad w = w(n)$$

According to (8.7), the *DFT* of a' is

$$b'_j = a_1 + a_3 u^j + a_5 u^{2j} + \cdots + a_{n-1} u^{(m-1)j}$$

which can be rewritten as

$$b'_j = a_1 + a_3 w^{2j} + a_5 w^{4j} + \cdots + a_{n-1} w^{(n-2)j} \qquad (8.8)$$

for $j = 0..m-1$.

Similarly, the *DFT* of a'' is

$$b_j'' = a_0 + a_2 w^{2j} + a_4 w^{4j} + \cdots + a_{n-2} w^{(n-2)j} \qquad (8.9)$$

for $j = 0..m-1$.

The *DFT* of all n points is

$$
\begin{aligned}
b_j \;=\;& a_0 \;+\; a_2 w^{2j} + \cdots + a_{n-2} w^{(n-2)j} \\
+\;& a_1 w^j + a_3 w^{3j} + \cdots + a_{n-1} w^{(n-1)j}
\end{aligned} \qquad (8.10)
$$

for $j = 0..n-1$. I have rearranged the terms by writing the even ones on the first line and the odd ones below.

By combining (8.8)–(8.10), you obtain a method of computing the first $n/2$ points of the complete *DFT* from the *DFT*s of the even and odd points:

$$b_j = b_j'' + w^j b_j' \qquad \text{for } j = 0..m-1 \qquad (8.11)$$

To compute the other half of the *DFT*, you need the following result:

$$w^m = (e^{i2\pi/n})^{n/2} = e^{i\pi} = -1$$

Consequently,

$$w^{k(j+m)} = (-1)^k w^{kj} \qquad (8.12)$$

If you replace j by $j+m$ in (8.10) and use (8.12), you get

$$
\begin{aligned}
b_{j+m} \;=\;& a_0 \;+\; a_2 w^{2j} + \cdots + a_{n-2} w^{(n-2)j} \\
-\;& a_1 w^j - a_3 w^{3j} - \cdots - a_{n-1} w^{(n-1)j}
\end{aligned}
$$

In short,

$$b_{j+m} = b_j'' - w^j b_j' \qquad \text{for } j = 0..m-1 \qquad (8.13)$$

The computational idea behind the *FFT* is the combination of (8.11) and (8.13):

$$
\begin{aligned}
b_j \;=\;& b_j'' + w^j b_j' \qquad \text{for } j = 0..m-1 \\
b_{j+m} \;=\;& b_j'' - w^j b_j' \qquad \text{where } m = n/2
\end{aligned} \qquad (8.14)
$$

Equation (8.14) shows that the *FFT b* of n points can be obtained by combining the *FFTs*, b'' and b', of the even and odd numbered points.

Since $n/2$ is also a power of two, you can use the same formula to compute b'' and b'. The *FFT* applies this rule recursively until it reaches a level that involves the transforms of single points only.

Consider the *FFT* of four points. First, you split the samples into two halves consisting of the even and odd numbered points, respectively. Each half is then split into two samples of one point each. Figure 8.5 illustrates the *recursive splitting* of the computation into smaller and smaller *FFTs*.

$$
\begin{array}{ccccc}
 & & & & \nearrow \quad \text{FFT}([a_0]) \\
 & & \text{FFT}([a_0 \ a_2]) & & \\
 & \nearrow & & \searrow \quad \text{FFT}([a_2]) & \\
\text{FFT}([a_0 \ a_1 \ a_2 \ a_3]) & & & & \\
 & \searrow & & \nearrow \quad \text{FFT}([a_1]) & \\
 & & \text{FFT}([a_1 \ a_3]) & & \\
 & & & & \searrow \quad \text{FFT}([a_3])
\end{array}
$$

Figure 8.5: Splitting the samples.

Since the transform of a single point is the point itself, the recursion stops when the *FFTs* are of length 1. The computation then combines four *FFTs* of length 1 into two *FFTs* of length 2 and, finally, two *FFTs* of length 2 into a single one of length 4. Figure 8.6 illustrates the *recursive combination* of *FFTs*.

a_0	$\searrow$	$a_0 + a_2$		$a_0 + a_2 + (a_1 + a_3)$
a_2	$\nearrow$	$a_0 - a_2$	$\searrow$	$a_0 - a_2 + i(a_1 - a_3)$
a_1	$\searrow$	$a_1 + a_3$	$\nearrow$	$a_0 + a_2 - (a_1 + a_3)$
a_3	$\nearrow$	$a_1 - a_3$		$a_0 - a_2 - i(a_1 - a_3)$

Figure 8.6: Combining the transforms.

Before writing an *FFT* algorithm, I will discuss several refinements.

In-Place Computation

It is possible to compute the *FFT* in place in a single array. The computation replaces the signal points by the corresponding transform.

In the splitting phase, the *FFT* computation operates on smaller and smaller slices of the same array. An array slice is split into halves by moving the even and odd numbered points to the upper and lower halves, respectively, as shown in Fig. 8.7.

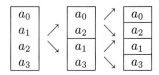

Figure 8.7: In-place splitting.

The transforms are then combined in place as shown in Fig. 8.6.

Let me for the moment just *assume* that it is possible to perform the *splitting* in place. You can then *prove* by induction that in-place *combination* is possible:

1. *Base step.* The *FFT* of a single point can be computed in place by leaving the point unchanged.

2. *Induction step.* Without loss of generality, I consider a slice of elements with indices from 0 to $n-1$. After splitting the slice into two halves, I assume that it is possible to compute the two *FFT*s in place. I will now show that this hypothesis also makes it possible to compute the combined *FFT* in place.

   Figure 8.8 shows the jth elements, b''_j and b'_j, of the left and right *FFT*s. Their indices are j and $j+m$, respectively.

   According to (8.14), b''_j and b'_j are used once only to compute elements b_j and b_{j+m} of the combined *FFT*. Since the two "output" elements have the same array indices as the "input" elements, they can replace them in the array.

Later, I will return to the problem of splitting the array.

b_j''	b_j'

b_j	b_{j+m}

0   j $j+m$ $n-1$

Figure 8.8: FFT elements.

The Recursive FFT

Figure 8.9 defines a recursive, in-place computation of the *FFT* in a single array *a*.

```
procedure fft(var a: table;
    first, last: integer);
var middle: integer;
begin
  if first < last then
    begin
      split(a, first, last, middle);
      fft(a, first, middle);
      fft(a, middle + 1, last);
      combine(a, first, last)
    end
end;
```

Figure 8.9: Recursive FFT.

Each activation of the procedure computes the *FFT* of a *slice* of the array *a*. The slice is defined by the indices of its *first* and *last* elements, where

$$1 \leq \text{first} \leq \text{last} \leq n$$

The procedure statement

$$\text{fft}(a, 1, n)$$

denotes the *FFT* computation involving all n points.

If an array slice holds one point only, it is left unchanged since the point is its own transform. Otherwise, the computation splits the slice into two halves, computes the *FFT* of each half separately, and combines them into a single *FFT*. The two *halves* have indices in the ranges

$$\text{first..middle} \qquad \text{middle+1..last}$$

respectively.

An array slice can be split into two halves using a local array b to rearrange the samples into even and odd numbered points. The *split* algorithm shown in Fig. 8.10 clearly does *not* define an in-place computation. However, it only serves as a pedagogical tool to explain the first version of the *fft* algorithm. It will shortly be replaced by a preprocessing step that takes place before the *FFT* computation.

```
procedure split(var a: table;
    first, last: integer;
    var middle: integer);
var even, half, j, size: integer;
    b: table;
begin
    middle := (first + last) div 2;
    size := last − first + 1;
    half := size div 2;
    for j := 1 to half do
       begin
          even := first + 2*(j − 1);
          b[j] := a[even];
          b[j + half] := a[even + 1]
       end;
    for j := 1 to size do
       a[first + j − 1] := b[j]
end;
```

Figure 8.10: Split algorithm.

The *combination* of two *FFTs* into one, based on (8.6) and (8.14), is defined by Fig. 8.11.

```
procedure combine(var a: table;
   first, last: integer);
const pi = 3.1415926536;
var even, half, odd, j: integer;
   w, wj, x: complex;
begin
   half := (last − first + 1) div 2;
   w := pair(cos(pi/half), sin(pi/half));
   wj := pair(1, 0);
   for j := 0 to half − 1 do
     begin
       even := first + j;
       odd := even + half;
       x := product(wj, a[odd]);
       a[odd] := difference(a[even], x);
       a[even] := sum(a[even], x);
       wj := product(wj, w)
     end
end;
```

Figure 8.11: Combine algorithm.

Initial Permutation

If you compare the left and right sides of Fig. 8.7, you will see that the net effect of recursive splitting is to permute the sampled points before the *FFT*s are combined. This suggests that splitting can be replaced by a single *permutation* of the array before the *FFT* combinations begin (Fig. 8.12).

Figure 8.13 defines the *simplified FFT* which is computed after the initial permutation.

How should you permute the array? You can get a hint from Fig. 8.14, which shows the end result of splitting eight sampled points in place.

In an array of n sampled points, the initial index of point a_j is j. The final index of a_j after the permutation is denoted

```
procedure dft(var a: table);
begin
  permute(a);
  fft(a, 1, n)
end;
```

Figure 8.12: Revised Fourier transform.

```
procedure fft(var a: table;
    first, last: integer);
var middle: integer;
begin
  if first < last then
    begin
      middle := (first + last) div 2;
      fft(a, first, middle);
      fft(a, middle + 1, last);
      combine(a, first, last)
    end
end;
```

Figure 8.13: Simplified FFT.

$$\text{index}(j,n) \qquad \text{for } j = 0..n-1$$

Table 8.2 shows the initial and final indices of eight points in decimal (and binary) form. The table suggests that the final index of a sampled

a_0	a_4	a_2	a_6	a_1	a_5	a_3	a_7
0	1	2	3	4	5	6	7

Figure 8.14: A permuted array.

point is obtained by reversing the order of the bits in the initial index:

$$\text{index}(j, n) = \text{reverse}(j, n) \qquad \text{for } j = 0..n-1 \qquad (8.15)$$

Table 8.2: Decimal and binary indices.

j	$\text{index}(j, 8)$
0 (000)	0 (000)
1 (001)	4 (100)
2 (010)	2 (010)
3 (011)	6 (110)
4 (100)	1 (001)
5 (101)	5 (101)
6 (110)	3 (011)
7 (111)	7 (111)

The reverse of a binary number consists of the last bit followed by the rest of the bits (if any) in reverse order:

$$
\begin{aligned}
\text{reverse}(0, 1) &= 0 \\
\text{reverse}(1, 1) &= 1 \\
\text{reverse}(2k, n) &= \text{reverse}(k, n/2) \\
\text{reverse}(2k+1, n) &= n/2 + \text{reverse}(k, n/2)
\end{aligned}
$$

These rules define a recursive function (Fig. 8.15).

I will prove (8.15) by induction:

1. *Base step.* In an array of size 1, the single point with index 0 is already correctly placed:

$$\text{index}(0,1) = 0 = \text{reverse}(0,1)$$

2. *Induction step.* I assume that (8.15) holds for arrays of size $n/2$ and will prove that it also holds for arrays of size n. Consider a sampled point a_j when an array of size n is split into two halves:

```
function reverse(j, n: integer): integer;
var half: integer;
begin
  if n = 1 then reverse := j
  else
    begin
      half := n div 2;
      reverse := (j mod 2)*half
                 + reverse(j div 2, half)
    end
end;
```

Figure 8.15: Bit reversal.

(a) If j is even, say $j = 2k$, a_j is placed in the left half with index k. The left half is then split in half. In formal terms,

$$\begin{aligned} \text{index}(2k, n) &= \text{index}(k, n/2) \\ &= \text{reverse}(k, n/2) \\ &= \text{reverse}(2k, n) \end{aligned}$$

(b) If j is odd, say $j = 2k+1$, a_j is placed in the right half with index $n/2 + k$. The right half is then split again. Consequently,

$$\begin{aligned} \text{index}(2k + 1, n) &= n/2 + \text{index}(k, n/2) \\ &= n/2 + \text{reverse}(k, n/2) \\ &= \text{reverse}(2k + 1, n) \end{aligned}$$

Bit reversal is obviously symmetric:

$$j = \text{reverse}(k, n) \quad \equiv \quad k = \text{reverse}(j, n)$$

So, the recursive splitting interchanges $a[j]$ and $a[k]$. This insight leads to the *permutation* algorithm shown in Fig. 8.16. The condition $j < k$ prevents a pair of points from being swapped twice. It also eliminates superfluous swapping when an index and its reverse are the same.

```
    procedure permute(var a: table);
    var j, k: integer; aj: complex;
    begin
      for j := 1 to n do
        begin
          k := reverse(j−1,n) + 1;
          if j < k then
            begin
              aj := a[j];
              a[j] := a[k];
              a[k] := aj
            end
        end
    end;
```

Figure 8.16: Initial permutation.

Since every index is reversed in time $O(\log n)$, the permutation takes $O(n\log n)$ time.

The *recursive FFT* consists of the algorithms shown in Figs. 8.11–13 and 8.15–16.

Fast Permutation

The *divide-and-conquer* nature of the *FFT* makes it well-suited for parallel computation [Fox 1988; Brinch Hansen 1991d and Chap. 9]. However, if a parallel *FFT* is preceded by a sequential $O(n\log n)$ permutation, the combination is still an $O(n\log n)$ algorithm.

Fortunately, it is possible to permute n points in $O(n)$ time. A fast permutation begins by constructing a map of size n that holds the bit-reversed values of the indices $0..n-1$.

I will illustrate the computational pattern for an array of eight points (see Table 8.2):

The first element of the permutation map is

$$rev_0 = 0$$

The next element is

$$\mathrm{rev}_1 = \mathrm{rev}_0 + 4 = 4$$

The next two elements are

$$\mathrm{rev}_2 = \mathrm{rev}_0 + 2 = 2$$
$$\mathrm{rev}_3 = \mathrm{rev}_1 + 2 = 6$$

The last four elements are

$$\mathrm{rev}_4 = \mathrm{rev}_0 + 1 = 1$$
$$\mathrm{rev}_5 = \mathrm{rev}_1 + 1 = 5$$
$$\mathrm{rev}_6 = \mathrm{rev}_2 + 1 = 3$$
$$\mathrm{rev}_7 = \mathrm{rev}_3 + 1 = 7$$

In each step, the length of the map is doubled by adding a power of two to each of the previous elements. The increment is halved after each step. A map of size n is constructed in $O(n)$ time, since

$$1 + 2 + 4 + \cdots + n/2 = n - 1$$

This method was suggested by Tapas Som.

The formal basis for the method is the rule

$$
\begin{aligned}
\mathrm{reverse}(j + 2^k, n) &= \mathrm{reverse}(j, n) + 2^{\log n - 1 - k} \\
&= \mathrm{reverse}(j, n) + n/2^{k+1}
\end{aligned}
$$

for $k = 0..\log n - 1$ and $j = 0..2^k - 1$. The *fast permutation* constructs a map according to this rule and uses it to swap pairs of points in a signal array of size n in $O(n)$ time (Fig. 8.17).

If a complex number is represented by two 64-bit reals and an index by a 32-bit integer, the permutation map increases the memory requirement by 25%.

The recursive *FFT* with fast permutation is defined by the algorithms shown in Figs. 8.11–13 and 8.17.

There are *FFT* algorithms that work when n is not a power of two. However, Press [1989] recommends using the *FFT* only when n is a power of two, if necessary by padding the data with zeros up to the next power of two.

```
procedure permute(var a: table);
type map = array [1..n] of integer;
var rev: map; half, incr, size,
   j, k: integer; aj: complex;
begin
  rev[1] := 1;
  half := n div 2;
  size := 1;
  while size <= half do
    begin
      incr := half div size;
      for j := 1 to size do
        rev[j + size] := rev[j] + incr;
      size := 2*size
    end;
  for j := 1 to n do
    begin
      k := rev[j];
      if j < k then
        begin
          aj := a[j];
          a[j] := a[k];
          a[k] := aj
        end
    end
end;
```

Figure 8.17: Fast permutation.

Iterative FFT

The *FFT* computation can also be defined by an iterative algorithm that transforms the entire array $\log n$ times. The first transformation combines n slices of size 1 into $n/2$ slices of size 2. The second transformation combines $n/2$ slices of size 2 into $n/4$ slices of size 4, and so on. The last transformation combines two slices of size $n/2$ into a single slice of size n (Fig. 8.18).

```
        procedure fft(var a: table;
           first, last: integer);
        var size, k, m: integer;
        begin
          m := last − first + 1;
          size := 2;
          while size <= m do
            begin
              k := first + size − 1;
              while k <= last do
                begin
                  combine(a, k − size + 1, k);
                  k := k + size
                end;
              size := 2*size
            end
        end;
```

Figure 8.18: Iterative FFT.

The Appendix includes the complete iterative *FFT*, which combines the algorithms in Figs. 8.11–12 and 8.17–18.

8.5   Final Remarks

I have explained the fast Fourier transform *(FFT)* and have illustrated the algorithm by examples and *SuperPascal* algorithms. The *FFT* is yet another example of a fundamental computation with a subtle theory and a short algorithm.

8.6   Appendix: Complete Algorithm

The complete *iterative FFT* with *fast permutation* is written in *SuperPascal*:

```
type
  complex = record re, im: real end;
```

```
    table = array [1..n] of complex;

procedure dft(var a: table);

    procedure permute(var a: table);
    type map = array [1..n] of integer;
    var rev: map; half, incr, size,
       j, k: integer; aj: complex;
    begin
       rev[1] := 1;
       half := n div 2;
       size := 1;
       while size <= half do
          begin
             incr := half div size;
             for j := 1 to size do
                rev[j + size] := rev[j] + incr;
             size := 2*size
          end;
       for j := 1 to n do
          begin
             k := rev[j];
             if j < k then
                begin
                   aj := a[j];
                   a[j] := a[k];
                   a[k] := aj
                end
          end
    end;

    procedure combine(var a: table;
       first, last: integer);
    const pi = 3.1415926536;
    var even, half, odd, j: integer;
       w, wj, x: complex;
    begin
```

```
      half := (last − first + 1) div 2;
      w := pair(cos(pi/half), sin(pi/half));
      wj := pair(1, 0);
      for j := 0 to half − 1 do
        begin
          even := first + j;
          odd := even + half;
          x := product(wj, a[odd]);
          a[odd] := difference(a[even], x);
          a[even] := sum(a[even], x);
          wj := product(wj, w)
        end
    end;


  procedure fft(var a: table;
      first, last: integer);
  var size, k, m: integer;
  begin
    m := last − first + 1;
    size := 2;
    while size <= m do
      begin
        k := first + size − 1;
        while k <= last do
          begin
            combine(a, k − size + 1, k);
            k := k + size
          end;
        size := 2*size
      end
  end;

begin
  permute(a);
  fft(a, 1, n)
end;
```

The following *SuperPascal* functions implement the *complex arithmetic* used by the *FFT* algorithm:

```
type complex = record re, im: real end;

function pair(re, im: real): complex;
var a: complex;
begin
   a.re := re; a.im := im;
   pair := a
end;

function sum(a, b: complex): complex;
begin
   a.re := a.re + b.re;
   a.im := a.im + b.im;
   sum := a
end;

function difference(a, b: complex): complex;
begin
   a.re := a.re − b.re;
   a.im := a.im − b.im;
   difference := a
end;

function product(a, b: complex): complex;
var c: complex;
begin
   c.re := a.re*b.re − a.im*b.im;
   c.im := a.re*b.im + a.im*b.re;
   product := c
end;
```

Chapter 9

Parallel Divide and Conquer

9.1 Introduction

In this chapter, I consider the *divide and conquer* paradigm for a parallel *tree machine* with distributed memory.

Divide and conquer is an elegant method for solving a problem: You divide the problem into smaller problems of the same kind, solve the smaller problems separately, and combine the partial results into a complete solution. The method is used recursively to split the problem into smaller and smaller problems until you reach a point where each problem is easy to solve.

This beautiful concept has led to fast sequential algorithms for sorting [Hoare 1961], Fourier transforms [Cooley 1965], matrix multiplication [Strassen 1969], spatial proximity [Bentley 1976], convex hulls [Eddy 1977], and *n*-body simulation [Barnes 1986].

Parallelism is a mechanism for splitting larger computations into smaller ones that can be performed simultaneously. For multicomputers, divide and conquer algorithms already exist for sorting, fast Fourier transforms, and matrix multiplication [Fox 1988].

I am more interested in the *programming methodology* of multicomputers than in solving specific problems. With this emphasis in mind, I develop a generic divide and conquer algorithm for a tree machine. From the generic algorithm, I derive balanced, parallel versions of *quicksort* and the *fast Fourier transform* by substitution of data types, variables, and sequential statements. The performance of these algorithms is analyzed and measured on a *Computing Surface* with 31 transputers configured as a tree machine.

9.2   Sequential Paradigm

Since I am interested in principles rather than detail, I concentrate on divide
and conquer algorithms with four simple properties:

1. A problem of size n and its solution are both defined by an array of n
   elements.

2. A problem of size 1 is its own solution.

3. A larger problem is solved by splitting it into halves, which are solved
   separately.

4. A problem is solved by an in-place computation that replaces the elements of a single array by the corresponding solution without using
   additional arrays.

I begin by writing a *sequential divide and conquer* algorithm in the programming language Pascal (Fig. 9.1). A complete problem and its solution
are defined by an array of n elements of some type T. The procedure generally solves a subproblem in a *slice* of the array a

$$a[first..last]$$

where

$$1 \leq first \leq last \leq n$$

A slice with one element only is left unchanged. A larger slice is *split*
into two smaller slices

$$a[first..middle] \qquad a[middle+1..last]$$

where

$$1 \leq first \leq middle < last \leq n$$

The subproblems are solved by *recursive* activations of the solution procedure, and the partial results are then *combined* into a single solution to the
original problem.

A complete problem is solved by transforming all the elements of an array
a of size n:

```
       type table = array [1..n] of T;

       procedure solve(var a: table;
         first, last: integer);
       var middle: integer;
       begin
         if first < last then
           begin
             split(a, first, last, middle);
             solve(a, first, middle);
             solve(a, middle + 1, last);
             combine(a, first, last, middle)
           end
       end;
```

Figure 9.1: Divide and conquer algorithm.

$$\text{solve}(a, 1, n)$$

The class of divide and conquer algorithms that I am considering is defined by Fig. 9.1. The procedures for splitting problems and combining solutions depend on the nature of a specific application, such as sorting or Fourier transformation. I assume that *split* and *combine* define *in-place* transformations of a single array slice.

9.3 Parallel Paradigm

The simplest parallel computer for divide and conquer computation is a *binary tree* of *processors* connected by communication *channels*. In Fig. 9.2, the processors and channels are shown as nodes and edges, respectively. The nodes at the top are the *leaves* of the tree. The single node at the bottom is the *main root*. Each node in the middle is the *root* of a *subtree*.

In the terminology of family trees, each root is called the *parent* of the two nodes immediately above it. These two nodes, in turn, are called the *children* of that parent.

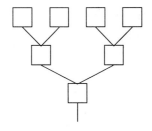

Figure 9.2: A tree machine.

Each node is connected to its parent by a *bottom* channel. In addition, each root is connected to its two children by a *left* and a *right* channel.

The main root inputs a complete problem from its bottom channel, splits it into two parts, and sends one part to its left child and the other part to its right child. The remaining roots repeat the splitting process. Eventually, each leaf inputs a problem through its channel, solves it, and outputs the solution through the same channel. Each root then inputs two partial solutions from its children and combines them into a single solution, which is output to its parent. Finally, the main root outputs the solution to the complete problem.

The number of processors p in a tree machine is related as follows to the *depth* of the tree:

$$p = 2^{depth+1} - 1$$

The tree in Fig. 9.2 is of depth 2 and uses 7 processors.

The tree machine will be programmed in *SuperPascal*. I assume that the parallel processes run on separate processors without shared memory.

The tree machine activates a *tree* of processes that run in parallel on p processors (Fig. 9.3). Initially, the main root executes the tree procedure as a sequential process. A tree with more than one processor consists of a root and two subtrees running in parallel. Each subtree has $(p-1)/2$ processors. The tree processes continue to split themselves recursively into parallel subtrees and roots until they reach the point where each process is a leaf process.

A *root* process inputs a problem, splits it into two problems, which are solved by its children, and outputs the combined result (Fig. 9.4).

```
            procedure tree(depth: integer;
               bottom: channel);
            var left, right: channel;
            begin
              if depth > 0 then
                begin
                  open(left, right);
                  parallel
                    tree(depth − 1, left)|
                    tree(depth − 1, right)|
                    root(bottom, left, right)
                  end
                end
              else leaf(bottom)
            end;
```

Figure 9.3: Parallel tree algorithm.

A *leaf* process inputs a problem, solves it by means of the sequential divide and conquer algorithm, and outputs the solution (Fig. 9.5).

The algorithms in Figs. 9.1 and 9.3–5 define the behavior of a tree machine solving a divide and conquer problem in parallel. I have deliberately ignored the system-dependent details of processor allocation.

9.4   Parallel Quicksort

The first divide and conquer example is the *quicksort* algorithm, which splits an array of integers into two parts and sorts the left and right parts separately (Fig. 9.6). The splitting is repeated recursively until the algorithm sorts a single element only (by an empty operation).

The *partition* algorithm selects an arbitrary key value from an array slice and splits the slice into two pieces, with the property that no element in the left piece is larger than the key, and no element in the right part is smaller than the key. The algorithm shown in Fig. 9.7 uses the value of the middle element as the key.

```
                    procedure root(bottom, left,
                       right: channel);
                    var a: table; first, last, middle,
                       middle2, i: integer;
                    begin
                       receive(bottom, first, last);
                       for i := first to last do
                          receive(bottom, a[i]);
                       split(a, first, last, middle);
                       send(left, first, middle);
                       for i := first to middle do
                          send(left, a[i]);
                       middle2 := middle + 1;
                       send(right, middle2, last);
                       for i := middle2 to last do
                          send(right, a[i]);
                       for i := first to middle do
                          receive(left, a[i]);
                       for i := middle2 to last do
                          receive(right, a[i]);
                       combine(a, first, last, middle);
                       for i := first to last do
                          send(bottom, a[i])
                    end;
```

Figure 9.4: Root algorithm.

The run time of partition is $O(n)$. The average run time of quicksort is $O(n\log n)$. The worst-case sorting time is $O(n^2)$.

Quicksort can be derived from Fig. 9.1 by making the following substitutions:

1. Type T is replaced by type *integer*.

2. Procedure *solve* is renamed *quicksort*.

3. The indices *middle* and *middle+1* are replaced by j and i, respectively.

```
procedure leaf(bottom: channel);
var a: table; first, last, i: integer;
begin
   receive(bottom, first, last);
   for i := first to last do
      receive(bottom, a[i]);
   solve(a, first, last);
   for i := first to last do
      send(bottom, a[i])
end;
```

Figure 9.5: Leaf algorithm.

```
type table = array [1..n] of integer;

procedure quicksort(var a: table;
   first, last: integer);
var i, j: integer;
begin
   if first < last then
      begin
         partition(a, i, j, first, last);
         quicksort(a, first, j);
         quicksort(a, i, last)
      end
end;
```

Figure 9.6: Standard quicksort.

4. The *split* operation is replaced by

$$partition(a, i, j, first, last)$$

5. The *combine* operation is empty.

It follows immediately that a *parallel quicksort* is obtained by making

```
procedure partition(var a: table;
    var i, j: integer; first, last: integer);
var ai, key: integer;
begin
  i := first; j := last;
  key := a[(i+j) div 2];
  while i <= j do
    begin
      while a[i] < key do i := i + 1;
      while key < a[j] do j := j − 1;
      if i <= j then
        begin
          ai := a[i]; a[i] := a[j];
          a[j]:=ai;
          i := i + 1; j := j − 1
        end
    end
end;
```

Figure 9.7: Partition algorithm.

the same substitutions in Figs. 9.4–5.

Unfortunately, the partition procedure produces array slices of unpredictable sizes. In the best case, the two slices are of equal size. In the worst case, the smallest slice has one element only. The unpredictable nature of quicksort causes *load imbalance* on a multicomputer [Fox 1988].

On a tree machine with 31 processors, each leaf receives a problem of size $n/16 = 0.06n$, provided the splitting is balanced. However, if partition on the average splits a problem of size m into two problems of size $0.6m$ and $0.4m$, respectively, two of the leaves receive problems of size $0.6^4 n = 0.13n$ and $0.4^4 n = 0.03n$. I will call this algorithm the *unbalanced parallel quicksort*.

Fortunately, quicksort can be balanced using a different splitting algorithm (Fig. 9.8).

The balanced quicksort can be derived from Fig. 9.1 as follows:

```
        procedure quicksort(var a: table;
            first, last: integer);
        var middle: integer;
        begin
          if first < last then
            begin
              middle := (first + last) div 2;
              find(a, first, last, middle);
              quicksort(a, first, middle);
              quicksort(a, middle+1, last)
            end
        end;
```

Figure 9.8: Balanced quicksort.

1. Type T is replaced by type *integer*.

2. Procedure *solve* is renamed *quicksort*.

3. *Split* is replaced by

$$middle := (first + last) \textbf{ div } 2;$$
$$find(a, first, last, middle)$$

4. *Combine* is empty.

The *find* algorithm repeatedly partitions an array slice into smaller and smaller pieces of unpredictable sizes until it has formed two halves with given first, last, and middle indices (Fig. 9.9).

If a single partitioning of n elements takes n time units, the average time required to find the middle element is

$$n + n/2 + n/4 + \cdots + 1 = 2n - 1$$

For large n, *find* is twice as slow as *partition*. That is why the balanced *sequential* quicksort is of academic interest only. (I remark in passing that it is possible to write an iterative version of the balanced quicksort without a stack!)

```
procedure find(var a: table;
   first, last, middle: integer);
var left, right, i, j: integer;
begin
   left := first; left := last;
   while left < right do
      begin
         partition(a, i, j, left, right);
         if middle <= j then right := j
         else if i <= middle then left := i
         else left := right
      end
end;
```

Figure 9.9: Find algorithm.

On a parallel tree machine, a sorting problem must be distributed evenly among the leaves to obtain the best possible performance. As a compromise, I will use the *find* algorithm in the roots only and the *partition* algorithm in the leaves. The resulting algorithm is called the *balanced parallel quicksort*. Measurements show that it consistently runs faster than the unbalanced algorithm.

The previous arguments are valid only for the *average* behavior of parallel quicksorting. In the *worst* case, both algorithms perform very poorly. The correctness of the standard quicksort, partition, and find algorithms is proven in Foley [1971] and Hoare [1971b].

9.5   Parallel FFT

The second example is the *fast Fourier transform* (*FFT*), which computes the frequency components of a signal that has been sampled n times [Cooley 1965]. The theory behind the *FFT* is explained in Chap. 8 and Brinch Hansen [1991c], which include sequential *FFT* procedures written in *Super-Pascal*.

The *FFT* computation is an in-line transformation of an array of n complex numbers (Fig. 9.10). This algorithm should be used only when n is a power of two, if necessary by padding the data with zeros up to the next power of two [Press 1989]. The array elements must be permuted in *bit-reversed* order before the *FFT* computation begins [Chap. 8 and Brinch Hansen 1991c].

```
type
    complex = record re, im: real end;
    table = array [1..n] of complex;

procedure fft(var a: table;
    first, last: integer);
var middle: integer;
begin
    if first < last then
        begin
            middle := (first + last) div 2;
            fft(a, first, middle);
            fft(a, middle + 1, last);
            combine(a, first, last)
        end
end;
```

Figure 9.10: Fast Fourier transform.

The transform of a single number is the number itself. The *FFT* splits a larger sequence into halves, computes the transform of each half separately, and combines the two transforms of size $n/2$ into a single transform of size n.

Figure 8.11 defines the combinations of two transforms into one. Since n is a power of two, this procedure does not require a *middle* parameter.

The run times of the *combine* and *fft* procedures are $O(n)$ and $O(n\log n)$, respectively.

The *fft* procedure can be obtained by making the following changes to Fig. 9.1:

1. Type T is replaced by type *complex*.

2. Procedure *solve* is renamed *fft*.

3. *Split* is replaced by

$$\text{middle} := (\text{first} + \text{last}) \textbf{ div } 2$$

4. *Combine* is replaced by

$$\text{combine(a, first, last)}$$

A *parallel fft* is obtained by making the same substitutions in Figs. 9.4–5.

9.6 Complexity

I will analyze the average performance of a parallel divide and conquer algorithm under the assumption that every problem is split into two subproblems of equal size.

The *sequential run time* $T(1,n)$ is the average time required to solve a divide and conquer problem of size n on a single processor. The processor inputs and outputs n data items in $O(n)$ time and transforms them in $O(n\log n)$ time. So,

$$T(1,n) = n(a\log n + b) \tag{9.1}$$

where a and b are system-dependent constants for computation and communication in a leaf processor.

The *parallel run time* $T(p,n)$ is the average time it takes to solve a problem of size n on a binary tree machine with p processors, where $p+1$ and n are powers of two.

The tree consists of a root and two subtrees. The root transforms n items in $O(n)$ time. The communication between the root and its parents also takes $O(n)$ time. The communication between the root and a subtree will be included in the run time of the subtree. Each subtree uses $(p-1)/2$ processors to solve a problem of size $n/2$. The root does not terminate until the subtrees have terminated. Since the subtrees solve problems of the same size in parallel, the parallel run time of the tree is

$$T(p,n) = T\left(\frac{p-1}{2}, \frac{n}{2}\right) + (b+c)n$$

where b and c are constants for communication and computation in a root processor.

This recurrence has the solution

$$T(p,n) = T(1,n/q) + 2(b+c)(n - n/q)$$

where

$$q = (p+1)/2$$

is the number of leaf processors.

So, the parallel run time is

$$T(p,n) = (n/q)(a\log(n/q) + b) + 2(b+c)(n - n/q) \qquad (9.2)$$

For $p = q = 1$, this formula reduces to (9.1).

I will use the abbreviations

$$T_1 = T(1,n) \qquad T_p = T(p,n) \qquad S_p = T_1/T_p$$

The *speedup* S_p defines how much faster a parallel divide and conquer algorithm runs on p processors compared to a single processor.

On a hypothetical tree machine of infinite size, the parallel run times of the roots would be

$$(b+c)(n + n/2 + n/4 + \cdots) = 2(b+c)n$$

I will call this time limit T_{min}, that is

$$T_{min} = 2(b+c)n \qquad (9.3)$$

From (9.2) and (9.3), it follows immediately that $T_p \geq T_{min}$, provided

$$a\log(n/q) + b \geq 2(b+c)$$

This assumption is satisfied by any nontrivial problem. For $a = b$ and $c = 2a$, the inequality is true if $n/q \geq 32$. In other words, each leaf node must solve a problem with at least 32 data items.

So, in practice, T_{min} is a *lower bound* on the parallel run time of a finite tree machine. It is also an *upper bound* on the cost of distributing a problem in a tree machine and collecting the results.

You can now rewrite (9.2) as follows:

$$T_p = T_1/q + (1 - 1/q)T_{min} - an\log q/q \qquad (9.4)$$

The parallel run time is the sum of three terms:

1. The first term T_1/q is the sequential run time T_1 divided by the number of leaf nodes q.

2. The second term $(1 - 1/q)T_{min}$ is the parallel run time of the roots.

3. The last term $anlogq/q$ is small compared to T_p. It reaches its maximum value $an/2$ for $q = 2$ (that is, $p = 3$). So,

$$\frac{anlogq/q}{T_p} \leq \frac{an/2}{T_{min}} = \frac{a}{4(b + c)}$$

For $a = b$ and $c = 2a$, the last term accounts for less than 8% of the run-time.

For large q, the parallel run time T_p approaches T_{min}.
The speedup cannot exceed T_1/T_{min}, that is

$$S_{max} = \frac{alogn + b}{2(b + c)} \tag{9.5}$$

Suppose you wish to achieve a speedup that is close to the maximum speedup in the following sense

$$S_p \geq S_{max}/(1 + f)$$

where f is a given fraction. This inequality can also be expressed as follows:

$$T_p \leq (1 + f)T_{min}$$

Using (9.4), you can extend the inequality further:

$$T_p \leq T_1/q + (1 - 1/q)T_{min} \leq (1 + f)T_{min}$$

From the second part of the inequality, you obtain the condition

$$q \geq (T_1/T_{min} - 1)/f$$

In other words,

$$S_p \geq S_{max}/(1 + f) \qquad \text{for } q \geq (S_{max} - 1)/f$$

Since S_{max} is $O(logn)$, this result shows that the tree machine achieves $O(logn)$ speedup with $O(logn)$ processors. Since the sequential run time is $O(nlogn)$, an $O(logn)$ speedup reduces the parallel run time to $O(n)$.

For $a = b$, $c = 2a$, and $n = 2^{20}$, the maximum speedup $S_{max} = 3.5$. For $p = 31$, the actual speedup $S_p = 3.1$ corresponding to $f = 0.16$. The last term in (9.4) is 4% of T_p only.

9.7 Performance

For the performance measurements, I replaced Figs. 9.6 and 9.10 by the *iterative quicksort* and *FFT* algorithms defined in Sedgewick [1984], Brinch Hansen [1991c] and Chap. 8. I reprogrammed the parallel algorithms in occam and ran them on a Computing Surface with T800 transputers configured as a binary tree machine. The input data were produced by a random number generator [Park 1988].

For *balanced parallel sorting* of 32-bit random integers, I measured

$$a = 3.8 \ \mu s \qquad b = 5.6 \ \mu s \qquad c = 2a$$

Table 9.1 shows measured (and predicted) sorting times for $n = 131072$ integers (in seconds). The performance limits are

$$T_{min} = 3.46 \ s \qquad S_{max} = 2.66$$

Table 9.1: Parallel balanced quicksort.

p	T_p		S_p	
1	9.25	(9.20)	1.00	(1.00)
3	6.02	(6.08)	1.54	(1.51)
7	4.56	(4.65)	2.03	(1.98)
15	3.96	(3.99)	2.34	(2.31)
31	3.63	(3.63)	2.55	(2.53)

Table 9.2 shows measured run times for the *unbalanced parallel quicksort*. ΔT_p is the relative time difference between the unbalanced and balanced algorithms. The unbalanced sort is 20–37% slower and is rather erratic.

For the *parallel FFT* of 128-bit random complex numbers, I found

$$a = 25 \ \mu s \qquad b = 22 \ \mu s \qquad c = a$$

Table 9.3 shows measured (and predicted) *FFT* times for $n = 32768$ complex numbers (in seconds). The performance limits are

$$T_{min} = 3.08 \ s \qquad S_{max} = 4.22$$

The run times for the parallel *FFT* do not include the *sequential permutation time* of the array:

$$8.5n \ \mu s = 0.28 \ s \qquad \text{for } n = 32768$$

Table 9.2: Parallel unbalanced quicksort.

p	T_p	S_p	ΔT_p
1	9.25	1.00	0%
3	8.20	1.13	36%
7	5.46	1.69	20%
15	5.41	1.71	37%
31	4.85	1.91	34%

Table 9.3: Parallel FFT.

p	T_p		S_p	
1	13.23	(13.01)	1.00	(1.00)
3	7.74	(7.64)	1.71	(1.70)
7	5.12	(5.15)	2.58	(2.53)
15	3.99	(4.01)	3.32	(3.24)
31	3.47	(3.50)	3.81	(3.72)

9.8   Final Remarks

I have presented a generic divide and conquer algorithm for a binary tree machine. From this algorithm, I have derived balanced, parallel algorithms for quicksort and fast Fourier transform.

For problems of size n, a tree machine achieves $O(\log n)$ speedup using $O(\log n)$ processors. The disappointing performance of parallel divide and conquer cannot be attributed solely to the overhead of processor communication. Even if communication was instant ($b = 0$), the maximum speedup of a balanced quicksort would still be $0.25 \log n$ only.

Although the degree of parallism grows exponentially as a tree machine repeatedly divides a problem, the wave of computation still spreads sequentially through the levels of the tree. In a large tree machine, the main root alone accounts for almost half of the parallel run time.

The parallel algorithms presented here have two obvious limitations:

1. When a tree machine with p processors solves a problem of size n, every node holds an array of size n. Consequently, the problem size is limited by the memory of a single node. This limitation can be

removed by having a large memory of $O(n)$ size in the main root and halving the memory size of each processor at each level in the tree. This limits the total size of the memory to $O(n\log p)$.

2. After dividing a sorting problem into smaller parts, a tree machine uses only half of its processors (the leaves) to reduce the sorting time. If I had used a *hypercube* instead of a tree machine, I could have written an algorithm that divides a sorting problem evenly among all nodes.

The latter observation is a valid criticism of small tree machines, but not of larger ones. If you use a multicomputer for large scientific computations, you probably have at least 32 or 64 processors. So, if you have to sort numbers, you may as well use all the processors you have.

A hypercube with p processors can solve a divide and conquer problem in the same time as a tree machine with $2p - 1$ processors [Chap. 10 and Brinch Hansen 1991e]. A tree machine with 31 transputers can sort a million numbers in 31 s. A hypercube with 32 transputers solves the same problem in 29 s, which is only 7% faster.

On a multicomputer with 32–64 processors, parallel tree algorithms are practically as fast as hypercube algorithms and are simpler to program.

Chapter 10

Hypercubes and Tree Machines

10.1 Introduction

Quicksort is probably the most widely used sequential method for sorting an array [Hoare 1961; Foley 1971]. On the average, it sorts n items in $O(n\log n)$ time. In the worst case, the sorting time is $O(n^2)$. The unpredictable nature of the algorithm makes it difficult to write an efficient, parallel quicksort for a multicomputer [Fox 1988; Brinch Hansen 1991d and Chap. 9].

In this chapter, I develop a *balanced parallel quicksort* for a *hypercube* and compare it with a similar algorithm for a binary *tree machine* [Chap. 9 and Brinch Hansen 1991d]. The performance of the hypercube algorithm is analyzed and measured on a Computing Surface.

10.2 Hypercube Sorting

Initially, I will discuss parallel sorting on a cube with only eight processor nodes (Fig. 10.1). Each node can communicate with its three nearest neighbors through bidirectional channels. A fourth channel (shown for node 0 only) connects a node with the environment of the cube.

The standard *quicksort* uses the familiar *partition* algorithm to split a sorting problem into two smaller sorting problems (Figs. 9.6–7). Since *partition* generally produces subproblems of unpredictable lengths, it may cause severe imbalance on a multicomputer. Later, I will show how to balance a

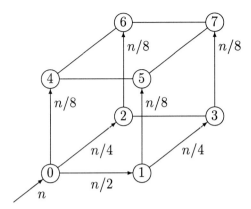

Figure 10.1: Data distribution in a cube.

parallel quicksort. In the following, I just assume that the nodes somehow always split sorting problems into smaller problems of equal (or nearly equal) size.

The cube sorts n numbers in three phases:

Splitting phase:

1. Node 0 inputs n numbers, splits them into two halves, sends one half to node 1, and keeps the other half.

2. Node 0 splits half of the numbers into two fourths, sends one fourth to node 2, and keeps the other fourth. Simultaneously, node 1 splits the other half, sends one fourth to node 3, and keeps the other fourth.

3. Nodes 0, 1, 2, and 3 simultaneously send one eighth of the numbers to nodes 4, 5, 6, and 7, respectively, and keep the remaining eighths.

Sorting phase:

4. All nodes work in parallel, while each of them sorts one eighth of the numbers.

Combining phase:

5. Node 0 inputs $n/8$ sorted numbers from node 4 and combines them with its own numbers into a sorted sequence of size $n/4$. At the same

time, nodes 1, 2, and 3 communicate with nodes 5, 6, and 7, respectively, and form sorted sequences of size $n/4$.

6. Nodes 0 and 1 simultaneously input $n/4$ sorted numbers from nodes 2 and 3, respectively, and form sorted sequences of size $n/2$.

7. Finally, node 0 inputs $n/2$ sorted numbers from node 1, combines them with its own numbers, and outputs a sorted sequence of size n to its environment.

A larger hypercube follows the same general pattern of splitting a sorting problem into smaller problems, solving them in parallel, and combining the results.

In general, a hypercube has p processors, where p is a power of two:

$$p = 2^d$$

The exponent, $d = \log p$, is called the *dimension* of the hypercube. For a cube, $p = 8$, and $d = 3$.

It is helpful to view a hypercube as a *hierarchical system*, where each *level* consists of a subset of the nodes. A cube has four levels of nodes:

level	nodes
0	0..0
1	1..1
2	2..3
3	4..7

A sorting problem is distributed through the cube, one level at a time. First, the node at level 0 inputs a problem, then the node at level 1 inputs a subproblem, followed by the nodes at level 2, and, finally, the nodes at level 3.

In general, a hypercube has $d+1$ node levels. Figure 10.2 defines the level number of node k, where

$$0 \le \text{level}(k) \le d \qquad \text{for } 0 \le k \le p - 1$$

I will program a hypercube node in *SuperPascal*.

The *input* of an array *slice* $a[i..j]$, including the bounds i and j, through a channel c is expressed as follows:

```
function level(k: integer): integer;
var j, kmax: integer;
begin
  kmax := 0; j := 0;
  while kmax < k do
    begin
      kmax := 2*kmax + 1;
      j := j + 1
    end;
  level := j
end;
```

Figure 10.2: Node level function.

```
receive(c, i, j);
for k := i to j do receive(c, a[k])
```

The corresponding *output* operation uses the *send* procedure in place of *receive*.

Each node is connected to its environment and nearest neighbors through a local array of $d+1$ channels. These channels can transmit messages of type *integer* only:

```
type
  channel = *(integer);
  channels = array [0..d] of channel;
```

A particular local channel is used to transmit a problem of a given size. For a cube, you have:

channel number	problem size
0	n
1	$n/2$
2	$n/4$
3	$n/8$

In general, channel number i carries a problem of size $n/2^i$, where $0 \le i \le d$.

The channel, through which a node inputs a sorting problem, is called its *bottom channel*. For the cube, you have:

nodes	problem size	bottom channel
0..0	n	0
1..1	$n/2$	1
2..3	$n/4$	2
4..7	$n/8$	3

In general, the index of the bottom channel is equal to the level of the corresponding node.

Figure 10.3 defines the behavior of hypercube node k for $n \geq p$. This is a *balanced parallel quicksort*. It maintains load balance by using the well-known *find* algorithm to split array slices in half [Hoare 1971b]. However, since *find* takes twice as long as *partition*, I use it during the splitting phase only. For the sorting phase, I use the standard quicksort (Fig. 9.6).

If you use *partition* instead of *find* in Fig. 10.3, you get an *unbalanced parallel quicksort*. Measurements show that such an algorithm is slower than the balanced sort and rather unpredictable.

10.3   Complexity

The *parallel run time* $T(p, n)$ is the average time required to sort n numbers on a hypercube with p processors, where n and p are powers of two, and $n \geq p$.

An initial node inputs n numbers and splits them into halves. Later, the same node combines the two sorted halves and outputs n sorted numbers. The node inputs, splits, combines, and outputs the n items in time $(b + c)n$, where b and c are system-dependent constants for communication and balanced splitting.

The initial node, which belongs to, say, the left half of the hypercube, sends $n/2$ items to the right half of the hypercube (see Fig. 10.1). The two halves of the hypercube now run in parallel. Each half uses $p/2$ processors to sort $n/2$ numbers. So the parallel run time of the complete hypercube is

$$T(p, n) = T(p/2, n/2) + (b + c)n$$

This recurrence has the solution

$$T(p, n) = T(1, n/p) + 2(b + c)(n - n/p)$$

```
procedure node(k: integer; c: channels);
var bottom, first, last, middle,
  i, j: integer;
begin
  bottom := level(k);
  receive(c[bottom], first, last);
  for j := first to last do
    receive(c[bottom], a[j]);
  for i := bottom + 1 to d do
    begin
      middle := (first + last) div 2;
      find(a, first, last, middle);
      send(c[i], first, middle);
      for j := first to middle do
        send(c[i], a[j]);
      first := middle + 1
    end;
  quicksort(a, first, last);
  for i := d downto bottom + 1 do
    begin
      receive(c[i], first, middle);
      for j := first to middle do
        receive(c[i], a[j])
    end;
  send(c[bottom], first, last);
  for j := first to last do
    send(c[bottom], a[j])
end;
```

Figure 10.3: Node algorithm

Eventually, each node inputs, sorts, and outputs n/p numbers in time

$$T(1, n/p) = (n/p)(a \log(n/p) + b)$$

where a and b are system-dependent constants for unbalanced splitting and communication.

Using the abbreviation $T_p = T(p, n)$, you have

$$T_p = (n/p)(a\log(n/p) + b) + 2(b + c)(n - n/p) \qquad (10.1)$$

The *sequential run time* T_1 is the average time it takes to sort n numbers on a single processor. For $p = 1$, (10.1) reduces to

$$T_1 = n(a\log n + b) \qquad (10.2)$$

On a hypothetical hypercube of infinite size, the parallel run time of the split and combine phases is

$$(b + c)(n + n/2 + n/4 + \cdots) = 2(b + c)n$$

This time limit is called T_{min}, that is

$$T_{min} = 2(b + c)n \qquad (10.3)$$

Using (10.1) and (10.3), it is easy to see that $T_p \geq T_{min}$ for any sorting problem that satisfies the inequality

$$a\log(n/p) + b \geq 2(b + c)$$

For $a = b$ and $c = 2a$, this assumption is satisfied as long as $n/p \geq 32$. So, for any nontrivial sorting problem, T_{min} is a *lower bound* on the parallel run time T_p.

The parallel run time can now be expressed as

$$T_p = T_1/p + (1 - 1/p)T_{min} - an\log p/p \qquad (10.4)$$

For a large hypercube, T_p approaches T_{min}.

The *speedup* $S_p = T_1/T_p$ cannot exceed T_1/T_{min}, that is

$$S_{max} = \frac{a\log n + b}{2(b + c)} \qquad (10.5)$$

If $a = b$, $c = 2a$, and $n = 2^{20}$, the maximum speedup $S_{max} = 3.5$. For $p = 32$, the actual speedup $S_p = 3.3$ only.

10.4 Performance

For the performance measurements, I replaced Fig. 9.6 by an iterative quicksort algorithm similar to the one defined in Sedgewick [1984]. I reprogrammed the parallel quicksort in occam and ran it on a Computing Surface with T800 transputers configured as a hypercube. The four channels of a transputer limits the hypercube to a maximum of eight nodes.

For *balanced parallel sorting* of 32-bit random integers, I found

$$a = 3.8 \ \mu s \qquad b = 5.6 \ \mu s \qquad c = 2a$$

Table 10.1 shows measured (and predicted) sorting times for $n = 131072$ integers (in seconds). The performance limits are

$$T_{min} = 3.46 \ s \qquad S_{max} = 2.66$$

Table 10.1: Parallel balanced quicksort.

p	T_p		S_p	
1	9.25	(9.20)	1.00	(1.00)
2	6.10	(6.08)	1.52	(1.51)
4	4.64	(4.65)	1.99	(1.98)
8	3.96	(3.99)	2.34	(2.31)

Table 10.2 shows measured run times for the *unbalanced parallel quicksort*. ΔT_p is the relative time difference between the unbalanced and balanced algorithms. The unbalanced sort is 20–36% slower and somewhat unpredictable.

Table 10.2: Parallel unbalanced quicksort.

p	T_p	S_p	ΔT_p
1	9.25	1.00	0%
2	8.31	1.11	36%
4	5.58	1.66	20%
8	5.24	1.77	32%

10.5 Hypercubes Versus Tree Machines

In Chap. 9 and Brinch Hansen [1991d], I analyzed parallel sorting on a Computing Surface configured as a binary tree machine. The only difference between the performance models of a hypercube and a tree machine is that for the tree machine, the number of nodes p is replaced by the number of leaf nodes

$$q = (p+1)/2$$

This difference is easy to understand. On a hypercube, every one of the p nodes sorts. On a tree machine, sorting is done by the q leaves only.

However, the performance limits, T_{min} and S_{max}, are the same for a hypercube and a tree machine.

Since a tree machine with $2p - 1$ processors has p leaves, it sorts as fast as a hypercube with p processors. In other words,

$$T_{cube}(p, n) = T_{tree}(2p - 1, n) \qquad (10.6)$$

This relationship is confirmed by the measurements reported here, and in Chap. 9 and Brinch Hansen [1991d].

In the following, I compare a hypercube with p processors and a tree machine with $p - 1$ processors, when both machines sort n numbers. The *time difference* between these machines is

$$\Delta T(p, n) = T_{tree}(p - 1, n) - T_{cube}(p, n)$$

If you replace p by $p/2$ in (10.6), you get

$$\Delta T(p, n) = T_{cube}(p/2, n) - T_{cube}(p, n)$$

which can be rewritten as follows, using (10.4)

$$\Delta T(p, n) = (T_1 - T_{min} - an(\log p - 2))/p$$

For $p \geq 4$, the following inequality holds:

$$\Delta T(p, n) \leq (T_1 - T_{min})/p$$

Since $T_{cube}(p, n) \geq T_{min}$, the *relative time difference* between a tree machine and a hypercube of similar size sorting the same numbers is bounded as follows:

$$\begin{aligned} \Delta T(p, n)/T_{cube}(p, n) &\leq \Delta T(p, n)/T_{min} \\ &\leq (T_1/T_{min} - 1)/p \end{aligned}$$

In short,

$$\Delta T(p,n)/T_{cube}(p,n) \leq (S_{max} - 1)/p$$

Table 10.3 compares parallel sorting on medium-sized hypercubes and tree machines for $a = b$, $c = 2a$, and $n = 2^{20}$, where $S_{max} = 3.5$. A hypercube with 32–64 nodes is only 3–6% faster than a tree machine with 31–63 nodes.

Table 10.3: Relative time difference.

p	$\Delta T(p,n)$
16	12%
32	6%
64	3%

10.6   Final Remarks

I have developed a balanced parallel quicksort for a hypercube and compared it with a similar algorithm for a binary tree machine. The performance of the hypercube quicksort was measured on a Computing Surface.

Part V

THE MONTE CARLO PARADIGM

Chapter 11

Simulated Annealing

11.1 Introduction

This chapter describes *simulated annealing*, an optimization method based on the principles of statistical mechanics. The method imitates the process by which melted metal forms an atomic lattice with minimal energy when it is cooled slowly. Simulated annealing finds near-optimal solutions to optimization problems, which cannot be solved exactly in reasonable amounts of computing time.

Simulated annealing was independently introduced by Kirkpatrick, Gelatt, and Vechi [1983], and Černy [1985]. The method has been applied to a large number of optimization problems in science and engineering [Aarts 1989].

The *traveling salesperson* problem is probably the most famous combinatorial optimization problem: A salesperson must visit each of n cities once and return to the initial city. The aim is to find the shortest possible tour [Lawler 1985].

The traveling salesperson, and many other optimization problems, belong to the class of *NP-complete* problems for which no efficient algorithms are believed to exist [Garey 1979]. For these intractable problems, you must be satisfied with approximation algorithms that find near-optimal solutions.

I will explain simulated annealing by developing a Pascal algorithm for the traveling salesperson problem. In a few minutes, this algorithm finds a near-optimal tour of 100 cities by sampling fewer than one million of the 5×10^{150} possible tours!

11.2 Naivete

For the traveling salesperson, the most obvious idea is to examine all the $(n-1)!/2$ possible tours. Suppose this computation takes $n!$ μs. In that case, you can find a minimum tour of 15 cities in about two weeks. However, a 24-city problem would require 20 billion years, which is about four times the age of Earth [Sagan 1980]. So *exhaustive search* is out of the question, except for very small problems.

Since it is impractical to consider all possible tours of n cities, I will examine only a *random sample* of tours. The idea is to make random changes of an initial tour in the hope of finding shorter and shorter tours. This statistical approach is an example of the *Monte Carlo* method of computing.

Consider first a *greedy search*, which always makes the choice that looks best at the moment. The initial tour is a randomly chosen sequence of the n cities. You now randomly select two cities and exchange them in the tour. The new tour is accepted if it is shorter than the previous one. The random exchange of cities continues until the tour no longer decreases.

Unfortunately, there is no guarantee that this algorithm will even come close to finding an optimum solution. In most cases, it will be trapped in a *local minimum* in the huge solution space.

11.3 Annealing

Annealing is the process of heating a metal until it melts and then lowering the temperature slowly to allow the atoms sufficient time to form a uniform lattice with *minimal energy*. If the metal is cooled too quickly, the atoms form a slighly irregular lattice with higher energy due to internal stress.

Annealing can be viewed as a stochastic process which finds an arrangement of the atoms that minimizes their energy. At high temperatures, the atoms move freely and will often move to positions that temporarily increase the total energy. As the temperature is lowered, the atoms gradually move toward a regular lattice and will only occasionally increase their energy.

The occasional increase of energy plays a crucial role in annealing. These *uphill changes* enable the atoms to escape from local minima by increasing their energy temporarily. At high temperatures, such jumps occur with high probability. At low temperatures, they seldom occur.

The temperature must be lowered slowly to maintain *thermal equilibrium*.

When the atoms are in equilibrium at temperature T, the probability that their total energy is E is proportional to $e^{-E/kT}$, where k is Bolzmann's constant [Feynman 1989].

Consequently, the probability that the energy is $E + dE$ can be expressed as follows:

$$\mathrm{Prob}(E + dE) = \mathrm{Prob}(E)e^{-dE/kT}$$

In other words, the probability that the energy changes from E to $E + dE$ is $e^{-dE/kT}$. As the temperature decreases, so does the probability of energy increases.

Simulated annealing is a computational method that imitates nature's way of finding a system configuration with minimum energy. I will discuss this method in the context of the traveling salesperson problem.

To emphasize the analogy between real and simulated annealing, I will use the terminology of statistical mechanics: Each tour is a possible *configuration* of the cities. The tour length represents the *energy* of the configuration. A variable T plays the role of *temperature*. Since T is a fictional entity, I replace Bolzmann's constant k by 1.

The aim is to lower the temperature slowly while changing the configuration until you reach near-minimal energy.

11.4   Configurations

In a plane, a *city* is defined by two real coordinates:

type city = **record** x, y: real **end**;

The algorithm in Fig. 11.1 defines the Euclidean *distance* between two cities p and q.

A *tour* of n cities is defined by an array of cities:

type tour = **array** [1..n] **of** city;

The salesperson visits the cities in numerical order 1,2...,n before returning to city number 1.

The *length* of a tour is the sum of the distances between successive cities (Fig. 11.2).

```
function distance(p, q: city): real;
var dx, dy: real;
begin
  dx := q.x − p.x;
  dy := q.y − p.y;
  distance := sqrt(dx*dx + dy*dy)
end;
```

Figure 11.1: Distance algorithm.

```
function length(a: tour): real;
var i: integer; sum: real;
begin
  sum := distance(a[n], a[1]);
  for i := 1 to n − 1 do
    sum := sum +
        distance(a[i], a[i+1]);
  length := sum
end;
```

Figure 11.2: Length algorithm.

11.5   Cooling

Simulated annealing begins at a high temperature T_{max}, which is lowered in a fixed number of *steps*. At each step, I keep the temperature T constant while searching for a shorter tour. The temperature is then reduced by a factor α (*alpha*), which is slightly less than 1 (Fig. 11.3). The parameters of the search procedure will be explained in the sequel.

11.6   Searching

In order to reach near-equilibrium at a given temperature T, you must examine many possible tours before lowering the temperature further. Figure 11.4 defines the Monte Carlo *search* for a shorter tour at temperature T.

```
procedure anneal(var a: tour;
    Tmax, alpha: real; steps,
    attempts, changes: integer);
var T: real; k: integer;
begin
  T := Tmax;
  for k := 1 to steps do
    begin
      search(a, T, attempts, changes);
      T := alpha*T
    end
end;
```

Figure 11.3: Annealing algorithm.

The search procedure randomly selects two cities, a_i and a_j, and considers the possibility of exchanging them:

$$select(a,\ i,\ j,\ dE)$$

The selection procedure also computes the resulting energy change dE.

The function value

$$accept(dE,\ T)$$

defines whether or not the energy change dE will be accepted at temperature T.

If the energy change is accepted, the tour is changed by exchanging cities a_i and a_j:

$$change(a,\ i,\ j)$$

The search continues until a fixed number of *changes* have been accepted. At high temperatures, most changes are accepted, and the tour looks quite random. At low temperatures, most random changes are likely to be rejected, since they increase a tour that is already fairly short. To limit the search for shorter tours at low temperatures, the search algorithm also limits the total number of *attempts*.

```
procedure search(var a: tour; T: real;
    attempts, changes: integer);
var i, j, na, nc: integer; dE: real;
begin
  na := 0; nc := 0;
  while (na < attempts)
    and (nc < changes) do
      begin
        select(a, i, j, dE);
        if accept(dE, T) then
          begin
            change(a, i, j);
            nc := nc + 1
          end;
        na := na + 1
      end
end;
```

Figure 11.4: Search algorithm.

11.7   Rearrangement

Preliminary experiments showed that random *city exchanges* produce longer tours than the random *path reversals* suggested by Lin [1965]. My final algorithm uses a variant of Lin's idea.

In a tour

$$a_1, a_2, \ldots, a_n$$

I randomly pick two cities, a_i and a_j. The successors of these cities are denoted a_{si} and a_{sj}, respectively:

$$\ldots, a_i, a_{si}, \ldots, a_j, a_{sj}, \ldots$$

A new tour is generated by reversing the order of the cities from a_{si} to a_j:

$$\ldots, a_i, a_j, \ldots, a_{si}, a_{sj}, \ldots$$

The *select* procedure generates two random city indices i and j, and computes the energy change dE, that will be caused by reversing the path from city number *si* to city number *j* (Fig. 11.5). The energy change is computed in constant time using the coordinates of the two cities and their successors. There is no need to compute the total length of any tour (except the final one).

```
procedure select(var a: tour;
    var si, j: integer;
    var dE: real);
var i, sj: integer;
begin
    generate(i, j);
    si := i mod n + 1;
    sj := j mod n + 1;
    if i <> j then
        dE := distance(a[i], a[j])
            + distance(a[si], a[sj])
            - distance(a[i], a[si])
            - distance(a[j], a[sj])
    else dE := 0.0
end;
```

Figure 11.5: Selection algorithm.

The *change* procedure defines a path reversal of cities number i through j (Fig. 11.6). The number of cities on the path is denoted n_{ij}. The path is reversed by swapping pairs of cities, starting at both ends of the path and working toward the middle. If n_{ij} is odd, the middle city is left alone.

Figure 11.7 defines the criterion for *accepting* an energy change dE at temperature T. A tour of shorter (or unchanged) length is always accepted. A longer tour is accepted with probability $e^{-dE/T}$. The latter possibility is simulated by comparing the probability with a random number between 0 and 1.

Moscato and Fontanari [1989] found a simpler *deterministic criterion* that works just as well (Fig. 11.8). This is the criterion used in my experiments.

```
procedure change(var a: tour;
    i, j: integer);
var k, nij: integer;
begin
    nij := (j − i + n) mod n + 1;
    for k := 1 to nij div 2 do
        swap(a,
            (i + k − 2) mod n + 1,
            (j − k + n) mod n + 1)
end;
```

Figure 11.6: Change algorithm.

```
function accept(dE, T: real): boolean;
begin
    if dE > 0.0 then
        accept := exp(−dE/T) > random
    else accept := true
end;
```

Figure 11.7: Probabilistic accept algorithm.

11.8 Parameters

The choice of annealing parameters requires educated guessing and experimentation.

Consider a volume uniformly filled with atoms of the same type and imagine that the volume is subdivided into subvolumes. When the atoms

```
function accept(dE, T: real): boolean;
begin accept := dE < T end;
```

Figure 11.8: Deterministic accept algorithm.

form a lattice during annealing, the same stochastic process takes place in every subvolume. From a macroscopic point of view, it is as if every subvolume goes through the same average number of energy changes.

For simulated annealing, this intuitive argument suggests that the total number of attempted and accepted energy *changes* should be proportional to the number of cities, that is $O(n)$.

The initial temperature T_{max} must be high enough to ensure that most energy changes are accepted. However, once the initial tour is random, it is a waste of computer time to attempt to make it "more random." So, T_{max} should not be too high.

I assume that the cities are placed on a square area. When you compare different tours, it is obviously the *relative* distances between cities that matter. You can therefore select a square of any dimension without changing the computation. I will use a square of n units. This choice makes the average density of cities independent of the problem size n.

On a square of area n, the distance between two successive cities cannot exceed the length of the diagonal, which is $O(\sqrt{n})$. A path reversal changes two distances in the tour. Assuming that the initial tour is random, the average energy changed caused by an initial path reversal is

$$dE_{max} = O(\sqrt{n})$$

I will use an initial temperature of the same order of magnitude to make sure that most initial changes will be accepted:

$$T_{max} = O(\sqrt{n})$$

The final temperature T_{min} must be so low that most energy increases will be rejected when we have found a near-optimal tour. Beyond that point, nothing is gained by considering further changes. So, T_{min} should not be too low.

If n cities are uniformly distributed on a square of area n, the average distances from each city to its nearest neighbors are $O(1)$. This is easy to see if you subdivide the square into n subsquares of area 1 and place a city on each subsquare.

When you are close to an optimal solution, the smallest energy increase is comparable to the distance between neighboring cities:

$$dE_{min} = O(1)$$

Most energy increases will be rejected if the final temperature is of the same order of magnitude:
$$T_{min} = O(1)$$
At this point, the algorithm soon gets trapped in a local (near-optimal) minimum.

After the last search, the final temperature is
$$T_{min} = T_{max}\alpha^{steps-1}$$

The termination condition, $T_{min} = O(1)$, is satisfied when
$$(1/\alpha)^{steps-1} = O(T_{max})$$

By taking the logarithm on both sides, you find
$$\begin{aligned} steps &= O(\log(T_{max})) \\ &= O(\log(\sqrt{n})) \\ &= O(\log n) \end{aligned}$$

These considerations and the folklore of simulated annealing led to the following *cooling schedule*:

$$\begin{aligned} T_{max} &= \sqrt{n} \\ \alpha &= 0.95 \\ steps &= 20 \ln n \\ attempts &= 100\ n \\ changes &= 10\ n \end{aligned}$$

The effect of the procedure statement
$$\text{anneal}(a, \text{sqrt}(n), 0.95, \text{trunc}(20*\ln(n)), 100*n, 10*n)$$
is to replace an initial tour a by a near-optimum tour (see Fig. 11.3).

11.9   Complexity

Simulated annealing goes through $O(\log n)$ temperature steps. For each temperature, the search examines $O(n)$ attempted or accepted changes. The computation rejects a change of the current tour in $O(1)$ time. If a change is accepted, the average path reversal involves $O(n)$ city exchanges. Consequently, the run time T_n of simulated annealing has the complexity

$$T_n = O((n^2 + n)\log n))$$

Since most steps take place at low temperatures, where most changes are rejected, the $O(n\log n)$ term is not negligible compared to the $O(n^2\log n)$ term.

11.10 Experiments

I reprogrammed simulated annealing in occam and tested it on a Computing Surface with T800 transputers using the random number generator of Park and Miller [1988].

The first test case was a *square grid* of n cities separated by horizontal and vertical distances of length 1 (Fig. 11.9).

Figure 11.9: A city grid.

A tour of the cities consists of n distances, each of which is at least of length 1. If n is the square of an even number, an optimal tour of length n exists, as shown in Fig. 11.9. This test case, which has a known optimal solution, gives an idea of the accuracy of simulated annealing.

Since the algorithm is probabilistic in nature, I tried each experiment ten times with different initial values of the random number generator. The trials were performed in parallel on a Computing Surface with ten transputers [Brinch Hansen 1992d].

Table 11.1 shows measured (and estimated) run time T_n (in minutes) for grids of 100 to 2500 cities. It also shows the shortest, average, and longest tours obtained from ten trials. The shortest tours are 0 to 4 percent longer than the optimal tours. The longest tours are 1 percent longer than the shortest ones.

Table 11.1: City grid.

n	T_n (m)		E_{min}	E_{aver}	E_{max}
100	2	(2)	100	101	101
400	14	(14)	406	407	410
900	50	(48)	921	924	927
1600	130	(129)	1651	1657	1665
2500	280	(290)	2602	2611	2619

The second test case was a *random distribution* of n cities on a square of n units (Table 11.2).

Table 11.2: Random cities.

n	T_n (m)		E_{min}	E_{aver}	E_{max}
100	2	(2)	76	78	80
400	14	(14)	307	310	314
900	50	(48)	717	723	728
1600	129	(129)	1276	1288	1297
2500	280	(290)	2009	2022	2037

The empirical formula

$$T_n = (0.26n + 240)n \ln n \ ms$$

defines the estimated run times shown in parentheses in Tables 11.1–2.

11.11   Final Remarks

Simulated annealing is an effective method for finding near-optimal solutions to optimization problems that cannot be solved exactly. When the method is applied to the NP-complete problem of the traveling salesperson, it finds short tours of hundreds of cities in 2–50 minutes.

Simulated annealing exploits an interesting analogy between combinatorial optimization and the statistical behavior of a physical system that slowly moves toward a state of minimal energy. It is yet another example of a fundamental computation with a subtle theory and a simple algorithm.

Chapter 12

Primality Testing

12.1 Introduction

This chapter describes a probabilistic method for testing the *primality* of large integers. The method was developed by Miller [1976] and Rabin [1980].

In the *RSA cryptosystem*, large primes play an essential role in the encoding and decoding of messages [Rivest 1978]. A user chooses two large random primes. These primes are used to compute a public encoding key and a secret decoding key. Both keys include the product of the primes. The user can receive encoded messages from anyone who knows the public key. But only the user (who knows the secret key) can decode the messages.

The crucial assumption is that it is feasible to generate large primes using a computer, but there is no known algorithm for finding the prime factors of large composite numbers in reasonable amounts of computer time. If that ever becomes possible, you will be able to break the code by factoring the public product of the secret primes.

The RSA cryptosystem is believed to be secure for keys of 150 decimal digits. The simplest way to find a 150-digit prime is to generate random 150-digit numbers until you discover a prime. The probability that a 150-digit number is a prime is about 1 in 150 ln10 [Courant 1941]. You must therefore expect to test about 350 numbers for primality before you find a prime. (Half of these tests can be skipped if you only examine odd numbers.)

So, the generation of primes is reduced to the problem of testing the primality of random numbers. Since it is not feasible to compute the prime factors of large numbers, I will use a probabilistic method that almost never fails to distinguish correctly between primes and composites.

I will describe the Miller-Rabin method of primality testing and illustrate it by a Pascal algorithm. The performance of the algorithm was tested on a Computing Surface.

12.2 Fermat's Theorem

The primality test uses a famous theorem discovered by Pierre de Fermat [1640].

Consider a prime p and any positive integer x that is not divisible by p. You can now define the following sequence of numbers:

$$0x \bmod p, \ 1x \bmod p, \ 2x \bmod p, \ \ldots, \ (p-1)x \bmod p$$

These numbers are obviously integers in the range from 0 to $p-1$. And they are distinct integers. For, if you assume that two of them are equal, say

$$jx \bmod p = ix \bmod \mathrm{p}$$

where $0 \leq \mathrm{i} < j \leq p-1$, then

$$(j-i)x \bmod p = 0$$

Since p is a prime, it cannot be expressed as a product of factors. Consequently, either $j - i$ or x (or both) must be divisible by p. But that is impossible, since $j - i$ is less than p, and x is not divisible by p.

Well, then you know that the sequence is simply a permutation of the integers $0, 1, \ldots, p-1$. Since the first number in the sequence is zero, the rest of it must be a permutation of the integers $1, 2, \ldots, p-1$. Consequently,

$$(1x \bmod p)(2x \bmod p) \cdots ((p-1)x \bmod p) = 1 * 2 * \cdots * (p-1)$$

which is equivalent to

$$(p-1)!(x^{p-1} - 1) \bmod p = 0$$

Since none of the factors of $(p-1)!$ are divisible by p, the rest of the product must be divisible by p:

$$(x^{p-1} - 1) \bmod p = 0$$

In short, if p is a prime and x is a positive integer that is not divisible by p, then

$$x^{p-1} \bmod p = 1 \qquad (12.1)$$

This is *Fermat's theorem.*

12.3 The Fermat Test

Fermat's theorem suggests a simple way to test the primality of a positive integer p:

1. Generate a random integer x in the range $1 \leq x \leq p - 1$. Since x is less than p, x is obviously not divisible by p.

2. Raise x to the power of $p - 1$ modulo p:

   (a) If the result is not 1, then p does not satisfy (12.1). This proves that p is not a prime. In that case, the integer x is called a *witness* to the compositeness of p.

   (b) If the result is 1, p may be a prime. But the Fermat test is not foolproof. For each base value x, there are an infinite number of composites p that satisfy (12.1). These composites are known as *pseudoprimes* [Burton 1980].

The algorithm shown in Fig. 12.1 defines the *Fermat test*. The boolean value of the function defines whether or not x is a witness to the compositeness of p.

The function defines *modular exponentiation* by repeated squaring. The loop maintains the invariant

$$my^e \bmod p = x^{p-1} \bmod p$$

where $1 \leq m \leq p - 1$ and $e \geq 0$.

When the loop terminates with $e = 0$, we have

$$m = x^{p-1} \bmod p$$

If m is not 1, then x is a witness; otherwise, it is not.

The algorithm assumes that numbers are represented by standard integers. This is obviously not possible for 150-digit decimal integers. In practice, the algorithm must be reprogrammed using multiple-length arithmetic. I will discuss this requirement later.

I will use three methods to reduce the probability that the primality test gives the wrong answer:

1. Test *large numbers*. It can be shown that the probability that a random number is a pseudoprime approaches zero as the number of digits goes toward infinity [Pomerance 1981].

```
function witness(x, p: integer): boolean;
var e, m, y: integer;
begin
  {1 <= x <= p − 1}
  m := 1; y := x; e := p − 1;
  while e > 0 do
    if e mod 2 = 1 then
      begin
        m := (m*y) mod p; e := e − 1
      end
    else
      begin
        y := sqr(y) mod p; e := e div 2;
      end;
  witness := (m <> 1)
end;
```

Figure 12.1: The Fermat test.

2. Repeat the Fermat test for *different base values x*. Although this helps, it is not watertight either. There are composite numbers p, which satisfy (12.1) for any base value x. Fortunately, these *Carmichael numbers* are extremely rare [Carmichael 1912].

3. Supplement the Fermat test with *another test*. The supplementary test is based on a theorem about quadratic remainders.

12.4   Quadratic Remainders

Consider the quadratic equation

$$y^2 \bmod p = 1 \tag{12.2}$$

where y and p are positive integers. This equation is equivalent to

$$(y - 1)(y + 1) \bmod p = 0$$

If p is a prime, either $y-1$ or $y+1$ (or both) must be divisible by p, that is

$$(y-1) \bmod p = 0$$

or

$$(y+1) \bmod p = 0$$

In that case, the only solutions to (12.2) are the *trivial* square roots of 1 modulo p:

$$y \bmod p = 1 \qquad y \bmod p = p-1$$

A *nontrivial* square root of 1 is an integer y modulo p in the range

$$1 < y \bmod p < p-1$$

which satisfies (12.2). If you can find such an integer y, then p is not a prime.

12.5 The Miller-Rabin Test

Figure 12.2 shows an extension of the Fermat test proposed by Miller [1976] and refined by Rabin [1980]. Every time the function squares the current value of y, it checks whether y modulo p is a nontrivial square root of 1. In that case, the function stops the Fermat test and returns the value true, indicating that p surely is composite.

The loop invariant is unchanged, but the termination condition is slightly different:

$$\text{sure or } (m = x^{p-1} \bmod p)$$

The Miller-Rabin test is also probabilistic.

12.6 A Probabilistic Algorithm

The Miller-Rabin test gives the wrong answer if it fails to discover a witness to a composite number. Rabin [1980] proved that the probability of failure is less than $\frac{1}{4}$. To improve the chance of finding the correct result, he suggested repeating the test m times with different random base values x.

The *test* algorithm, shown in Fig. 12.3, initializes a random number generator with a *seed* equal to 1.

```
function witness(x, p: integer): boolean;
var e, m, p1, r, y: integer;
    sure: boolean;
begin
    {1 <= x <= p − 1}
    m := 1; y := x; e := p − 1;
    p1 := e; sure := false;
    while not sure and (e > 0) do
        if e mod 2 = 1 then
            begin
                m := (m*y) mod p; e := e − 1
            end
        else
            begin
                r := y;
                y := sqr(y) mod p; e := e div 2;
                if y = 1 then
                    sure := (1 < r) and (r < p1)
            end;
    witness := sure or (m <> 1)
end;
```

Figure 12.2: The Miller-Rabin test.

If the algorithm discovers a single witness, then p is definitely composite. At this point, I could skip further testing. Instead, I let the algorithm complete the sequence of trials to make it obvious that the m trials can be performed simultaneously on a parallel computer.

If the algorithm finds no witness in, say, 40 trials, then p is a prime with overwhelming probability. The probability that the algorithm fails to detect a composite is less than $(1/4)^{40} \approx 10^{-24}$.

This is far less than the probability of a computer error. A computer that performs one million operations per second, with the same probability of failure per operation, will fail once in thirty billion years. That is roughly the age of the universe since the Big Bang [Sagan 1980]!

```
var seed: real;

procedure test(p, m: integer;
    var sure: boolean);
var trial, x: integer;
begin
  seed := 1; sure := false;
  for trial := 1 to m do
    begin
      randomno(x, p − 1);
      { 1 <= x <= p − 1 }
      if witness(x, p) then
        sure := true
    end
end;
```

Figure 12.3: Primality testing algorithm.

12.7 Complexity

The algorithms in Figs. 12.2–3 must be reprogrammed to perform *multiple-length arithmetic* on large natural numbers. Multiple-length division turns out to be a problem of surprising difficulty [Chap. 13 and Brinch Hansen 1992c].

Consider primality testing of an integer p with N *decimal digits*. During the computation, an integer with $O(N)$ decimal digits is represented by an array of $O(n)$ digits in a *radix b*, which is a power of ten:

$$b = 10^{\log b} \qquad n \approx N/\log b$$

The witness test performs $O(N)$ iterations (unless it is interrupted by the discovery of a nontrivial square root of 1). Each iteration involves multiplication and division of $O(n^2)$ complexity. Each step also requires operations of $O(n)$ complexity, including the time-consuming computation of trial digits during division [Brinch Hansen 1992c].

Consequently, primality testing has the complexity

$$T = O((n^2 + n)N) = O((n + 1)nN)$$

In other words,

$$T \approx (cN/\mathrm{log}b + d)N^2/\mathrm{log}b \qquad (12.3)$$

where c and d are system-dependent constants of decimal arithmetic.

12.8   Experiments

I programmed Rabin's algorithm in occam and tested it on a Computing Surface with T800 transputers using the random number generator of Park and Miller [1988].

After systematic testing of the multiple-length arithmetic, I performed several experiments. In each experiment, a random integer p was tested 40 times for primality using different random base values x. The trials were performed in parallel by 40 transputers [Chap. 14 and Brinch Hansen 1992d].

The program correctly identified the 121-digit *Mersenne number*

$$2^{400} - 1$$

as a composite, and confirmed that

$$2^{400} - 593$$

almost certainly is a prime [Rabin 1980].

Table 12.1 shows measured (and predicted) run times T in seconds for a random integer p with $N = 120$ decimal digits. The integer is represented by an array of random digits in radix b. In theory, radix 10,000 reduces the run time by a factor of 16 (or less) compared to radix 10. In practice, it makes the program run 13 times faster.

Table 12.1: Run times.

b	T (s)	
10	219	(226)
100	59	(61)
1,000	29	(29)
10,000	17	(18)

Table 12.2 shows measured (and predicted) run times T for primality testing of random numbers with N decimal digits represented in radix 10,000.

Table 12.2: More run times.

N	$T\ (s)$	
120	17	(18)
160	39	(39)
200	73	(73)
240	124	(122)
280	190	(190)

The empirical formula

$$T \approx (0.12N/\log b + 1.3)N^2/\log b \ \text{ms}$$

defines the estimated run times shown in parentheses in Tables 12.1–2.

12.9   Final Remarks

I have described a probabilistic algorithm for testing the primality of a large integer without factorizing it. The Miller-Rabin algorithm is always right when it identifies a number as composite. A number that is not recognized as composite is prime with extremely high probability. On a Computing Surface, the algorithm tests the primality of a 150-digit decimal integer 40 times in about 30 seconds.

Chapter 13

Multiple-Length Division Revisited

13.1   Introduction

Long division of natural numbers plays a crucial role in *Cobol arithmetic* [Brinch Hansen 1966], *cryptography* [Rivest 1978], and *primality testing* [Rabin 1980]. While writing a program for primality testing, I learned two lessons the hard way [Chap. 12 and Brinch Hansen 1992b]:

1. Only a handful of textbooks discuss the theory and practice of long division, and none of them do it satisfactorily.

2. A correct, efficient algorithm for long division cannot be reinvented with minimal effort.

   This chapter attempts to fill this surprising gap in the literature on computer algorithms.

   A helpful description of an algorithm should include three elements:

1. An informal introduction that illustrates the problem and its solution by well-chosen examples.

2. A concise definition of the general problem and an explanation of the computational theory.

3. A well-structured complete algorithm written in a standard programming language using the same terminology as the theoretical discussion.

The best textbooks on algorithms satisfy all three requirements. However, computer scientists do not always appreciate that a professional programmer cannot rely on a complex algorithm unless it is written in a programming language that runs on an available computer. There are too many pitfalls in purely theoretical arguments about "pseudocode" that cannot be compiled and executed on any computer.

I am aware of only four texts that deal with multiple-length arithmetic. I will briefly discuss how well they satisfy the above criteria.

In 1969, *Donald Knuth* published a volume on *Seminumerical Algorithms*. This work contains the most comprehensive treatment of multiple-length arithmetic:

1. In his introduction to long division, Knuth gives a three-line hint of an example and remarks: "It is clear that this same idea works in general."

2. Knuth covers most of the relevant theory from the literature.

3. Knuth presents a division algorithm in three different ways. The first version is a mixture of English, mathematical notation, and *goto* statements. The second one is an informal flowchart that merely shows the flow of control. The third attempt is written in the assembly language MIX with informal comments. Each of these versions conveys insight, but none of them inspire complete confidence in the finer details. They are obviously not well-structured algorithms written in a standard programming language.

However, you must keep in mind that Knuth wrote the first edition of his book in the late 1960s, when structured programming was still in its infancy.

Ten years later, *Suad Alagić* and *Michael Arbib* wrote a book on *The Design of Well-Structured and Correct Programs* [1978]. This text has two pages on long division:

1. Alagić and Arbib do not illustrate long division by examples.

2. They state four theorems from Knuth without motivation, proof, or reference.

3. Their algorithm for long division consists of 56 lines written in Pascal. The entire program is a single compound statement composed of shorter statements according to the principles of structured programming. However, the lack of procedures makes it hard to study the algorithm bottom-up (or top-down) at different levels of detail. The program assumes that array dimensions correspond exactly to the lengths of operands. As it stands, the program cannot be compiled and executed. (It has one syntax error and two undeclared names.) The algorithm is helpful, but not sufficiently developed for software design.

Clearly, this program could have been developed further. If the authors had finished the job, there would have been no need to write this tutorial. Alagić and Arbib make a devastating remark about this part of their book: "The reader who has struggled through [our program]—which is typical of the way in which programs are presented and documented—may come to understand the advantages of a top-down approach to presenting a program."

This brings me to *Derick Wood's* textbook on *Paradigms and Programming with Pascal* [1984], which presents a slightly different form of long division:

1. Wood carefully explains long division by an example.

2. His method underestimates quotient digits and corrects them by a slow loop that uses multiple-length arithmetic. The main problem is the lack of a theory that predicts the maximum number of corrections required.

3. Wood's algorithm consists of seven procedures, three of which are left as exercises. With one exception, the remaining procedures are well-structured and well-explained. However, the main procedure for long division contains a complicated *while* statement that tests and prepares its own termination in the middle of the loop.

In his book on *Prime Numbers and Computer Methods for Factorization*, *Hans Riesel* [1985] makes the following observation: "Unfortunately...the performance of exact computations on large integers has a limited appeal, and computer manufacturers do not find it profitable to include such facilities in the software that goes with their hardware. This means that the reader

may have to construct such a package himself for the computer he is using...
[We] shall discuss ways in which this can be done."

1. Riesel gives no examples of long division.

2. According to Riesel: "Division is by far the most complicated of the four elementary operations." In spite of that, he immediately adds: "We shall only sketch...division." This warning is followed by a single page of hints with no theoretical analysis.

3. Without further explanation, Riesel presents a Pascal procedure of 45 lines, which uses *goto* statements (instead of *while* and *for* statements) to implement iteration. Although written in a standard language, this procedure is too hard to follow.

These evaluations of existing textbooks are written not for the sake of criticizing the authors, but to explain why it is necessary to discuss a fundamental algorithm that has been known for five centuries [Smith 1988]. When you need multiple-length division on a computer, you will look in vain for a textbook that combines an elegant algorithm with a simple explanation.

In the following, I illustrate the subtleties of long division by examples, define the problem concisely, summarize the theory, and develop a complete *SuperPascal* algorithm using a consistent terminology. I also derive the complexity of the algorithm and explain how the radix is selected. The Appendix contains proofs of the theorems on which the algorithm is based.

13.2 Long Division

Most computers limit integer arithmetic to operands of 32–64 bits, corresponding to 8–17 decimal digits. A larger integer must be represented by an array of digits, each occupying a single machine word. The arithmetic operations on multiple-length integers are serial operations that imitate paper-and-pencil methods.

If a machine word represents a decimal digit, a 100-digit decimal number requires 100 machine words. However, if you use radix 1000 (instead of ten), the same number occupies only 34 words. A large radix reduces both the memory space of multiple-length integers and the execution time of serial arithmetic.

Multiple-length division is surprisingly difficult. The following example illustrates *long division* of decimal numbers, as we learned it in school.

Example 1:

$$
\begin{array}{r}
3098 \\
102\overline{)0316097} \\
\underline{0306} \\
0100 \\
\underline{0000} \\
1009 \\
\underline{0918} \\
0917 \\
\underline{0816} \\
101
\end{array}
$$

The initial remainder is the dividend 316097 extended with a leading zero: 0316097. (The purpose of the extra digit will soon become apparent.) The quotient digits are computed one at a time:

1. Since the divisor has three digits, you divide the four leading digits of the remainder by the divisor:

$$0316 \ \mathbf{div} \ 102 = 3$$

This gives you the leading digit of the quotient. The remainder is then reduced to 010097, as shown.

2. You divide the four leading digits of the new remainder by the divisor to get the next quotient digit:

$$0100 \ \mathbf{div} \ 102 = 0$$

This leaves a remainder of 10097.

3. You use the same method to compute the last two digits of the quotient:

$$1009 \ \mathbf{div} \ 102 = 9$$
$$0917 \ \mathbf{div} \ 102 = 8$$

The final remainder is 101.

In each step, you treat the four leading digits of the remainder r as an integer $r\{4\}$ and use the divisor d to compute a *quotient digit* q_k:

$$q_k = r\{4\} \textbf{ div } d$$

The integer $r\{4\}$ is called a *prefix* of the remainder.

The following table is a different representation of the division steps in Example 1:

k	$r\{4\}$	q_k
3	0316	3
2	0100	0
1	1009	9
0	0917	8

Without a zero in front of the initial remainder, the computation of the first quotient digit would be a special case

$$316 \textbf{ div } 102 = 3$$

requiring three digits of the remainder (instead of four).

If the divisor has many digits, a quotient digit can seldom be computed directly, but must be estimated and corrected, if necessary. The main challenge is to replace human intuition about this process by an efficient iterative algorithm.

The three leading digits of the remainder define a shorter *prefix* $r\{3\}$. Similarly, the two leading digits of the divisor define a *prefix* $d\{2\}$. I will use

$$r\{3\} \textbf{ div } d\{2\}$$

as an *initial estimate* of the quotient digit q_k. Since a decimal digit must be less than 10, the initial estimate q_e is defined as follows:

$$q_e = \min(r\{3\} \textbf{ div } d\{2\}, 9)$$

The *error* of the initial estimate is the difference

$$\Delta q = q_e - q_k$$

In Example 1, where $d\{2\} = 10$, the initial estimate produces the following sequence of digits:

k	$r\{4\}$	q_k	$r\{3\}$	q_e	Δq
3	0316	3	031	3	0
2	0100	0	010	1	1
1	1009	9	100	9	0
0	0917	8	091	9	1

In every step,

$$0 \le \Delta q \le 1$$

Later, you will see that this inequality always holds. So, the most obvious idea is to correct a *trial digit* q_t as follows:

$q_t := q_e;$
if $r\{4\} < d * q_t$ **then** $q_t := q_t - 1$

At the end of this iteration, $q_t = q_k$.

In Example 1, half of the initial guesses require a single correction. The number of corrections can be reduced dramatically by *scaling* the operands before the division: You multiply the divisor and the dividend by the same digit. The scaling must make the leading digit of the divisor at least equal to half of the radix without changing the length of the divisor. This is called *normalization*.

Example 2:

Example 1 is normalized by multiplying both operands by five:

$$102 * 5 = 510$$
$$0316097 * 5 = 1580485$$

The leading digit of the normalized divisor is equal to 5, which is half of the radix 10. The normalized divisor still has only three digits. Since the original dividend already has an extra digit-position, normalization does not change its length either. This is another reason for adding the extra digit.

After normalization, division proceeds as usual:

$$\begin{array}{r} 3098 \\ \hline 510\overline{)1580485} \\ \underline{1530} \\ 0504 \\ \underline{0000} \\ 5048 \\ \underline{4590} \\ 4585 \\ \underline{4080} \\ 505 \end{array}$$

Finally, the remainder is divided by the scaling factor to obtain the remainder of the original problem:

$$505 \text{ div } 5 = 101$$

In each step, the initial estimate q_e is the prefix $r\{3\}$ divided by the prefix $d\{2\} = 51$:

k	$r\{4\}$	q_k	$r\{3\}$	q_e	Δq
3	1580	3	158	3	0
2	0504	0	050	0	0
1	5048	9	504	9	0
0	4585	8	458	8	0

In this example, the initial estimates are exact estimates of the corresponding quotient digits. However, in general, normalized division occasionally requires correction of an initial estimate. In decimal arithmetic, the average number of corrections is less than 20%. For higher radices, corrections are rarely necessary.

After this intuitive exploration, I am ready to analyze the problem concisely.

13.3   The Essence of the Problem

I am considering long division of two natural numbers, x and y

$$q = x \text{ div } y \qquad\qquad (13.1)$$
$$r = x \text{ mod } y$$

where $x \geq 0$ and $y > 0$.

The quotient q and the remainder r are natural numbers which satisfy the constraints:

$$x = y * q + r \qquad (13.2)$$

$$0 \leq r \leq y - 1 \qquad (13.3)$$

Each number is represented by an array of digits in *radix b*. The *dividend* x has n digits

$$x = x_{n-1}b^{n-1} + x_{n-2}b^{n-2} + \cdots + x_0 \qquad (13.4)$$

while the *divisor* y has m digits

$$y = y_{m-1}b^{m-1} + y_{m-2}b^{m-2} + \cdots + y_0 \qquad (13.5)$$

Two *special cases* immediately arise:

1. $m = 1$: If the divisor is a single-digit number, I will use a very simple division algorithm. Since zero is a single-digit number, this algorithm will also detect overflow.

2. $m > n$: If the divisor is longer than the dividend, the quotient is zero, and the remainder is x.

In the theoretical analysis, I will concentrate on the remaining case

$$2 \leq m \leq n \qquad (13.6)$$

where the divisor has at least two digits, and the dividend has at least as many digits as the divisor.

Before the division, the operands are multiplied by a *scaling factor, $f \geq 1$,* that will be defined later. The following abstract program defines *normalized division:*

```
var x, y, q, r, d, f: integer;
begin
    r := x * f;
    d := y * f;
    q := r div d;
    r := (r mod d) div f
end
```

The *normalized divisor*, $d = y * f$, has m digits

$$d = d_{m-1}b^{m-1} + d_{m-2}b^{m-2} + \cdots + d_0 \qquad (13.7)$$

Since $y > 0$, and $f \geq 1$, you also have $d > 0$.

The *quotient* q has $n - m + 1$ digits:

$$q = q_{n-m}b^{n-m} + q_{n-m-1}b^{n-m-1} + \cdots + q_0 \qquad (13.8)$$

The initial *remainder*, $r = x * f$, has $n + 1$ digits. Immediately before the computation of quotient digit q_k, the remainder has been reduced to $k + m + 1$ digits

$$r = r_{k+m}b^{k+m} + r_{k+m-1}b^{k+m-1} + \cdots + r_0 \qquad (13.9)$$

where $0 \leq k \leq n - m$.

The leading $m + 1$ digits of the remainder define a *prefix* $r\{m + 1\}$:

$$r\{m + 1\} = r_{k+m}b^m + r_{k+m-1}b^{m-1} + \cdots + r_k \qquad (13.10)$$

The essence of multiple-length division is the computation of a single *quotient digit* q_k

$$q_k = r\{m + 1\} \ \mathbf{div} \ d \qquad (13.11)$$

by iteration.

To simplify the algebra a bit, I will assume that the *radix* b is *even*, say, a power of two or ten:

$$b \ \mathbf{div} \ 2 = b/2 \geq 1 \qquad (13.12)$$

13.4   Trial Iteration

The Initial Estimate

The computation of a quotient digit q_k is an iteration that decrements an initial estimate until it equals q_k. The most conservative guess is $b - 1$, which requires $O(b)$ corrections. Fortunately, there is a much better choice.

The three leading digits of the remainder r define a *prefix* $r\{3\}$:

$$r\{3\} = r_{k+m}b^2 + r_{k+m-1}b + r_{k+m-2} \qquad (13.13)$$

The *prefix* $d\{2\}$ consists of the two leading digits of the divisor d

$$d\{2\} = d_{m-1}b + d_{m-2} \qquad (13.14)$$

where

$$2 \le m \le k + m \le n \qquad (13.15)$$

I assume that $r\{3\}$ and $d\{2\}$ can be represented as single-length integers.

I will use

$$q_e = \min(r\{3\} \textbf{ div } d\{2\}, b - 1) \qquad (13.16)$$

as the *initial estimate* of q_k. Obviously $0 \le q_e \le b - 1$.

The following theorems show that q_e is an excellent guess. They are due to Krishnamurthy and Nandi [1967]. (The Appendix includes the proofs of all theorems used.)

Theorem 1: $q_k \le q_e$

Theorem 2: $q_e \le q_k + 1$

By combining Theorems 1 and 2 with the assumption that q_k is a digit, you obtain the inequality:

$$0 \le q_k \le q_e \le q_k + 1 \le b \qquad (13.17)$$

So, the initial estimate q_e is either correct or off by 1.

Trial Correction

The computation of a *quotient digit* q_k is based on two simple theorems about any *trial digit* q_t:

Theorem 3: *If* $r\{m+1\} < d * q_t$ *then* $q_k < q_t$

Theorem 4: *If* $r\{m+1\} \ge d * q_t$ *then* $q_t \le q_k$

These theorems and (13.17) suggest the following *trial iteration:*

$$q_t := q_e;$$
$$\textbf{if } r\{\text{m+1}\} < d * q_t \textbf{ then } q_t := q_t - 1$$

Here is the same algorithm with assertions added:

$$\{\ 0 \le q_k \le q_e \le q_k + 1 \le b \ \text{by (13.17)}\ \}$$
$$q_t := q_e;$$
$$\{\ 0 \le q_k \le q_t \le q_k + 1 \le b\ \}$$
if $r\{m{+}1\} < d * q_t$ **then**
$$\quad \{\ 0 \le q_k < q_t \le q_k + 1 \le b \ \text{by Theorem 3}\ \}$$
$$\quad q_t := q_t - 1$$
$$\quad \{\ 0 \le q_k \le q_t < q_k + 1 \le b\ \}$$
else
$$\quad \{\ 0 \le q_k \le q_t \le q_k < b \ \text{by Theorem 4}\ \}$$

The *if* statement terminates with the postcondition

$$0 \le q_k \le q_t' \le q_k \le b - 1$$

which implies that $q_t = q_k$.

I will show that the frequency of trial corrections depends on the *leading digit* $d\{1\}$ of the divisor d

$$d\{1\} = d_{m-1} \tag{13.18}$$

where $1 \le d\{1\} \le b - 1$.

The computation of quotient digit q_k is equivalent to the integer division

$$q_k = r\{m + 1\} \ \textbf{div} \ d$$

which leaves a remainder

$$r\{m + 1\} \ \textbf{mod} \ d = r\{m + 1\} - d * q_k$$

where $0 \le r\{m + 1\} \ \textbf{mod} \ d < d$.

I assume that the relative remainder

$$z_k = (r\{m + 1\} \ \textbf{mod} \ d)/d = r\{m + 1\}/d - q_k$$

is a random variable with a uniform distribution between 0 and 1.

At this point, another theorem is needed:

Theorem 5: *If* $q_k = q_e - 1$ *then* $r\{m + 1\}/d - q_k > 1 - 1/d\{1\}$

The probability that a correction is required is

$$\text{Prob}(q_k = q_e - 1) = \text{Prob}(z_k > 1 - 1/d\{1\})$$

In other words,

$$\text{Prob}(q_k = q_e - 1) \; < \; 1/d\{1\} \tag{13.19}$$

To reduce the number of corrections, you should obviously make the leading digit of the divisor as large as possible. This requires normalization of the operands.

Normalization

The divisor d is *normalized* if its leading digit is at least half of the radix b:

$$1 \le b/2 \le d\{1\} \le b - 1 \tag{13.20}$$

This requirement implies that

$$1 \le b^m/2 \le d \le b^m - 1 \tag{13.21}$$

The *leading digit* $y\{1\}$ of the original divisor y is

$$y\{1\} = y_{m-1} \tag{13.22}$$

where $1 \le y\{1\} \le b - 1$. This digit determines the *scaling factor* f:

$$f = b \; \textbf{div} \; (y\{1\} + 1) \tag{13.23}$$

Obviously, $1 \le f \le b/2$.

The following theorem shows that normalization is done correctly:

Theorem 6: $b^m/2 \le y * f \le b^m - 1$

From now on, I assume that the divisor, $d = y * f$, is normalized. By (13.19) and (13.20), the probability that an initial estimate q_e needs to be decremented is bounded as follows:

$$\text{Prob}(q_k = q_e - 1) < 2/b$$

In decimal division, at least 80% of the initial estimates are correct. For radix 1,000, each guess is correct with probability 0.998.

13.5   SuperPascal Algorithm

With this background, I will describe a *SuperPascal* algorithm for multiple-length division. The theoretical discussion introduced names for the most important constants and variables. The algorithm uses exactly the same terminology and is presented in bottom-up form. (If you prefer top-down design, please read the rest of this section backwards.)

Number Representation

A natural *number* x is represented by an array of $w + 1$ digits in *radix b*, say

> **const** b = 1000; w = 100;
> **type** number = **array** [0..w] **of** integer;
> **var** x: number;

The algorithm can divide natural numbers with 1 to w digits. During division, the remainder is extended with an additional position.

Every *digit* $x[k]$ is an integer in the range

$$0 \le x[k] \le b - 1 \qquad \text{for } 0 \le k \le w$$

The kth digit of x represents the integer $x[k] * b^k$. I will use the words *left* and *right* to refer to the high-order and low-order positions of a number.

SuperPascal extends Pascal with structured function types. The function, shown in Fig. 13.1, defines the conversion of a single-length integer x to a multiple-length integer of type *number*.

The *length* of a natural number is the number of significant digits in the corresponding array. The algorithm in Fig. 13.2 determines the length of a number x by a linear search from left to right. The search stops at the first nonzero digit or at the rightmost digit, whichever is reached first. This variant of linear searching was derived in Brinch Hansen [1990a].

Partial Arithmetic

The simplest part of multiple-length division is the multiplication or division of a natural number by a single digit. To avoid confusing these *partial operations* with complete multiple-length operations, they are called *product, quotient,* and *remainder* (instead of multiply, divide, and modulo):

```
function value(x: integer): number;
var y: number; i: integer;
begin
  for i := 0 to w do
    begin
      y[i] := x mod b;
      x := x div b
    end;
  value := y
end;
```

Figure 13.1: Value algorithm.

```
function length(x: number): integer;
var i, j: integer;
begin
  i := w; j := 0;
  while i <> j do
    if x[i] <> 0 then j := i
    else i := i − 1;
  length := i + 1
end;
```

Figure 13.2: Length algorithm.

Function	Result
product(x,k)	x * k
quotient(x,k)	x div k
remainder(x,k)	x mod k

Each operation involves a natural number x and a digit k. The functions are straightforward implementations of familiar paper-and-pencil methods.

A partial *product* is computed, digit by digit, from right to left using a *carry* (Fig. 13.3). The effect of the *assume* statement is to halt the execution if *overflow* occurs.

```
function product(x: number;
  k: integer): number;
var carry, i, m, temp: integer;
begin
  m := length(x); carry := 0;
  for i := 0 to m − 1 do
    begin
      temp := x[i]*k + carry;
      x[i] := temp mod b;
      carry := temp div b
    end;
  if m <= w then x[m] := carry
  else assume carry = 0;
  product := x
end;
```

Figure 13.3: Product algorithm.

The *quotient* of a partial division is calculated serially from left to right (Fig. 13.4).

The *remainder* of a partial division is the last carry (compare Figs. 13.4 and 13.5).

Prefix Arithmetic

The computation of a quotient digit $q[k]$ breaks down into simpler *prefix operations*. In the following, $x[i..j]$ denotes digits i through j of a natural number x.

The assignment

$$q_t := \text{trialdigit}(r, d, k, m)$$

defines a *trial digit*, $q_t = q_e$, which is an initial estimate of q_k. The operands of the *trial digit* function are prefixes of the remainder r and the divisor d

$$r\{3\} = r[k + m..k + m − 2] \qquad d\{2\} = d[m − 1..m − 2]$$

where

$$2 \leq m \leq k + m \leq w \tag{13.24}$$

```
function quotient(x: number;
   k: integer): number;
var carry, i, m, temp: integer;
begin
  m := length(x); carry := 0;
  for i := m − 1 downto 0 do
    begin
      temp := carry*b + x[i];
      x[i] := temp div k;
      carry := temp mod k
    end;
  quotient := x
end;
```

Figure 13.4: Quotient algorithm.

```
function remainder(x: number;
   k: integer): number;
var carry, i, m: integer;
begin
  m := length(x); carry := 0;
  for i := m − 1 downto 0 do
    carry := (carry*b + x[i]) mod k;
  remainder := value(carry)
end;
```

Figure 13.5: Remainder algorithm.

The initial estimate is computed as described earlier (Fig. 13.6). Strictly speaking, the trial function should verify that its *precondition* holds. However, since (13.24) turns out to be an invariant of long division, this assumption is described by a comment only.

Two functions define prefix comparison and subtraction:

```
function trialdigit(r, d: number;
    k, m: integer): integer;
var d2, km, r3: integer;
begin
    { 2 <= m <= k+m <= w }
    km := k + m;
    r3 := (r[km]*b + r[km−1])*b + r[km−2];
    d2 := d[m−1]*b + d[m−2];
    trialdigit := min(r3 div d2, b − 1)
end;
```

Figure 13.6: Trial-digit algorithm.

Function	Result
smaller(r, dq, k, m)	$r\{m+1\} < dq$
difference(r, dq, k, m)	$r - dq * b^k$

The (m+1)-place operands are

$$r\{m+1\} = r[k+m..k] \qquad d * q_t = dq[m..0]$$

where

$$0 \le k \le k+m \le w \tag{13.25}$$

Since the division invariant (13.24) implies the precondition (13.25), these functions do not verify this assumption.

The boolean function that determines if the prefix $r\{m+1\}$ is *smaller* than the product dq is a variant of the *length* function (see Figs. 13.2 and 13.7).

The subtraction of the product dq from the $m+1$ high-order digits of the remainder r proceeds from right to left using a *borrow*. If the *difference* is negative, the execution halts (Fig. 13.8).

Division Algorithms

Figure 13.9 defines *long division*

$$x \text{ div } y$$

```
function smaller(r, dq: number;
    k, m: integer): boolean
{ r[k+m..k] < dq[m..0] };
var i, j: integer;
begin
    { 0 <= k <= k+m <= w }
    i := m; j := 0;
    while i <> j do
        if r[i+k] <> dq[i]
            then j := i
            else i := i − 1;
    smaller := r[i+k] < dq[i]
end;
```

Figure 13.7: Smaller algorithm.

of two natural numbers

$$x[n-1..0] \qquad y[m-1..0]$$

where

$$2 \leq m \leq n \leq w \qquad (13.26)$$

After normalization of the operands, the *quotient q* is computed, digit by digit, from left to right. The quotient iteration maintains the invariant

$$2 \leq m \leq k+m \leq n \leq w \qquad (13.27)$$

The *long modulo* operation

$$x \ \mathbf{mod} \ y$$

is very similar (Fig. 13.10). Notice that the final *remainder r* is divided by the *scaling factor f*.

The complete algorithm for computing the quotient of a *multiple-length division* uses simpler methods for the special cases, where the *divisor y* has only a single digit or is longer than the *dividend x* (Fig. 13.11). In all other cases, the algorithm uses long division after establishing the precondition (13.26).

Figure 13.12 shows the complete algorithm for computing the remainder of a multiple-length division.

```
function difference(r, dq: number;
  k, m: integer): number;
{ r[k+m..k] :=
    r[k+m..k] − dq[m..0];
  difference := r }
var borrow, diff, i: integer;
begin
  { 0 <= k <= k+m <= w }
  borrow := 0;
  for i := 0 to m do
    begin
      diff := r[i+k] − dq[i]
        − borrow + b;
      r[i+k] := diff mod b;
      borrow := 1 − diff div b
    end;
  assume borrow = 0;
  difference := r
end;
```

Figure 13.8: Difference algorithm.

Complexity

The complexity of long division is determined by the $n-m+1$ quotient steps. Each step is dominated by product and difference operations on $(m+1)$-place operands. Consequently, the complexity is

$$O((n - m + 1)(m + 1))$$

For random divisors with uniformly distributed lengths between 2 and n, the average run time T is close to

$$T \approx \frac{1}{n} \int_2^n (n - m + 1)(m + 1)dm = O(n^2) \quad \text{for } n \gg 2$$

Since

$$10^N \approx b^n \quad \text{for } n \approx N/\mathrm{log}b$$

```
function longdiv(x, y: number;
    n, m: integer): number;
{ longdiv = x div y }
var d, dq, q, r: number;
    f, k, qt: integer;
begin
  { 2 <= m <= n <= w }
  f := b div (y[m−1] + 1);
  r := product(x, f);
  d := product(y, f);
  q := value(0);
  for k := n − m downto 0 do
    begin
      { 2 <= m <= k+m <= n <= w }
      qt := trialdigit(r, d, k, m);
      dq := product(d, qt);
      if smaller(r, dq, k, m) then
        begin
          qt := qt − 1;
          dq := product(d, qt)
        end;
      q[k] := qt;
      r := difference(r, dq, k, m)
    end;
  longdiv := q
end;
```

Figure 13.9: Long divide algorithm.

a decimal number with N digits corresponds to a radix-b number with $N/\log b$ digits. Consequently,

$$T \approx O\left((N/\log b)^2\right)$$

Using radix 1000, instead of ten, reduces the average division time by a factor of 9. Radix 10,000 makes multiple-length division 16 times faster than decimal division.

```
function longmod(x, y: number;
    n, m: integer): number;
{ longmod = x mod y }
var d, dq, r: number;
    f, k, qt: integer;
begin
    { 2 <= m <= n <= w }
    f := b div (y[m−1] + 1);
    r := product(x, f);
    d := product(y, f);
    for k := n − m downto 0 do
        begin
            { 2 <= m <= k+m <= n <= w }
            qt := trialdigit(r, d, k, m);
            dq := product(d, qt);
            if smaller(r, dq, k, m) then
                begin
                    qt := qt − 1;
                    dq := product(d, qt)
                end;
            r := difference(r, dq, k, m)
        end;
    longmod := quotient(r, f)
end;
```

Figure 13.10: Long modulo algorithm.

Radix Selection

The algorithms in Figs. 13.4–5 include integer expressions of the form

$$d * b + d$$

where the d's denote arbitrary digits. The corresponding values can be represented by standard integers if you choose a radix b that satisfies the inequality

$$d * b + d \leq b^2 - 1 \leq maxint$$

```
function divide(x, y: number): number;
var m, n, y1: integer; q: number;
begin
  m := length(y);
  if m = 1 then
    begin
      y1 := y[m−1];
      assume y1 > 0;
      q := quotient(x, y1)
    end
  else
    begin
      n := length(x);
      if m > n then q := value(0)
      else { 2 <= m <= n <= w }
        q := longdiv(x, y, n, m)
    end;
  divide := q
end;
```

Figure 13.11: Divide algorithm.

where *maxint* is the largest standard integer.

For 32-bit integers, this means

$$b^2 \leq 2^{31}$$

or $b \leq 46{,}340$. A possible choice is $b = 10{,}000$.

However, the *trial digit* function (Fig. 13.6) has an expression of the form

$$(d * b + d) * b + d$$

The corresponding inequality is

$$(d * b + d) * b + d \leq b^3 - 1 \leq maxint$$

For 32-bit integers, you must therefore use a smaller radix, for which

$$b^3 \leq 2^{31}$$

```
function modulo(x, y: number): number;
var m, n, y1: integer; r: number;
begin
   m := length(y);
   if m = 1 then
      begin
         y1 := y[m−1];
         assume y1 > 0;
         r := remainder(x, y1)
      end
   else
      begin
         n := length(x);
         if m > n then r := x
         else { 2 <= m <= n <= w }
            r := longmod(x, y, n, m)
      end;
   modulo := r
end;
```

Figure 13.12: Modulo algorithm.

that is, $b \leq 1,290$. For example, $b = 1,000$.

If the available computer supports both 32 and 64-bit integers, a radix of 10,000 is feasible if you use *double-precision arithmetic* in the trial digit function.

13.6 Final Remarks

I have developed a Pascal algorithm for long division of natural numbers and have explained the theory behind the algorithm. This chapter is merely an interpretation and formalization of the original ideas of the authors referenced in the text. It was written only because I was unable to find an elegant, complete algorithm described with convincing clarity in the literature.

13.7   Appendix: Proof of Theorems

The appendix summarizes the laws of prefixes and integer division and proves
the theorems about long division.

Prefix Laws

By (13.5), (13.22):

$$y\{1\}b^{m-1} \leq y < (y\{1\}+1)b^{m-1} \tag{13.28}$$

By (13.7), (13.18):

$$d\{1\}b^{m-1} \leq d < (d\{1\}+1)b^{m-1} \tag{13.29}$$

By (13.7), (13.14):

$$d\{2\}b^{m-2} \leq d < (d\{2\}+1)b^{m-2} \tag{13.30}$$

By (13.10), (13.13):

$$r\{3\}b^{m-2} \leq r\{m+1\} < (r\{3\}+1)b^{m-2} \tag{13.31}$$

Division Laws

Any integer division, $q = x$ **div** y, satisfies three equivalent laws:

$$x/y - 1 < q \leq x/y \tag{13.32}$$

$$x < y(q+1) \leq x+y \tag{13.33}$$

$$x - y + 1 \leq y*q \leq x \tag{13.34}$$

The following instances of these laws apply to the integer divisions that
define the quotients, f, q_e, and q_k, where

$$\begin{aligned} f &= b \textbf{ div } (y\{1\}+1) \\ q_e &= \min(r\{3\} \textbf{ div } d\{2\}, b-1) \\ q_k &= r\{m+1\} \textbf{ div } d \end{aligned}$$

By (13.32):

$$b/(y\{1\}+1) - 1 < f \leq b/(y\{1\}+1) \tag{13.35}$$

If $q_e = r\{3\}$ **div** $d\{2\}$, then by (13.34):

$$r\{3\} - d\{2\} + 1 \;\leq\; d\{2\} * q_e \;\leq\; r\{3\} \tag{13.36}$$

By (13.34):

$$r\{m+1\} - d + 1 \;\leq\; d * q_k \;\leq\; r\{m+1\} \tag{13.37}$$

By (13.33):

$$r\{m+1\} \;<\; d(q_k + 1) \;\leq\; r\{m+1\} + d \tag{13.38}$$

Proof of Theorem 1

Theorem: $q_k \leq q_e$

Proof:

1. If $q_e = r\{3\}$ **div** $d\{2\}$, then

$$
\begin{aligned}
d(q_k - q_e) \;&\leq\; r\{m+1\} - d\{2\}q_e b^{m-2} \\
&\qquad \text{by (13.30), (13.37)} \\
&<\; ((r\{3\} + 1) - (r\{3\} - d\{2\} + 1))b^{m-2} \\
&\qquad \text{by (13.31), (13.36)} \\
&=\; d\{2\}b^{m-2} \\
&\leq\; d \qquad \text{by (13.30)}
\end{aligned}
$$

Since $d > 0$, you have $q_k - q_e < 1$, which implies $q_k - q_e \leq 0$.

2. If $q_e = b - 1$, then

$$q_k \;\leq\; q_e \qquad \text{by } q_k \;\leq\; b - 1$$

Proof of Theorem 2

Theorem: $q_e \;\leq\; q_k + 1$

Proof by contradiction: If $q_e \;\geq\; q_k + 2$, then

$$
\begin{aligned}
r\{m+1\} \;&<\; d(q_k + 1) & &\text{by (13.38)} \\
&\leq\; d(q_e - 1) & &\text{by } q_e \geq q_k + 2 \\
&<\; (d\{2\} + 1)q_e b^{m-2} - d & &\text{by (13.30)} \\
&\leq\; (r\{3\} + q_e)b^{m-2} - d & &\text{by (13.36)} \\
&<\; (r\{3\} + b)b^{m-2} - d & &\text{by } q_e < b \\
&\leq\; r\{3\}b^{m-2} & &\text{by } d \geq b^{m-1} \\
&\leq\; r\{m+1\} & &\text{by (13.31)}
\end{aligned}
$$

that is, $r\{m+1\} \, < \, r\{m+1\}$, a contradiction.

Proof of Theorem 3

Theorem: *If $r\{m+1\} \, < \, d * q_t$ then $q_k \, < \, q_t$*

Proof:

$$
\begin{aligned}
d(q_k - q_t) \;\; &\le \;\; r\{m+1\} - d * q_t \quad \text{by (13.37)} \\
&< \;\; 0 \qquad\qquad\qquad\quad \text{by } r\{m+1\} \, < \, d * q_t
\end{aligned}
$$

Since $d > 0$, you have $q_k - q_t < 0$.

Proof of Theorem 4

Theorem: *If $r\{m+1\} \, \ge \, d * q_t$ then $q_t \, \le \, q_k$*

Proof by contradiction: If $q_t \, \ge \, q_k + 1$, then

$$
\begin{aligned}
r\{m+1\} \;\; &< \;\; d(q_k + 1) \quad \text{by (13.38)} \\
&\le \;\; d * q_t \qquad\quad \text{by } q_t \, \ge \, q_k + 1 \\
&\le \;\; r\{m+1\} \quad\; \text{by } r\{m+1\} \, \ge \, d * q_t
\end{aligned}
$$

that is, $r\{m+1\} \, < \, r\{m+1\}$, a contradiction.

Proof of Theorem 5

Theorem: *If $q_k = q_e - 1$ then $r\{m+1\}/d - q_k \, > \, 1 - 1/d\{1\}$*

Proof:

$$
\begin{aligned}
r\{m+1\} - d * q_k \;\; &= \;\; d + r\{m+1\} - d * q_e \\
&\qquad \text{by } q_k = q_e - 1 \\
&> \;\; d + (r\{3\} - (d\{2\} + 1)q_e)b^{m-2} \\
&\qquad \text{by (13.30), (13.31)} \\
&\ge \;\; d - q_e b^{m-2} \qquad \text{by (13.36)} \\
&> \;\; d - b^{m-1} \qquad\; \text{by } q_e \, < \, b \\
&= \;\; d(1 - b^{m-1}/d) \qquad \text{by } d \, > \, 0 \\
&\ge \;\; d(1 - 1/d\{1\}) \qquad \text{by (13.29)}
\end{aligned}
$$

Consequently, $r\{m+1\}/d - q_k \, > \, 1 - 1/d\{1\}$.

Proof of Theorem 6

Theorem: $b^m/2 \leq y * f \leq b^m - 1$

1. Upper bound:

$$
\begin{aligned}
y * f &\leq ((y\{1\} + 1)b^{m-1} - 1)f && \text{by (13.28)} \\
&\leq (y\{1\} + 1)f * b^{m-1} - 1 && \text{by } f \geq 1 \\
&\leq b^m - 1 && \text{if } f \leq b/(y\{1\} + 1)
\end{aligned}
$$

The largest possible scaling factor is

$$
f = b \textbf{ div } (y\{1\} + 1)
$$

2. Lower bound:

   (a) If $y\{1\} < b/2$, then

$$
\begin{aligned}
y\{1\}f &> y\{1\}(b/(y\{1\} + 1) - 1) && \text{by (13.35)} \\
&= (b/2 - y\{1\} - 1)(y\{1\} - 1)/(y\{1\} + 1) + b/2 - 1 \\
& \quad \text{by algebra} \\
&\geq b/2 - 1 && \text{by } 1 \leq y\{1\} \leq b/2 - 1
\end{aligned}
$$

   Since $y\{1\}f > b/2 - 1$ and $b/2$ is an integer, you have $y\{1\}f \geq b/2$. Consequently,

$$
\begin{aligned}
y * f &\geq y\{1\}f * b^{m-1} && \text{by (13.28)} \\
&\geq b^m/2 && \text{by } y\{1\}f \geq b/2
\end{aligned}
$$

   (b) If $y\{1\} \geq b/2$, then

$$
\begin{aligned}
y * f &\geq y\{1\}b^{m-1} && \text{by } f \geq 1, \text{ (13.28)} \\
&\geq b^m/2 && \text{by } y\{1\} \geq b/2
\end{aligned}
$$

Chapter 14

Parallel Monte Carlo Trials

14.1   Introduction

Monte Carlo methods are probabilistic algorithms for problems that cannot be solved exactly.

The classic problem of the *traveling salesperson* is to find the shortest tour through n cities. A computer cannot examine the vast number of possible tours through, say, 100 cities. Instead, I will use a Monte Carlo method which has a high probability of finding a near-optimal tour in reasonable time. This method is known as *simulated annealing* [Kirkpatrick 1983; Brinch Hansen 1992a and Chap. 11]. The chance of finding a good solution can be increased by selecting the shortest tour found in, say, 10 annealing runs.

Primality testing of a large integer is another problem which has a huge number of possible solutions, that is, divisors. In practice, this problem can also be solved by Monte Carlo trials. The Miller-Rabin algorithm uses random numbers to test the same integer repeatedly [Rabin 1980; Brinch Hansen 1992b and Chap. 12]. The algorithm either proves that a number is composite or makes it highly probable that it is prime.

Simulated annealing and primality testing illustrate a general characteristic of Monte Carlo methods: Since there is an element of chance in a Monte Carlo computation, a result can often be improved by repeating the same computation with different random numbers. A multicomputer can perform parallel *Monte Carlo trials* very efficiently without any communication between the processors [Ulam 1986].

I will develop a generic algorithm for parallel Monte Carlo trials on a multicomputer. I will then show how the generic algorithm can be adapted for simulated annealing and primality testing by simple substitution of data types and procedures. The performance of the parallel algorithms is measured on a *Computing Surface*.

14.2 Sequential Paradigm

I assume that a Monte Carlo method is defined by a Pascal procedure of the form:

> **procedure** solve(a: problem; **var** b: solution; trial: integer)

The procedure parameters define a *problem a* of some type, a *solution b* of some type, and a *trial number* used as an initial seed of a random number generator. Since this procedure and its parameters vary from one Monte Carlo method to another, I deliberately leave them unspecified at this point.

The algorithm, shown in Fig. 14.1, defines a sequential paradigm for Monte Carlo trials. The same problem is solved m times using the trial numbers $1, 2, \ldots, m$ as distinct initial seeds. The m solutions are collected in a table.

```
const m = ...{ trials };
type table = array [1..m] of solution;

procedure compute(a: tour; var b: table);
var trial: integer;
begin
   for trial := 1 to m do
      solve(a, b[trial], trial)
end;
```

Figure 14.1: Sequential Monte Carlo trials.

14.3 Parallel Paradigm

I will rewrite the algorithm in Fig. 14.1 for a multicomputer. First, the same problem is broadcast to p processors. Each processor then performs m/p

trials. Finally, m solutions are collected from the processors. To simplify things a bit, I will assume that the number of trials m is divisible by the number of processors p. The local *quota*, $q = m/p$, is the number of trials per processor.

The parallel program uses a *pipeline* with p *nodes* controlled by a *master* process (Fig. 14.2). The parallel processes will be programmed in *Super-Pascal*. I assume that parallel processes run on separate processors without shared memory and communicate through synchronous channels only.

pipeline

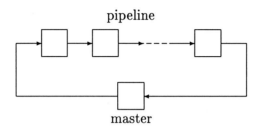

master

Figure 14.2: Master and pipeline.

A channel c, that only transmits messages of types *problem* and *solution*, is declared and opened as follows:

type channel = *(problem, solution);
var c: channel;
open(c)

The master and node processes each have a *left* and a *right* channel. The master process outputs a problem a to the pipeline and inputs m solutions from the pipeline (Fig. 14.3).

The m trials are distributed as follows among the p nodes:

Node	First trial	Last trial
1	1	q
2	$q+1$	$2q$
...	...	...
i	$(i-1)q+1$	iq
...	...	...
p	$(p-1)q+1$	$pq\ (=m)$

```
procedure master(a: tour; var b: table;
  left, right: channel);
var trial: integer;
begin
  send(left, a);
  for trial := 1 to m do
    reccive(right, b[trial])
end;
```

Figure 14.3: Master algorithm.

Pipeline node number i goes through two major phases:

1. *Broadcasting phase:* The node inputs a problem a. If the node is followed by another node, it outputs the problem to its successor:

```
receive(left, a);
if i < p then send(right, a)
```

2. *Trial phase:* The node solves the same problem q times:

```
q := m div p;
for j := 1 to q do
  begin
    trial := (i − 1)*q + j;
    solve(a, b, trial);
    collection phase
  end
```

After every iteration, each node holds a single solution. The nodes now go through a minor phase:

- *Collection phase:* Each node outputs its most recent solution b, and copies the most recent solutions produced by its predecessors in the pipeline:

```
            send(right, b);
            for k := 1 to i − 1 do
               begin
                  receive(left, b);
                  send(right, b)
               end
```

In short, the pipeline outputs p solutions at a time to the master.

Together these pieces define the complete algorithm for a pipeline node (Fig. 14.4).

```
         procedure node(i: integer;
            left, right: channel);
         { 1 <= i <= p }
         var a: problem; b: solution;
            j, k, q, trial: integer;
         begin
            receive(left, a);
            if i < p then send(right, a);
            q := m div p;
            for j := 1 to q do
               begin
                  trial := (i − 1)*q + j;
                  solve(a, b, trial);
                  send(right, b);
                  for k := 1 to i − 1 do
                     begin
                        receive(left, b);
                        send(right, b)
                     end
               end
         end;
```

Figure 14.4: Node algorithm.

The algorithm in Fig. 14.5 defines the parallel network shown in Fig. 14.2. The computation opens $p+1$ channels and runs the master and the pipeline nodes in parallel.

```
const m = ...{ trials };
  p = ...{ processors };
type table = array [1..m] of solution;

procedure compute(a: tour; var b: table);
type net = array [0..p] of channel;
var c: net; i: integer;
begin
  for i := 0 to p do open(c[i]);
  parallel
    master(a, b, c[0], c[p])|
    forall i := 1 to p do
      node(i, c[i−1], c[i])
  end
end;
```

Figure 14.5: Parallel Monte Carlo trials.

I have developed a generic algorithm for parallel execution of Monte Carlo trials on a multicomputer (Figs. 14.3–5). I will now use this paradigm to solve two different problems.

14.4   Simulated Annealing

The first Monte Carlo method I will consider is simulated annealing. In Chap. 11 and Brinch Hansen [1992a], I discussed simulated annealing and illustrated the method by a sequential Pascal algorithm for the traveling salesperson's problem:

```
procedure anneal(var a: tour;
  Tmax, alpha: real; steps,
  attempts, changes: integer)
```

This procedure replaces an initial random tour of n cities by a near-optimal tour.

Parallel annealing trials can be implemented by making the following substitutions in Figs. 14.3–5:

1. The problem and solution types are both replaced by the type *tour* defined as follows:

   const n = ...{ cities };
   type city = **record** x, y: real **end**;
      tour = **array** [1..n] **of** city;

2. The solution procedure is replaced by

   procedure solve(a: tour; **var** b: tour; trial: integer);
   begin
      newseed(trial); b := a;
      anneal(b, sqrt(n), 0.95, trunc(20*ln(n)), 100*n, 10*n)
   end

The programming details are explained in Chap. 11 and Brinch Hansen [1992a].

I reprogrammed simulated annealing in occam for a Computing Surface with T800 transputers. Table 14.1 shows the run time T_p for parallel computation of 10 different tours of 400 cities on 1, 5, and 10 transputers. The processor efficiency, $E_p = T_1/(pT_p)$, is very close to 1.

Table 14.1: Run times.

p	T_p (s)	E_p
1	8367.2	1.0000
5	1674.8	0.9992
10	838.3	0.9981

14.5   Primality Testing

The second Monte Carlo method is primality testing of a large integer p. (This integer should not be confused with the number of processors, which is also called p.)

I discussed the Miller-Rabin algorithm in Chap. 12 and Brinch Hansen [1992b], and illustrated it by a sequential Pascal function:

   function witness(x, p: integer): boolean

The boolean value of this function defines whether or not a random integer x is a *witness* to the compositeness of the integer p.

Parallel primality trials can be implemented by making the following substitutions in Figs. 14.3–5:

1. The problem type is replaced by type integer.

2. The solution type is replaced by type boolean.

3. The solution procedure is replaced by

```
procedure solve(p: integer; var sure: boolean; trial: integer);
var x: integer;
begin
    newseed(trial); randomno(x, p − 1);
    { 1 <= x <= p − 1 }
    sure := witness(x, p)
end
```

In practice, this procedure must be reprogrammed to perform *multiple-length arithmetic* on integers represented by arrays of digits [Chap. 13 and Brinch Hansen 1992c].

The parallel primality trials were also tested on a Computing Surface. Table 14.2 shows the run time T_p for 40 primality tests of a random integer with 160 decimal digits. (Here p denotes the number of processors.) The trials were performed in parallel on 1, 10, 20, and 40 transputers. The processor efficiency E_p is practically 1.

Table 14.2: More run times.

p	T_p (s)	E_p
1	1503.3	1.0000
10	150.4	0.9995
20	75.2	0.9995
40	37.7	0.9969

14.6 Final Remarks

In this chapter, I developed a generic algorithm for parallel execution of Monte Carlo trials on a multicomputer. I then modified this algorithm to solve two different problems: Finding a near-optimal tour of n cities by simulated annealing, and testing the primality of an n-digit integer by the Miller-Rabin method [Chaps. 11–12 and Brinch Hansen 1992a, 1992b]. The parallel algorithms were implemented in occam for a Computing Surface. The processor efficiency was close to 1.

The parallel primality testing algorithm inspired my student, Jonathan Greenfield [1994], to write his PhD thesis on *Distributed Programming Paradigms with Cryptography Applications.*

Part VI

THE CELLULAR
AUTOMATA PARADIGM

Chapter 15

Laplace's Equation

15.1 Introduction

Physical phenomena that vary continuously in space and time are described by *partial differential equations*. The most important of these is *Laplace's equation*, which defines gravitational and electrostatic potentials as well as stationary flow of heat and ideal fluid [Feynman 1989].

This chapter discusses Laplace's equation for steady-state heat flow in a two-dimensional region with fixed temperatures on the boundaries. The equilibrium temperatures are computed on a square grid using *successive overrelaxation* with *parity ordering* of the grid elements [Young 1971; Press 1989].

The numerical method is illustrated by a Pascal algorithm. A parallel version of this algorithm has been tested on a Computing Surface [Chap. 16 and Brinch Hansen 1992f].

I assume that you are familiar with elementary calculus.

15.2 The Heat Equation

I will illustrate Laplace's equation by defining the equilibrium temperatures in a thin plate of homogenous material and uniform thickness. The faces of the plate are perfectly insulated. On the boundaries of the plate, each point is kept at a known fixed temperature. As heat flows through the plate from warm towards cold boundaries, the plate eventually reaches a state where each point has a steady (time-independent) temperature maintained by the heat flow. The problem is to define the equilibrium temperature $u(x, y)$ for every point (x, y) on the plate.

I will study the heat flow through a small rectangular element of the plate with origin (x, y) and sides of lengths Δx and Δy (Fig. 15.1).

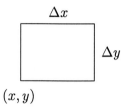

Figure 15.1: A small element.

Due to the insulation of the faces, the heat flows only in two dimensions. At every point (x, y), the velocity v of the heat flow has a horizontal component v_x and a vertical component v_y (Fig. 15.2). I will examine the horizontal and vertical flows separately.

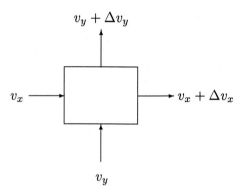

Figure 15.2: Horizontal and vertical flow.

The horizontal flow enters the element through the left boundary with velocity v_x and leaves the element through the right boundary with velocity $v_x + \Delta v_x$. Since these boundaries have length Δy, the element receives heat at the rate

$$v_x \Delta y$$

and loses heat at the rate

$$(v_x + \Delta v_x)\Delta y$$

So, the horizontal flow removes heat from the element at the rate

$$\Delta v_x \Delta y = \frac{\partial v_x}{\partial x}\Delta x \Delta y$$

Similarly, the vertical flow removes heat from the element at the rate

$$\Delta v_y \Delta x = \frac{\partial v_y}{\partial y}\Delta y \Delta x$$

The combined rate of heat loss is the sum of the horizontal and vertical loss rates:

$$\left(\frac{\partial v_x}{\partial x} + \frac{\partial v_y}{\partial y}\right)\Delta x \Delta y$$

In equilibrium, the element holds a constant amount of heat, which keeps its temperature $u(x, y)$ constant. Since the rate of heat loss is zero in the steady-state, you have the *heat conservation* law:

$$\frac{\partial v_x}{\partial x} + \frac{\partial v_y}{\partial y} = 0 \tag{15.1}$$

Now, heat flows towards decreasing temperatures at a rate proportional to the temperature gradient

$$v_x = -k\frac{\partial u}{\partial x} \qquad v_y = -k\frac{\partial u}{\partial y} \tag{15.2}$$

where k is a constant [Feynman 1989]. This is the law of the *velocity potential.*

By combining the conservation and potential laws, you obtain *Laplace's equation* for equilibrium temperatures:

$$\frac{\partial^2 u}{\partial x^2} + \frac{\partial^2 u}{\partial y^2} = 0 \tag{15.3}$$

This partial differential equation is also known as the *heat equation* or the *equilibrium equation*. It is often abbreviated as follows:

$$\nabla^2 u = 0 \qquad\qquad (15.4)$$

A function $u(x, y)$ that satisfies this equation is called a *potential function*. The *boundary conditions* determine a potential function.

15.3 Difference Equations

As an example, I will solve the heat equation for a *square region*, where the temperature is fixed at each boundary (Fig. 15.3).

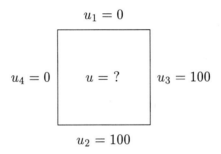

Figure 15.3: A square region.

A numerical solution can be found only for a *discrete* form of the heat equation. The first step is to divide the square region into a *square grid* of elements with uniform *spacing* h (Fig. 15.4). The center of each element represents a single point in the region.

There are three kinds of grid elements:

1. *Interior elements*, marked "?", have unknown temperatures, which satisfy a discrete heat equation.

2. *Boundary elements*, marked "+", have fixed, known temperatures.

3. *Corner elements*, marked "−", are not used.

A numerical solution to the heat equation is based on the observation that the heat flow through an interior element is driven by *temperature differences*

−	+	+	+	+	+	+	−
+	?	?	?	?	?	?	+
+	?	?	?	?	?	?	+
+	?	?	?	?	?	?	+
+	?	?	?	?	?	?	+
+	?	?	?	?	?	?	+
+	?	?	?	?	?	?	+
−	+	+	+	+	+	+	−

Figure 15.4: A square grid.

between the element and its immediate neighbors. Figure 15.5 shows an interior element and four adjacent elements. The five elements are called c (center), n (north), s (south), e (east), and w (west).

	n	
w	c	e
	s	

Figure 15.5: Adjacent elements.

These elements have the following *coordinates* and *temperatures:*

$$u_n = u(x, y + h)$$

$$u_w = u(x - h, y) \qquad u_c = u(x, y) \qquad u_e = u(x + h, y)$$

$$u_s = u(x, y - h)$$

If the grid spacing h is small enough, you can approximate the temperature u_e by the first three terms of a *Taylor expansion* of the function u in the neighborhood east of (x, y) [Courant 1989]:

$$u_e \approx u_c + h \frac{\partial u}{\partial x} + \frac{1}{2} \frac{\partial^2 u}{\partial x^2}$$

A Taylor expansion in the western neighborhood of (x, y) gives an approximation of the temperature u_w:

$$u_w \approx u_c - h\frac{\partial u}{\partial x} + \frac{1}{2}h^2\frac{\partial^2 u}{\partial x^2}$$

Consequently,

$$u_e + u_w \approx 2u_c + h^2\frac{\partial^2 u}{\partial x^2} \tag{15.5}$$

Similarly,

$$u_n + u_s \approx 2u_c + h^2\frac{\partial^2 u}{\partial y^2} \tag{15.6}$$

From (15.5) and (15.6), you obtain the important approximation

$$\nabla^2 u \approx (u_n + u_s + u_e + u_w - 4u_c)/h^2$$

According to the heat equation (15.4), the left-hand side is zero for steady-state heat flow. Consequently, the discrete heat equation is a system of *difference equations* of the form

$$4u_c - u_n - u_s - u_e - u_w \approx 0 \tag{15.7}$$

There is a separate equation for each of the $n{\times}n$ interior elements.

In *thermal equilibrium*, the temperature of each grid element is simply the *average* of the temperatures of the four surrounding elements:

$$u_c \approx (u_n + u_s + u_e + u_w)/4 \tag{15.8}$$

15.4   Numerical Solution

On an $n{\times}n$ grid, the heat equation is replaced by n^2 linear equations in the unknown temperatures. Solving this system by a direct method requires $O(n^6)$ run-time on a sequential computer. For a grid of, say $250{\times}250$ elements, you obtain 62,500 linear equations with $4{\times}10^9$ coefficients. If the run time is measured in units of 1 μsec, the computation takes eight years. This is clearly impractical.

Each equation (15.7) has five nonzero coefficients only. For such a *sparse* linear system, *iterative* methods are far more efficient than direct methods. Iterative solution of linear equations is known as *relaxation*. In the following,

I develop a Pascal algorithm that uses relaxation to solve the discrete heat equation on a square grid with fixed boundary values.

A *grid u* is represented by an $(n + 2) \times (n + 2)$ real array:

```
const n = 250;
type row = array [0..n+1] of real;
     grid = array [0..n+1] of row;
var u: grid;
```

It consists of $n \times n$ interior elements surrounded by a border of $4n$ boundary elements, as shown in Fig. 15.4.

The *Laplace procedure* initializes the boundary elements with fixed temperatures u_1, u_2, u_3, and u_4, and the interior elements with the tentative temperature u_5. This is followed by a fixed number of relaxation steps (Fig. 15.6).

```
procedure laplace(var u: grid;
    u1, u2, u3, u4, u5: real;
    steps: integer);
var k: integer;
begin
    newgrid(u);
    for k := 1 to steps do relax(u)
end;
```

Figure 15.6: Laplace algorithm.

A *new grid* holds known values in the boundary elements and reasonable values in the interior elements based on educated guessing (Fig. 15.7).

The known and estimated temperatures, shown in Fig. 15.3, are defined by the same *initial* function (Fig. 15.8). The temperatures of the four corner elements are arbitrary (and irrelevant).

The procedure statement

laplace(u, 0.0, 100.0, 100.0, 0.0, 50.0, n)

denotes a computation that solves the heat flow problem shown in Fig. 15.3. As a reasonable guess, the interior elements are initially set at the average of the boundary temperatures:

```
procedure newgrid(var u: grid);
var i, j: integer;
begin
  for i := 0 to n + 1 do
    for j := 0 to n + 1 do
      u[i,j] := initial(i, j)
end;
```

Figure 15.7: Newgrid algorithm.

```
function initial(
    i, j: integer): real;
begin
  if i = 0 then
    initial := u1
  else if i = n + 1 then
    initial := u2
  else if j = n + 1 then
    initial := u3
  else if j = 0 then
    initial := u4
  else
    initial := u5
end;
```

Figure 15.8: Initial algorithm.

$$(0 + 100 + 100 + 0)/4 = 50$$

15.5   Relaxation Methods

A relaxation step replaces the temperature of every interior element by a better approximation based on the previous temperatures of the element and the temperatures of its neighbors (see Fig. 15.5).

The simplest method is *Jacoby relaxation*, which conceptually updates every temperature simultaneously. This procedure must keep a copy of the current grid until the next temperatures have been computed (Fig. 15.9).

```
procedure relax(var u: grid);
var u0: grid; i, j: integer;
begin
  u0 := u;
  for i := 1 to n do
    for j := 1 to n do
      u[i,j] :=
        nextstate(
          u0[i-1,j], u0[i+1,j],
          u0[i,j+1], u0[i,j-1])
end;
```

Figure 15.9: Jacobi relaxation.

The most obvious idea is to replace every temperature u_c by the average of the surrounding approximate temperatures u_n, u_s, u_e, and u_w (Fig. 15.10).

```
function nextstate(
    un, us, ue, uw: real): real;
begin
  nextstate :=
    (un + us + ue + uw)/4.0
end;
```

Figure 15.10: Simple state transition.

The relaxation algorithm, shown in Fig. 15.11, uses a new temperature as soon as it has been computed. This in-place computation cuts the memory requirement in half. The method is called *Gauss-Seidel relaxation*, "even though Gauss didn't know about it and Seidel didn't recommend it" [Strang 1986].

Since new values are better approximations than old ones, Gauss-Seidel converges twice as fast as Jacobi. However, both methods require $O(n^2)$ re-

```
procedure relax(var u: grid);
var i, j: integer;
begin
   for i := 1 to n do
      for j := 1 to n do
         u[i,j] :=
            nextstate(
               u[i−1,j], u[i+1,j],
               u[i,j+1], u[i,j−1])
end;
```

Figure 15.11: Gauss-Seidel relaxation.

laxation steps and $O(n^4)$ run time [Press 1989]. If the run time is measured in units of, say 10 μsec, the computation of 250×250 equilibrium temperatures takes 11 hours. The slow *convergence* of these methods makes them impractical for scientific computing.

By 1950, engineers had discovered that convergence is much faster if temperatures are *overrelaxed*. Instead of approximating a new temperature by the average temperature

$$aver = (u_n + u_s + u_e + u_w)/4.0$$

you make the next temperature a weighted sum of the old temperature and the surrounding temperatures:

$$next = (1 - f) * u_c + f * aver$$

The *relaxation factor* f is 1 for Gauss-Seidel. For overrelaxation, $f > 1$. This *ad hoc* method converges only if $f < 2$ [Press 1989].

It was a breakthrough when David Young [1954] developed a theory of overrelaxation. For the heat equation with fixed boundary values on a large $n \times n$ square grid, the fastest convergence is obtained with the following *optimal* relaxation factor:

$$f_{opt} = 2 - 2\pi/n$$

For $n = 250$, the optimal factor is $f_{opt} = 1.97$.

It is illuminating to look at overrelaxation from a different point of view. The *residual*

$$res = aver - u_c$$

is a measure of how well an approximate temperature u_c satisfies the discrete heat equation (15.7). In overrelaxation, the correction of each temperature is proportional to its residual

$$next = u_c + f * res$$

where $1 < f < 2$.

The method of *successive overrelaxation* is based on this accidental discovery supported by Young's theory (Fig. 15.12). The method requires n *steps* and $O(n^3)$ run time to achieve 3-figure accuracy [Press 1989]. If the run time is measured in units of 10 μsec, a 250×250 grid requires less than three minutes of computing.

```
function nextstate(
    uc, un, us, ue, uw: real): real;
var res: real;
begin
  { fopt = 2.0 − 2.0*pi/n }
  res :=
      (un + us + ue + uw)/4.0 − uc;
  nextstate := uc + fopt*res
end;
```

Figure 15.12: Optimal state transition.

The theory of optimal overrelaxation is valid only if the grid elements are updated in an appropriate order. The row-wise updating of Gauss-Seidel is acceptable, but is inherently a sequential method. Instead, I will use an *ordering* that can be adapted for parallel computing [Young 1971; Barlow 1982; Brinch Hansen 1992f and Chap. 16].

Every element $u[i,j]$ has a *parity*

$$(i + j) \bmod 2$$

which is either *even* (0) or *odd* (1). Even and odd elements alternate on the grid like black and white squares on a chessboard. Every interior element is surrounded by four elements of the opposite parity (Fig. 15.13). So, the updating of the even elements depends only on the odd elements, and vice versa.

−	1	0	1	0	1	0	−
1	0	1	0	1	0	1	0
0	1	0	1	0	1	0	1
1	0	1	0	1	0	1	0
0	1	0	1	0	1	0	1
1	0	1	0	1	0	1	0
0	1	0	1	0	1	0	1
−	0	1	0	1	0	1	−

Figure 15.13: Parity ordering.

Figure 15.14 defines *successive overrelaxation with parity ordering*. A relaxation step consists of a scan of the even elements followed by a scan of the odd elements. A single scan updates all elements with the same *parity* b. I assume that n is *even*.

Successive overrelaxation can be refined further by *Chebyshev acceleration*, which changes the relaxation factor after each scan [Press 1989]. However, the fastest relaxation method is the *multigrid* technique, which computes n^2 temperatures recursively on finer and finer grids in $O(n^2)$ time [Press 1991].

15.6 Pascal Algorithm

The complete Pascal algorithm, shown below, is composed of Figs. 15.6–8, 15.12, and 15.14.

```
          procedure relax(var u: grid);
          var b, i, j, k: integer;
          begin
            for b := 0 to 1 do
              for i := 1 to n do
                begin
                  k := (i + b) mod 2;
                  j := 2 − k;
                  while j <= n − k do
                    begin
                      u[i,j] :=
                        nextstate(u[i,j],
                            u[i−1,j], u[i+1,j],
                            u[i,j+1], u[i,j−1]);
                      j := j + 2
                    end
                end
          end;
```

Figure 15.14: Successive overrelaxation.

```
const n = 250 { even };
type row = array [0..n+1] of real;
     grid = array [0..n+1] of row;

procedure laplace(var u: grid;
    u1, u2, u3, u4, u5: real;
    steps: integer);
const pi = 3.14159265358979;
var k: integer; fopt: real;

  function initial(
      i, j: integer): real;
  begin
    if i = 0 then
      initial := u1
```

```
    else if i = n + 1 then
       initial := u2
    else if j = n + 1 then
       initial := u3
    else if j = 0 then
       initial := u4
    else
       initial := u5
end;

function nextstate(
    uc, un, us, ue, uw: real): real;
var res: real;
begin
    res :=
       (un + us + ue + uw)/4.0 − uc;
    nextstate := uc + fopt*res
end;

procedure newgrid(var u: grid);
var i, j: integer;
begin
    for i := 0 to n + 1 do
       for j := 0 to n + 1 do
          u[i,j] := initial(i, j)
end;

procedure relax(var u: grid);
var b, i, j, k: integer;
begin
    for b := 0 to 1 do
       for i := 1 to n do
          begin
             k := (i + b) mod 2;
             j := 2 − k;
             while j <= n − k do
                begin
```

```
                    u[i,j] :=
                        nextstate(u[i,j],
                            u[i−1,j], u[i+1,j],
                            u[i,j+1], u[i,j−1]);
                    j := j + 2
                end
            end
    end;

    begin
        fopt := 2.0 − 2.0*pi/n;
        newgrid(u);
        for k := 1 to steps do relax(u)
    end;
```

15.7 Final Remarks

I have derived Laplace's equation for steady-state heat flow in two dimensions and have explained how the equation is solved by successive overrelaxation on a discrete grid. The numerical method was illustrated by a Pascal algorithm.

Chapter 16

Parallel Cellular Automata

16.1 Introduction

The theme of this chapter is *parallel cellular automata*. The numerous applications of cellular automata include forest infestation [Hoppensteadt 1978], fluid flow [Frisch 1986], earthquakes [Bak 1989], forest fires [Bak 1990], and sandpile avalanches [Hwa 1989].

Cellular automata are ideally suited for parallel computing. My goal is to explore *programming methodology for multicomputers*. I will illustrate this theme by developing a generic program for parallel execution of cellular automata on a multicomputer with a square matrix of processor nodes. I will then show how easy it is to adapt the generic program for two different applications: (1) simulation of a *forest fire*, and (2) numerical solution of *Laplace's equation* for stationary heat flow. On a *Computing Surface* with transputer nodes, the parallel efficiency of these model programs is close to one.

16.2 Cellular Automata

A *cellular automaton* is an array of parallel processes, known as *cells*. At discrete moments in *time*, the cells update their states *simultaneously*. The state *transition* of a cell depends only on its previous state and the states of the *adjacent* cells.

I will program a *two-dimensional* cellular automaton with *fixed boundary states* (Fig. 16.1). The automaton is a square matrix with three kinds of cells:

1. *Interior cells*, marked "?", may change their states dynamically.

2. *Boundary cells*, marked "+", have fixed states.

3. *Corner cells*, marked "−", are not used.

−	+	+	+	+	+	+	−
+	?	?	?	?	?	?	+
+	?	?	?	?	?	?	+
+	?	?	?	?	?	?	+
+	?	?	?	?	?	?	+
+	?	?	?	?	?	?	+
+	?	?	?	?	?	?	+
−	+	+	+	+	+	+	−

Figure 16.1: A cellular automaton.

Figure 16.2 shows an interior cell and the four neighbors that may influence its state. These five cells are labeled c (central), n (north), s (south), e (east), and w (west).

Figure 16.2: Adjacent cells.

The cellular automaton will be programmed in *SuperPascal*.

A cellular automaton is a set of parallel communicating cells. If you ignore boundary cells and communication details, a two-dimensional automaton is defined as follows:

```
forall i := 1 to n do
    forall j := 1 to n do
        cell(i,j)
```

After initializing its own state, every interior cell goes through a fixed number of state transitions before outputting its final state:

    initialize own state;
    for k := 1 **to** steps **do**
      begin
        exchange states with
          adjacent cells;
        update own state
      end
    output own state

The challenge is to transform this fine-grained parallel model into an efficient program for a *multicomputer* with distributed memory.

16.3   Initial States

Consider a cellular automaton with 36 interior cells and 24 boundary cells. In a sequential computer, the combined state of the automaton can be represented by an 8×8 matrix, called a *grid* (Fig. 16.3). For reasons that will be explained later, the grid elements are indicated by 0's and 1's.

$-$	1	0	1	0	1	0	$-$
1	0	1	0	1	0	1	0
0	1	0	1	0	1	0	1
1	0	1	0	1	0	1	0
0	1	0	1	0	1	0	1
1	0	1	0	1	0	1	0
0	1	0	1	0	1	0	1
$-$	0	1	0	1	0	1	$-$

Figure 16.3: A square grid.

Figure 16.4 shows the *initial values* of the elements. The boundary elements have fixed values u_1, u_2, u_3, and u_4. Every interior element has the same initial value u_5.

In general, a grid u has $n \times n$ interior elements and $4n$ boundary elements:

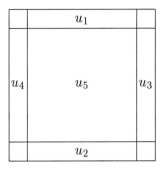

Figure 16.4: Initial values.

const n = ...;
type state = (...);
  row = **array** [0..n+1] **of** state;
  grid = **array** [0..n+1] **of** row;
var u: grid;

Since the possible *states* of every cell vary from one application to another, I deliberately leave them unspecified. The grid dimension n and the initial states u_1, u_2, u_3, u_4, and u_5 are also application dependent.

On a sequential computer, the grid is initialized as follows:

for i := 0 **to** n + 1 **do**
  for j := 0 **to** n + 1 **do**
    u[i,j] := initial(i,j)

The algorithm, shown in Fig. 16.5, defines the *initial* value of the element $u[i, j]$. The values of the corner elements are arbitrary (and irrelevant).

16.4 Data Parallelism

For simulation of a cellular automaton, the ideal *multicomputer architecture* is a square matrix of identical processor *nodes* (Fig. 16.6). Every node is connected to its nearest neighbors (if any) by four communication *channels*.

Figure 16.7 shows a grid with 36 interior elements divided into 9 subgrids. You now have a 3×3 matrix of nodes and a 3×3 matrix of subgrids. The two matrices define a one-to-one correspondence between subgrids and nodes. I

```
function initial(i, j: integer): state;
begin
  if i = 0 then
    initial := u1
  else if i = n + 1 then
    initial := u2
  else if j = n + 1 then
    initial := u3
  else if j = 0 then
    initial := u4
  else
    initial := u5
end;
```

Figure 16.5: Initial algorithm.

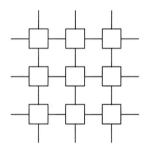

Figure 16.6: Processor matrix.

will assign each subgrid to the corresponding node and let the nodes update the grids simultaneously. This form of distributed processing is called *data parallelism*.

Every processor holds a 4×4 *subgrid* with four interior elements and eight boundary elements (Fig. 16.8). Every boundary element holds either an interior element of a neighboring subgrid or a boundary element of the entire grid. (I will say more about this later.)

–	1	0	1	0	1	0	–
1	0	1	0	1	0	1	0
0	1	0	1	0	1	0	1
1	0	1	0	1	0	1	0
0	1	0	1	0	1	0	1
1	0	1	0	1	0	1	0
0	1	0	1	0	1	0	1
–	0	1	0	1	0	1	–

Figure 16.7: A subdivided grid.

–	1	0	–
1	0	1	0
0	1	0	1
–	0	1	–

Figure 16.8: A subgrid.

16.5 Processor Nodes

With this background, I am ready to program a cellular automaton that runs on a $q \times q$ *processor matrix*. The *nodes* follow the same script (Fig. 16.9).

A node is identified by its row and column numbers (q_i, q_j) in the processor matrix, where

$$1 \le q_i \le q \qquad 1 \le q_j \le q$$

Four communication channels, labeled *up, down, left,* and *right,* connect a node to its nearest neighbors (if any).

Every node holds a subgrid with $m \times m$ interior elements and $4m$ boundary elements (Fig. 16.8):

```
const m = ...;
type
    subrow = array [0..m+1] of state;
    subgrid = array [0..m+1] of subrow;
```

```
procedure node(qi, qj, steps: integer;
   up, down, left, right: channel);
var u: subgrid; k: integer;
begin
   newgrid(qi, qj, u);
   for k := 1 to steps do
      relax(qi, qj, up, down,
         left, right, u);
   output(qi, qj, right, left, u)
end;
```

Figure 16.9: Node algorithm.

The grid dimension n is a multiple of the subgrid dimension m:

$$n = m * q$$

After initializing its subgrid, a node updates the subgrid a fixed number of times before outputting the final values. In numerical analysis, grid iteration is known as *relaxation*.

Node (q_i, q_j) holds the following subset

$$u[i_0..i_0 + m + 1,\ j_0..j_0 + m + 1]$$

of the complete grid $u[0..n + 1,\ 0..n + 1]$, where

$$i_0 = (q_i - 1)m \qquad j_0 = (q_j - 1)m$$

The initialization of a subgrid is straightforward (Fig. 16.10).

16.6   Parallel Relaxation

In each time step, every node updates its own subgrid. The next value of an interior element is a function of its current value u_c and the values u_n, u_s, u_e, and u_w of the four adjacent elements (Fig. 16.2). Every application of a cellular automaton requires a different set of *state transitions*. In some

```
procedure newgrid(qi, qj: integer;
    var u: subgrid);
var i, i0, j, j0: integer;
begin
    i0 := (qi − 1)*m;
    j0 := (qj − 1)*m;
    for i := 0 to m + 1 do
        for j := 0 to m + 1 do
            u[i,j] := initial(i0+i, j0+j)
end;
```

Figure 16.10: Newgrid algorithm.

applications, *probabilistic* state transitions require the use of a random number generator that updates a global seed variable. Since functions cannot have side-effects in *SuperPascal*, the *next state* of a cell $u[i, j]$ is defined by a procedure (Fig. 16.11).

```
procedure nextstate(var u: subgrid;
    i, j: integer);
{ 1 <= i <= m, 1 <= j <= m }
begin u[i,j] := ... end;
```

Figure 16.11: State transition algorithm.

Parallel relaxation is not quite as easy as it sounds. When a node updates row number 1 of its subgrid, it needs access to row number m of the subgrid of its northern neighbor (Fig. 16.7). To relax its subgrid, a node must share a single row or column with each of its four neighbors.

The solution to this problem is to let neighboring grids *overlap* by one row or column vector. Before a node updates its interior elements, it exchanges a pair of vectors with each of the adjacent nodes. The overlapping vectors are kept in the boundary elements of the subgrids (Fig. 16.8). If a neighboring node does not exist, a local boundary vector holds the corresponding boundary elements of the entire grid (Figs. 16.4 and 16.7).

The northern neighbor of a node outputs row number m of its own subgrid to the node, which inputs it in row number 0 of its own subgrid (Fig. 16.8). In return, the node outputs its row number 1 to its northern neighbor, which inputs it in row number $m + 1$ of its subgrid. Similarly, a node exchanges rows with its southern neighbor, and columns with its eastern and western neighbors (Fig. 16.6).

The *shared elements* raise the familiar concern about time-dependent errors in parallel programs. *Race conditions* are prevented by a rule of *mutual exclusion:* While a node updates an element, another node cannot access the same element. This rule is enforced by an ingenious method [Barlow 1982].

Every grid element $u[i,j]$ is assigned a *parity*

$$(i + j) \bmod 2$$

that is either *even* (0) or *odd* (1), as shown in Figs. 16.3 and 16.7. To eliminate tedious (and unnecessary) programming details, I assume that the subgrid dimension m is *even*. This guarantees that every subgrid has the same *parity ordering* of the elements (Figs. 16.7–8).

Parity ordering reveals a simple property of grids: The next values of the even interior elements depend only on the current values of the odd elements, and vice versa. This observation suggests a reliable method for parallel relaxation.

In each relaxation step, the nodes scan their grids twice:

1. *First scan:* The nodes exchange odd elements with their neighbors and update all even elements simultaneously.

2. *Second scan:* The nodes exchange even elements and update all odd elements simultaneously.

The key point is this: In each scan, the simultaneous updating of local elements depends only on shared elements with constant values! In the terminology of parallel programming, the nodes are *disjoint processes* during a scan.

The *relaxation* procedure uses a local variable to update elements with the same *parity* b after exchanging elements of the opposite parity $1 - b$ with its neighbors (Fig. 16.12).

```
            procedure relax(qi, qj: integer;
              up, down, left, right: channel;
              var u: subgrid);
          var b, i, j, k: integer;
          begin
            for b := 0 to 1 do
              begin
                exchange(qi, qj, 1 − b,
                  up, down, left, right, u);
                for i := 1 to m do
                  begin
                    k := (i + b) mod 2;
                    j := 2 − k;
                    while j <= m − k do
                      begin
                        nextstate(u, i, j);
                        j := j + 2
                      end
                  end
              end
          end;
```

Figure 16.12: Relaxation algorithm.

16.7 Local Communication

The nodes communicate through *synchronous channels* with the following properties:

1. Every channel connects exactly two nodes.

2. The communications on a channel take place one at a time.

3. A communication takes place when a node is ready to output a value through a channel and another node is ready to input the value through the same channel.

4. A channel can transmit a value in either direction between two nodes.

5. The four channels of a node can transmit values simultaneously.

These requirements are satisfied by *transputer* nodes programmed in *occam* [Cok 1991].

The identical behavior of the nodes poses a subtle problem. Suppose the nodes simultaneously attempt to input from their northern neighbors. In that case, the nodes will *deadlock*, since none of them are ready to output through the corresponding channels. There are several solutions to this problem. I use a method that works well for transputers.

Before the nodes scan elements of the same parity, they communicate with their neighbors in two phases (Fig. 16.13).

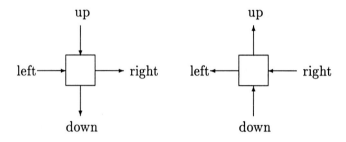

Figure 16.13: Communication phases.

In each phase, every node communicates simultaneously on its four channels as shown below. Phases 1 and 2 correspond to the left and right halves of Fig. 16.13.

Channel	Phase 1	Phase 2
up	input	output
down	output	input
left	input	output
right	output	input

Since every input operation on a channel is matched by a simultaneous output operation on the same channel, this *protocol* is *deadlock free*. It is also very *efficient*, since every node communicates simultaneously with its four neighbors.

Figure 16.14 defines the *exchange* of elements of parity b between a node and its four neighbors.

```
procedure exchange(qi, qj, b: integer;
    up, down, left, right: channel;
    var u: subgrid);
begin
    phase1(qi, qj, b,
        up, down, left, right, u);
    phase2(qi, qj, b,
        up, down, left, right, u)
end;
```

Figure 16.14: Exchange algorithm.

Phase 1 is defined by Fig. 16.15. The *if* statements prevent boundary nodes from communicating with nonexisting neighbors (Fig. 16.6).

Phase 2 is similar (Fig. 16.16).

I have used this protocol on a *Computing Surface* with transputer nodes. Since transputer links can communicate in both directions simultaneously, the two communication phases run in parallel. So, every transputer inputs and outputs simultaneously through all four links!

If the available processors cannot communicate simultaneously with their neighbors, a sequential protocol must be used [Dijkstra 1982]. This is also true if the overhead of parallelism and communication is substantial. However, the replacement of one protocol by another should only change Figs. 16.14–16 and leave the rest of the program unchanged.

16.8 Global Output

At the end of a simulation, the nodes output their final values to a *master* processor that assembles a complete grid. The boundary channels of the processor matrix are not used for grid relaxation (Fig. 16.6). I use the horizontal boundary channels to connect the nodes and the master M into a *pipeline* for *global output* (Fig. 16.17).

The boundary elements of the entire grid have known fixed values (see Fig. 16.4). These elements are needed only during relaxation. The final output is an $n \times n$ matrix of interior elements only. Every element defines the final state of a single cell.

```
procedure phase1(qi, qj, b: integer;
    up, down, left, right: channel;
    var u: subgrid);
var k, last: integer;
begin
  k := 2 − b;
  last := m − b;
  while k <= last do
    begin
      { 1 <= k <= m }
      [sic] parallel
        if qi > 1 then
          receive(up, u[0,k])|
        if qi < q then
          send(down, u[m,k])|
        if qj > 1 then
          receive(left, u[k,0])|
        if qj < q then
          send(right, u[k,m])
      end;
      k := k + 2
    end
end;
```

Figure 16.15: Phase 1 algorithm.

So, I will redefine the full grid, omitting the boundary elements:

```
type
    row = array [1..n] of state;
    grid = array [1..n] of row;
```

The *master* inputs the final grid row by row, one element at a time (Fig. 16.18).

The nodes use a common procedure to *output* interior elements in row order (Fig. 16.19). Every row of elements is distributed through a row of nodes (Figs. 16.6–7). For each of its subrows, node (q_i, q_j) outputs the m

```
                    procedure phase2(qi, qj, b: integer;
                       up, down, left, right: channel;
                       var u: subgrid);
                 var k, last: integer;
                 begin
                    k := b + 1;
                    last := m + b - 1;
                    while k <= last do
                       begin
                          { 1 <= k <= m }
                          [sic] parallel
                             if qi > 1 then
                                send(up, u[1,k])|
                             if qi < q then
                                receive(down, u[m+1,k])|
                             if qj > 1 then
                                send(left, u[k,1])|
                             if qj < q then
                                receive(right, u[k,m+1])
                          end;
                          k := k + 2
                       end
                 end;
```

Figure 16.16: Phase 2 algorithm.

interior elements, and copies the remaining $(q - q_j)m$ elements of the same row from its eastern neighbor. This completes the output of the rows of elements, which are distributed through row q_i of the processor matrix. The node then copies the remaining $(q - q_i)m$ complete rows of n elements each.

A simple procedure is used to *copy* a fixed number of elements from one channel to another (Fig. 16.20).

In my program for the Computing Surface, I extended the copy procedure with parallel input/output. I also modified the algorithms in Figs. 16.9 and 16.18 slightly to enable the program to output intermediate grids at fixed intervals.

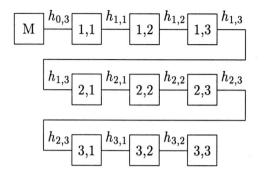

Figure 16.17: Output pipeline.

```
procedure master(right: channel;
    var u: grid);
var i, j: integer;
begin
  for i := 1 to n do
    for j := 1 to n do
      receive(right, u[i,j])
end;
```

Figure 16.18: Master algorithm.

16.9   Processor Network

Figure 16.21 illustrates the *network* that ties the processors together. The network consists of a horizontal channel matrix h and a vertical channel matrix v.

Figure 16.22 defines parallel *simulation* of a cellular automaton that computes a relaxed grid u. Execution of the parallel statement activates (1) the master, (2) the first column of nodes, and (3) the rest of the nodes.

This completes the development of the generic program. I will now demonstrate how easily the program can be adapted to different applications of cellular automata.

```
procedure output(qi, qj: integer;
   inp, out: channel; var u: subgrid);
var i, j: integer;
begin
  for i := 1 to m do
    begin
      for j := 1 to m do
        send(out, u[i,j]);
      copy((q − qj)*m, inp, out)
    end;
  copy((q − qi)*m*n, inp, out)
end;
```

Figure 16.19: Output algorithm.

```
procedure copy(no: integer;
   inp, out: channel);
var k: integer; uk: state;
begin
  for k := 1 to no do
    begin
      receive(inp, uk);
      send(out, uk)
    end
end;
```

Figure 16.20: Copy algorithm.

16.10   Example: Forest Fire

A typical application of a cellular automaton is simulation of a *forest fire*. Every cell represents a *tree* that is either *alive, burning,* or *dead.* In each time-step, the next state of every tree is defined by *probabilistic rules* similar to the ones proposed by Bak [1990]:

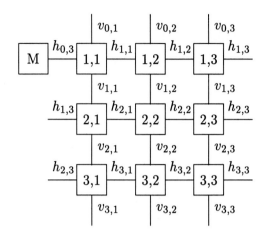

Figure 16.21: Processor network.

1. If a live tree is next to a burning tree, it burns; otherwise, it catches
   fire with probability p_b.

2. A burning tree dies.

3. A dead tree has probability p_a of being replaced by a live tree.

   Parallel simulation of a forest fire requires only minor changes of the
generic program:

1. The possible *states* are:

$$\textbf{type state} = (\text{alive, burning, dead});$$

2. The *initial* states may, for example, be:

$$u_1 = u_2 = u_3 = u_4 = \text{dead} \qquad u_5 = \text{alive}$$

3. Figure 16.23 defines state *transitions*.

4. A *random number* generator is added.

```
procedure simulate(
  steps: integer; var u: grid);
type
  line = array [1..q] of channel;
  matrix = array [0..q] of line;
var h, v: matrix; i, j: integer;
begin
  open(h[0,q]);
  for i := 1 to q do
    for j := 1 to q do
      open(h[i,j]);
  for i := 0 to q do
    for j := 1 to q do
      open(v[i,j]);
  parallel
    master(h[0,q], u)|
    forall j := 1 to q do
      node(j, 1, steps,
           v[j−1,1], v[j,1],
           h[j−1,q], h[j,1])|
    forall i := 1 to q do
      forall j := 2 to q do
        node(i, j, steps,
             v[i−1,j], v[i,j],
             h[i,j−1], h[i,j])
  end
end;
```

Figure 16.22: Simulation algorithm.

16.11   Example: Laplace's Equation

A cellular automaton can also solve *Laplace's equation* for *equilibrium temperatures* in a square region with fixed temperatures at the boundaries. Every cell represents the temperature at a single point in the region. In each time-step, the next temperature of every cell is defined by a simple *deter-*

```
procedure nextstate(var u: subgrid;
   i, j: integer);
{ 1 <= i <= m, 1 <= j <= m }
var x: real;
begin
  case u[i,j] of
    alive:
      if
         (u[i−1,j] = burning) or
         (u[i+1,j] = burning) or
         (u[i,j+1] = burning) or
         (u[i,j−1] = burning)
      then u[i,j] := burning
      else
        begin
          random(x);
          if x <= pb then
             u[i,j] := burning
        end;
    burning:
      u[i,j] := dead;
    dead:
      begin
        random(x);
        if x <= pa then
           u[i,j] := alive
      end
  end
end;
```

Figure 16.23: Forest fire state transition.

ministic rule.

Parallel simulation of heat flow requires the following changes of the generic program:

1. The *states* are temperatures represented by reals.

2. A possible choice of *initial* temperatures is:

$$u_1 = 0$$
$$u_2 = 100$$
$$u_3 = 100$$
$$u_4 = 0$$
$$u_5 = 50$$

3. Figure 16.24 defines the *next* temperature of an interior cell $u[i, j]$. In steady-state, the temperature of every interior cell is the average of the neighboring temperatures:

$$u_c = (u_n + u_s + u_e + u_w)/4.0$$

   This is the discrete form of Laplace's equation. The *residual, res,* is a measure of how close a temperature is to satisfying this equation. The correction of a temperature u_c is proportional to its residual.

4. A *relaxation factor*, f_{opt}, is added. For a large square grid relaxed in parity order, the relaxation factor

$$f_{opt} = 2 - 2\pi/n$$

   ensures the fastest possible convergence towards stationary temperatures. In numerical analysis, this method is called *successive overrelaxation* with *parity ordering*. The method requires n relaxation *steps* to achieve 3-figure accuracy of the final temperatures [Young 1954; Press 1989].

The sequential Laplace algorithm is explained in Chap. 15 and Brinch Hansen [1992e]. Numerical solution of Laplace's equation on multicomputers is also discussed in Barlow [1982], Evans [1984], Pritchard [1987], Saltz [1987], and Fox [1988].

```
procedure nextstate(var u: subgrid;
  i, j: integer);
{ 1 <= i <= m, 1 <= j <= m }
var res: real;
begin
  res :=
    (u[i−1,j] + u[i+1,j] +
     u[i,j+1] + u[i,j−1])/4.0
    − u[i,j];
  u[i,j] := u[i,j] + fopt*res
end;
```

Figure 16.24: Laplace state transition.

16.12   Complexity

In each time-step, every node exchanges overlapping elements with its neighbors in $O(m)$ time, and updates its own subgrid in $O(m^2)$ time. The final output takes $O(n^2)$ time. The *parallel run time* required to relax an $n \times n$ grid n times on p processors is

$$T(n,p) = n(am^2 + O(m)) + O(n^2)$$

where a is a system-dependent constant of relaxation and

$$n = m\sqrt{p} \tag{16.1}$$

The complexity of parallel simulation can be rewritten as follows:

$$T(n,p) = n^2(an/p + O(1) + O(1/\sqrt{p}))$$

For $1 \le p \ll n$, the communication times are insignificant compared to the relaxation time, and you have approximately

$$T(n,p) \approx an^3/p \qquad \text{for } n \gg p \tag{16.2}$$

If the same simulation runs on a single processor, the *sequential run time* is obtained by setting $p = 1$ in (16.2):

$$T(n,1) \approx an^3 \qquad \text{for } n \gg 1 \tag{16.3}$$

The *processor efficiency* of the parallel program is

$$E(n,p) = \frac{T(n,1)}{p\,T(n,p)} \tag{16.4}$$

The nominator is proportional to the number of processor cycles used in a sequential simulation. The denominator is a measure of the total number of cycles used by p processors performing the same computation in parallel.

By (16.2), (16.3), and (16.4), you find that the parallel efficiency is close to one, when the problem size n is large compared to the machine size p:

$$E(n,p) \approx 1 \qquad \text{for } n \gg p$$

Since this analysis ignores the (insignificant) communication times, it cannot predict how close to one the efficiency is.

In theory, the efficiency can be computed from (16.4) by measuring the sequential and parallel run times for the same value of n. Unfortunately, this is not always feasible. When 36 nodes relax a 1500×1500 grid of 64-bit reals, every node holds a subgrid of $250 \times 250 \times 8 = 0.5$ Mbytes. However, on a single processor, the full grid occupies 18 Mbytes.

A more realistic approach is to make the $O(n^2)$ grid proportional to the machine size p. Then every node has an $O(m^2)$ subgrid of constant size independent of the number of nodes. And the nodes always perform the same amount of computation per time-step.

When a *scaled simulation* runs on a single processor, the run time is approximately

$$T(m,1) \approx am^3 \qquad \text{for } m \gg 1 \tag{16.5}$$

since $p = 1$ and $n = m$.

From (16.1), (16.3), and (16.5), you obtain

$$T(n,1) \approx p^{3/2}\,T(m,1) \qquad \text{for } m \gg 1 \tag{16.6}$$

The computational formula you need follows from (16.4) and (16.6):

$$E(n,p) \approx \frac{\sqrt{p}\,T(m,1)}{T(n,p)} \qquad \text{for } m \gg 1 \tag{16.7}$$

This formula enables you to compute the efficiency of a parallel simulation by running a scaled-down version of the simulation on a single node.

16.13   Performance

I reprogrammed the model program in *occam2* and ran it on a *Computing Surface* with T800 transputers configured as a square matrix with a master node [Meiko 1987; Inmos 1988; McDonald 1991]. The program was modified to solve *Laplace's equation* as explained in Sec. 16.11.

Table 16.1 shows measured (and predicted) run times $T(n, p)$ in seconds for n relaxations of an $n \times n$ grid on p processors. In every run, the subgrid dimension $m = 250$.

Table 16.1: Run times.

p	n	$T(n,p)$ (s)		E_p
1	250	278	(281)	1.00
4	500	574	(563)	0.97
9	750	863	(844)	0.97
16	1000	1157	(1125)	0.96
25	1250	1462	(1406)	0.95
36	1500	1750	(1688)	0.95

The predicted run times, shown in parentheses, are defined by (16.2) using

$$a = 18 \ \mu s$$

The processor efficiency $E(n, p)$ was computed from (16.7) using the measured run times.

16.14   Final Remarks

I have developed a generic program for parallel execution of cellular automata on a multicomputer with a square matrix of processor nodes. From the generic program, I have derived two model programs for simulation of a forest fire and numerical solution of Laplace's equation for stationary heat flow. On a Computing Surface with 36 transputers, the program performs 1500 relaxations of a 1500×1500 grid of 64-bit reals in 29 minutes, with an efficiency of 0.95.

Part VII

PARALLEL MODEL PROGRAMS

Chapter 17

Complete SuperPascal Programs

17.1 Introduction

The following is a collection of complete *SuperPascal* programs discussed in this book. Each program generates a test case, executes a parallel algorithm, and displays the results. The programs were tested using a portable implementation of *SuperPascal* under Unix. The portable code was executed by a slow interpreter on a Sun workstation. Consequently, the *SuperPascal* programs only solve small instances of the scientific applications. Each program was rewritten in *occam2* and used to solve much larger instances of the same problems on a Computing Surface with T800 transputers.

17.2 The Householder Pipeline

The Householder pipeline solves n linear equations. The program is discussed in Chaps. 3–4. The pipeline is *not* folded as described in Chap. 5. The procedure *ring* ensures that the numbers of computational steps per node differ by at most one.

Test case:

$$
\begin{bmatrix}
1 & \cdots & 1 & 1 & 2 \\
1 & \cdots & 1 & 2 & 1 \\
1 & \cdots & 2 & 1 & 1 \\
\cdots & \cdots & \cdots & \cdots & \cdots \\
2 & \cdots & 1 & 1 & 1
\end{bmatrix}
\begin{bmatrix}
x_1 \\ x_2 \\ x_3 \\ \cdots \\ x_n
\end{bmatrix}
=
\begin{bmatrix}
s - 1 \\ s - 2 \\ s - 3 \\ \cdots \\ s - n
\end{bmatrix}
$$

where $s = (n+1)(n+2)/2$.

Input/output sequences:

$$
\begin{aligned}
\text{left}(r) &= \ < b >< a_r..a_n > \textbf{ rev } < a_1..a_{r-1} > \\
\text{right}(s) &= \ < b >< a_{s+1}..a_n > \textbf{ rev } < a_1..a_s > \\
\text{left}(1) &= \ < b >< a_1..a_n > \\
\text{right}(n-1) &= \ < b > \textbf{ rev } < a_1..a_n >
\end{aligned}
$$

```
program householder(input, output);
const
   n = 50 { equations };
   p = 3 { pipeline nodes };
   qmin = 16 { (n−1) div p steps/node };
type
   column = array [1..n] of real;
   matrix = array [1..n] of column;

procedure reduce(var a: matrix;
   var b: column);
type channel = *(column);

   function product(i: integer;
      a, b: column): real;
   { the scalar product of
      elements i..n of a and b }
   var ab: real; k: integer;
   begin
      ab := 0.0;
      for k := i to n do
```

```
        ab := ab + a[k]*b[k];
      product := ab
   end;

   procedure eliminate(i: integer;
      var ai, vi: column);
   var anorm, dii, fi, wii: real;
      k: integer;
   begin
      anorm := sqrt(product(i, ai, ai));
      if ai[i] > 0.0
         then dii := −anorm
         else dii := anorm;
      wii := ai[i] − dii;
      fi := sqrt(−2.0*wii*dii);
      vi[i] := wii/fi;
      ai[i] := dii;
      for k := i + 1 to n do
         begin
            vi[k] := ai[k]/fi;
            ai[k] := 0.0
         end
   end;

   procedure transform(i: integer;
      var aj, vi: column);
   var fi: real; k: integer;
   begin
      fi := 2.0*product(i, vi, aj);
      for k := i to n do
         aj[k] := aj[k] − fi*vi[k]
   end;

   procedure node(r, s: integer;
      left, right: channel);
   type block =
      array [0..qmin] of column;
```

```
var a, v: block; aj, b: column;
  i, j: integer;
begin
  { 1 <= r <= s <= n − 1 }
  receive(left, b);
  for i := 0 to s − r do
    begin
      receive(left, a[i]);
      for j := 0 to i − 1 do
        transform(j + r, a[i], v[j]);
      eliminate(i + r, a[i], v[i]);
      transform(i + r, b, v[i])
    end;
  send(right, b);
  for j := s + 1 to n do
    begin
      receive(left, aj);
      for i := 0 to s − r do
        transform(i + r, aj, v[i]);
      send(right, aj)
    end;
  for i := s − r downto 0 do
    send(right, a[i]);
  for j := r − 1 downto 1 do
    begin
      receive(left, aj);
      send(right, aj)
    end
end;

procedure master(var a: matrix;
  var b: column; left, right: channel);
var i: integer;
begin
  send(left, b);
  for i := 1 to n do
    send(left, a[i]);
```

```
      receive(right, b);
      for i := n downto 1 do
         receive(right, a[i])
   end;

   procedure ring(var a: matrix;
      var b: column);
   type net = array [0..p] of channel;
   var k, long, qmax: integer; c: net;
   begin
      qmax := qmin + 1;
      long := (n − 1) mod p;
      for k := 0 to p do open(c[k]);
      parallel
         master(a, b, c[0], c[p])|
         forall k := 1 to long do
            node((k − 1)*qmax + 1,
               k*qmax, c[k−1], c[k])|
         forall k := long + 1 to p do
            node((k − 1)*qmin + long
               + 1, k*qmin + long,
                  c[k−1], c[k])
      end
   end;

begin ring(a, b) end { reduce };

procedure substitute(var a: matrix;
   var b, x: column);
var i, j: integer;
begin
   for i := n downto 1 do
      begin
         x[i] := b[i]/a[i,i];
         for j := i − 1 downto 1 do
            b[j] := b[j] − a[i,j]*x[i]
      end
```

```
  end;

procedure run;
var a: matrix; b, x: column;

  procedure initialize(var a: matrix;
    var b: column);
  var i, j, s: integer;
  begin
    s := (n + 1)*(n + 2) div 2;
    for i := 1 to n do
      begin
        for j := 1 to n − i do
          a[i,j] := 1.0;
        a[i,n−i+1] := 2.0;
        for j := n − i + 2 to n do
          a[i,j] := 1.0;
        b[i] := s − i
      end
  end;

  procedure display(x: column);
  const m = 10 { items/line };
  var i, j, k: integer;
  begin
    k := n div m;
    for i := 0 to k − 1 do
      begin
        for j := 1 to m do
          write(x[i∗m+j]:6:1);
        writeln
      end;
    for j := 1 to n mod m do
      write(x[k∗m+j]:6:1);
    writeln
  end;
```

```
begin
   initialize(a, b);
   reduce(a, b);
   substitute(a, b, x);
   display(x)
end;


begin
   writeln('Householder pipeline:',
      ' n = ', n:1, ', p = ', p:1);
   writeln; run
end.
```

17.3 The N-Body Pipeline

The *n*-body pipeline simulates the movements of *n* bodies in space. The program is discussed in Chap. 6. The procedure *ring* ensures that the numbers of computational steps per node differ by at most one.

Test case: *n* bodies with identical masses and randomly distributed initial positions and velocities in a sphere with a given average mass density. Distance is measured in astronomical units, mass in solar masses, and time in years. Consequently, the gravitational constant $G = 4\pi^2$.

```
program nbody(input, output);
const
   n = 12 { bodies };
   p = 3 { pipeline nodes };
   qmin = 3 { (n−1) div p };
   steps = 50;
   twopi = 6.2831853072;
   G = 39.4784176044;
   d = 8.0e−18 { mass density };
   r0 = 7.0e5 { max initial distance };
   v0 = 10.0 { max initial velocity };
   dt = 10.0 { time step };
type
   vector = record x, y, z: real end;
```

```
    body = record m: real; r, v, f: vector end;
    system = array [1..n] of body;

{ vector arithmetic }

function newvector(ax, ay, az: real): vector;
var a: vector;
begin
    a.x := ax; a.y := ay; a.z := az;
    newvector := a
end;

function length(a: vector): real;
begin
    length :=
        sqrt(sqr(a.x) + sqr(a.y) + sqr(a.z))
end;

function sum(a, b: vector): vector;
begin
    a.x := a.x + b.x;
    a.y := a.y + b.y;
    a.z := a.z + b.z;
    sum := a
end;

function difference(a, b: vector): vector;
begin
    a.x := a.x − b.x;
    a.y := a.y − b.y;
    a.z := a.z − b.z;
    difference := a
end;

function product(a: vector; b: real): vector;
begin
    a.x := a.x*b;
```

```
    a.y := a.y*b;
    a.z := a.z*b;
    product := a
end;
```

{ n-body simulation }

```
procedure findforces(var a: system);
type channel = *(body);

    function force(pi, pj: body): vector;
    var eij, rij: vector; fm, rm: real;
    begin
      rij := difference(pj.r, pi.r);
      rm := length(rij);
      fm := G*pi.m*pj.m/sqr(rm);
      eij := product(rij, 1/rm);
      force := product(eij, fm)
    end;

    procedure addforces(var pi, pj: body);
    var fij: vector;
    begin
      fij := force(pi, pj);
      pi.f := sum(pi.f, fij);
      pj.f := difference(pj.f, fij)
    end;

    procedure node(r, s: integer;
      left, right: channel);
    type block =
      array [0..qmin] of body;
    var p: block; pj: body;
      i, j: integer;
    begin
      { 1 <= r <= s <= n - 1 }
      for i := 0 to s - r do
```

```
        begin
          receive(left, p[i]);
          for j := 0 to i − 1 do
          [sic] { i <> j }
             addforces(p[i], p[j])
        end;
      for j := s + 1 to n do
        begin
          receive(left, pj);
          for i := 0 to s − r do
             addforces(pj, p[i]);
          send(right, pj)
        end;
      for i := s − r downto 0 do
        send(right, p[i]);
      for j := r − 1 downto 1 do
        begin
          receive(left, pj);
          send(right, pj)
        end
    end;

    procedure master(var p: system;
      left, right: channel);
    var i: integer;
    begin
      for i := 1 to n do
        send(left, p[i]);
      for i := n downto 1 do
        receive(right, p[i])
    end;

    procedure ring(var a: system);
    type net = array [0..p] of channel;
    var k, long, qmax: integer; c: net;
    begin
      qmax := qmin + 1;
```

```
    long := (n − 1) mod p;
    for k := 0 to p do open(c[k]);
    parallel
      master(a, c[0], c[p])|
      forall k := 1 to long do
        node((k − 1)*qmax + 1,
          k*qmax, c[k−1], c[k])|
      forall k := long + 1 to p do
        node((k − 1)*qmin + long
          + 1, k*qmin + long,
            c[k−1], c[k])
    end
  end;

begin ring(a) end { findforces };

procedure integrate(var p: system; dt: real);
var i: integer;

  procedure movebody(
    var pi: body; dt: real);
  var ai, dvi, dri: vector;
  begin
    ai := product(pi.f, 1/pi.m);
    dvi := product(ai, dt);
    dri :=
      product(sum(pi.v,
        product(dvi, 0.5)), dt);
    pi.v := sum(pi.v, dvi);
    pi.r := sum(pi.r, dri);
    pi.f := newvector(0, 0, 0)
  end;

begin
  for i := 1 to n do movebody(p[i], dt)
end { integrate };
```

```
procedure simulate(var p: system;
  dt: real; steps: integer);
var i: integer;
begin
  for i := 1 to steps do
    begin
      findforces(p);
      integrate(p, dt)
    end
end;

procedure run;
var p: system; seed: real;

  procedure random(var value: real;
    max: real);
  { 0 <= value <= max }
  const a = 16807.0; m = 2147483647.0;
  var temp: real;
  begin
    temp := a*seed;
    seed := temp − m*trunc(temp/m);
    value := (seed/m)*max
  end;

  procedure getvector(
    var a: vector; max: real);
  var m, u, v: real; e: vector;
  begin
    random(m, max);
    random(u, twopi);
    random(v, twopi);
    e :=
      newvector(
        cos(u)*cos(v),
        cos(u)*sin(v),
        sin(u));
```

```
      a := product(e, m)
    end;


    procedure getbody(
      var pi: body; mi: real);
    begin
      pi.m := mi;
      getvector(pi.r, r0);
      getvector(pi.v, v0);
      pi.f := newvector(0, 0, 0)
    end;


    procedure getsystem(var p: system);
    var m, volume: real; i: integer;
    begin
      seed := 1;
      volume := (2.0/3.0)*twopi*r0*r0*r0;
      m := d*volume/n;
      for i := 1 to n do
        getbody(p[i], m)
    end;


    procedure display(var p: system);
    var i: integer;
    begin
      for i := 1 to n do
        writeln(
          p[i].r.x:11, ' ',
          p[i].r.y:11, ' ',
          p[i].r.z:11);
      writeln
    end;

begin
  getsystem(p);
  display(p);
  simulate(p, dt, steps);
```

```
      display(p)
   end { run };

   begin
      writeln('N-body pipeline:');
      writeln('n = ', n:1, ', p = ', p:1,
         ', steps = ', steps:1);
      writeln; run
   end.
```

17.4   The Multiplication Pipeline

The multiplication pipeline multiplies two $n \times n$ real matrices. The program
is discussed in Chap. 7. The procedure *ring* ensures that the numbers of
rows per node differ by at most one.

   Test Case:

$$
a \;=\; \begin{bmatrix}
1 & 0 & 0 & \cdots & 0 \\
1 & 1 & 0 & \cdots & 0 \\
1 & 1 & 1 & \cdots & 0 \\
\cdots & \cdots & \cdots & \cdots & \cdots \\
1 & 1 & 1 & \cdots & 1
\end{bmatrix}
$$

$$
a \times a^{T} \;=\; \begin{bmatrix}
1 & 1 & 1 & \cdots & 1 \\
1 & 2 & 2 & \cdots & 2 \\
1 & 2 & 3 & \cdots & 3 \\
\cdots & \cdots & \cdots & \cdots & \cdots \\
1 & 2 & 3 & \cdots & n
\end{bmatrix}
$$

```
   program multiplication(input, output);
   const
      n = 20 { n x n matrices };
      p = 3 { pipeline nodes };
      qmin = 6 { n div p };
   type
      vector = array [1..n] of real;
      matrix = array [1..n] of vector;
```

```
procedure multiply(var a, b, c: matrix);
{ c := a*b }
type channel = *(vector);

  function f(ai, bj: vector): real;
  var cij: real; k: integer;
  begin
    cij := 0.0;
    for k := 1 to n do
      cij := cij + ai[k]*bj[k];
    f := cij
  end;

  procedure node(r, s: integer;
    left, right: channel);
  type block =
    array [0..qmin] of vector;
  var a, c: block; i, j: integer;
    ai, bj, ci: vector;
  begin
    { 1 <= r <= s <= n }
    for i := 0 to s − r do
      receive(left, a[i]);
    for i := s + 1 to n do
      begin
        receive(left, ai);
        send(right, ai)
      end;
    for j := 1 to n do
      begin
        receive(left, bj);
        if s < n then
          send(right, bj);
        for i := 0 to s − r do
          c[i,j] := f(a[i], bj)
      end;
```

```
for i := 1 to r − 1 do
  begin
    receive(left, ci);
    send(right, ci)
  end;
for i := 0 to s − r do
  send(right, c[i])
end;

procedure master(var a, b, c: matrix;
  left, right: channel);
var i, j: integer; bj: vector;
begin
  for i := 1 to n do send(left, a[i]);
  for j := 1 to n do
    begin
      for i := 1 to n do bj[i] := b[i,j];
      send(left, bj)
    end;
  for i := 1 to n do receive(right, c[i])
end;

procedure ring(var a, b, c: matrix);
type net = array [0..p] of channel;
var k, long, qmax: integer; d: net;
begin
  qmax := qmin + 1;
  long := n mod p;
  for k := 0 to p do open(d[k]);
  parallel
    master(a, b, c, d[0], d[p])|
    forall k := 1 to long do
      node((k − 1)*qmax + 1,
        k*qmax, d[k−1], d[k])|
    forall k := long + 1 to p do
      node((k − 1)*qmin + long
        + 1, k*qmin + long,
```

```
                  d[k−1], d[k])
      end
  end;

  begin ring(a, b, c) end { multiply };

  procedure transpose(var a, b: matrix);
  { b := aT }
  var i, j: integer;
  begin
    for i := 1 to n do
      for j := 1 to n do
        b[i,j] := a[j,i]
  end;

  procedure run;
  var a, b, c: matrix;

    procedure initialize(var a, b: matrix);
    var i, j: integer;
    begin
      for i := 1 to n do
        begin
          for j := 1 to i do
            a[i,j] := 1.0;
          for j := i + 1 to n do
            a[i,j] := 0.0
        end;
      transpose(a, b)
    end;

    procedure display(var c: matrix);
    var i, j: integer;
    begin
      for i := 1 to n do
        begin
          for j := 1 to n do
```

```
                  write(round(c[i,j]):3);
               writeln
            end
      end;

   begin
      initialize(a, b);
      multiply(a, b, c);
      display(c)
   end { run };

   begin
      writeln('Matrix multiplication:');
      writeln('n = ', n:1, ', p = ', p:1);
      writeln; run
   end.
```

17.5   The Shortest Paths Pipeline

The shortest paths pipeline solves the all-pairs shortest paths problem for a directed graph with n nodes labeled $1, 2, \cdots, n$. The program is discussed in Chap. 7. The procedure *ring* ensures that numbers of rows per node differ by at most one.

Test graph:

$$1 \to 2 \to \cdots \to n - 1 \to n$$

Test matrices:

$$a \; = \; \begin{bmatrix} 0 & 1 & \infty & \cdots & \infty \\ \infty & 0 & 1 & \cdots & \infty \\ \infty & \infty & 0 & \cdots & \infty \\ \cdots & \cdots & \cdots & \cdots & \cdots \\ \infty & \infty & \infty & \cdots & 0 \end{bmatrix}$$

$$a^{n-1} \; = \; \begin{bmatrix} 0 & 1 & 2 & \cdots & n-1 \\ \infty & 0 & 1 & \cdots & n-2 \\ \infty & \infty & 0 & \cdots & n-3 \\ \cdots & \cdots & \cdots & \cdots & \cdots \\ \infty & \infty & \infty & \cdots & 0 \end{bmatrix}$$

```
program shortestpaths(input, output);
const
  n = 20 { n x n matrices };
  p = 3 { pipeline nodes };
  qmin = 6 { n div p };
  infinity = 1.0e300;
type
  vector = array [1..n] of real;
  matrix = array [1..n] of vector;

procedure multiply(var a, b, c: matrix);
{ c := a*b }
type channel = *(vector);

  function min(a, b: real): real;
  begin
    if a <= b then min := a
    else min := b
  end;

  function sum(a, b: real): real;
  begin
    if (a < infinity) and (b < infinity)
      then sum := a + b
      else sum := infinity
  end;

  function f(ai, bj: vector): real;
  var cij: real; k: integer;
  begin
    cij := infinity;
    for k := 1 to n do
      cij := min(cij, sum(ai[k],bj[k]));
    f := cij
  end;

  procedure node(r, s: integer;
```

```
      left, right: channel);
  type block =
    array [0..qmin] of vector;
  var a, c: block; i, j: integer;
    ai, bj, ci: vector;
  begin
    { 1 <= r <= s <= n }
    for i := 0 to s − r do
      receive(left, a[i]);
    for i := s + 1 to n do
      begin
        receive(left, ai);
        send(right, ai)
      end;
    for j := 1 to n do
      begin
        receive(left, bj);
        if s < n then
          send(right, bj);
        for i := 0 to s − r do
          c[i,j] := f(a[i], bj)
      end;
    for i := 1 to r − 1 do
      begin
        receive(left, ci);
        send(right, ci)
      end;
    for i := 0 to s − r do
      send(right, c[i])
  end;

  procedure master(var a, b, c: matrix;
    left, right: channel);
  var i, j: integer; bj: vector;
  begin
    for i := 1 to n do send(left, a[i]);
    for j := 1 to n do
```

```
    begin
      for i := 1 to n do bj[i] := b[i,j];
      send(left, bj)
    end;
    for i := 1 to n do receive(right, c[i])
  end;

  procedure ring(var a, b, c: matrix);
  type net = array [0..p] of channel;
  var k, long, qmax: integer; d: net;
  begin
    qmax := qmin + 1;
    long := n mod p;
    for k := 0 to p do open(d[k]);
    parallel
      master(a, b, c, d[0], d[p])|
      forall k := 1 to long do
        node((k − 1)*qmax + 1,
          k*qmax, d[k−1], d[k])|
      forall k := long + 1 to p do
        node((k − 1)*qmin + long
          + 1, k*qmin + long,
            d[k−1], d[k])
    end
  end;

begin ring(a, b, c) end { multiply };

procedure square(var a: matrix);
{ a := a*a }
var b, c: matrix;
begin
  c := a; b := a;
  multiply(c, b, a)
end;

procedure allpaths(var a, d: matrix);
```

```
    var m: integer;
begin
  d := a; m := 1;
  while m < n − 1 do
    begin square(d); m := 2∗m end
end;

procedure run;
var a, d: matrix;

  procedure initialize(var w: matrix);
  var i, j: integer;
  begin
    for i := 1 to n do
      for j := 1 to n do
        w[i,j] := infinity;
    for i := 1 to n do
      w[i,i] := 0.0;
    for i := 1 to n − 1 do
      w[i,i+1] := 1.0
  end;

  procedure display(
    var a: matrix);
  var i, j: integer;
    aij: real;
  begin
    for i := 1 to n do
      begin
        for j := 1 to n do
          begin
            aij := a[i,j];
            if aij < infinity
              then write(round(aij):3)
              else write(' −')
          end;
        writeln
```

```
        end;
      writeln
    end;

  begin
    initialize(a);
    allpaths(a, d);
    display(d)
  end { run };

  begin
    writeln('Shortest paths:');
    writeln('n = ', n:1, ', p = 1', p:1);
    writeln; run
  end.
```

17.6   The Quicksort Tree

The binary quicksort tree sorts n integers. The program is discussed in Chap. 9.

Test case: n random integers.

```
  program sorting(input, output);
  const
    d = 2 { tree depth: log(p+1)−1 };
    p = 7 { tree nodes: 2**(d+1)−1 };
    n = 500 { items: >=2**d };
  type table = array [1..n] of integer;

  procedure sort(var a: table);
  type channel = *(integer);
  var bottom: channel;

    procedure partition(var a: table;
      var i, j: integer; first, last: integer);
    var ai, key: integer;
    begin
```

```
    i := first; j := last;
    key := a[(i+j) div 2];
    while i <= j do
      begin
        while a[i] < key do i := i + 1;
        while key < a[j] do j := j - 1;
        if i <= j then
          begin
            ai := a[i]; a[i] := a[j];
            a[j]:=ai;
            i := i + 1; j := j - 1
          end
      end
  end;

  procedure find(var a: table;
    first, last, middle: integer);
  var left, right, i, j: integer;
  begin
    left := first; right := last;
    while left < right do
      begin
        partition(a, i, j, left, right);
        if middle <= j then right := j
        else if i <= middle then left := i
        else left := right
      end
  end;

  procedure quicksort(var a: table;
    first, last: integer);
  var i, j: integer;
  begin
    if first < last then
      begin
        partition(a, i, j, first, last);
        quicksort(a, first, j);
```

```
        quicksort(a, i, last)
      end
  end;

  procedure leaf(bottom: channel);
  var a: table; first, last, i: integer;
  begin
    receive(bottom, first, last);
    for i := first to last do
      receive(bottom, a[i]);
    quicksort(a, first, last);
    for i := first to last do
      send(bottom, a[i])
  end;

  procedure root(bottom, left,
    right: channel);
  var a: table; first, last, middle,
    middle2, i: integer;
  begin
    receive(bottom, first, last);
    for i := first to last do
      receive(bottom, a[i]);
    middle := (first + last) div 2;
    find(a, first, last, middle);
    send(left, first, middle);
    for i := first to middle do
      send(left, a[i]);
    middle2 := middle + 1;
    send(right, middle2, last);
    for i := middle2 to last do
      send(right, a[i]);
    for i := first to middle do
      receive(left, a[i]);
    for i := middle2 to last do
      receive(right, a[i]);
    for i := first to last do
```

```
            send(bottom, a[i])
      end;

      procedure tree(depth: integer;
         bottom: channel);
      var left, right: channel;
      begin
         if depth > 0 then
            begin
               open(left, right);
               parallel
                  tree(depth − 1, left)|
                  tree(depth − 1, right)|
                  root(bottom, left, right)
               end
            end
         else leaf(bottom)
      end;

      procedure master(var a: table;
         bottom: channel);
      var i: integer;
      begin
         send(bottom, 1, n);
         for i := 1 to n do
            send(bottom, a[i]);
         for i := 1 to n do
            receive(bottom, a[i])
      end;

   begin
      open(bottom);
      parallel
         tree(d, bottom)|
         master(a, bottom)
      end
   end { sort };
```

```
procedure run;
var a: table; seed: real;

    procedure random(var value: integer);
    { 0 <= value <= max−1 }
    const max = 10000; a = 16807.0;
      m = 2147483647.0;
    var temp: real;
    begin
      temp := a*seed;
      seed := temp − m*trunc(temp/m);
      value := trunc((seed/m)*max)
    end;

    procedure initialize(var a: table);
    var i: integer;
    begin
      seed := 1.0;
      for i := 1 to n do random(a[i])
    end;

    procedure display(a: table);
    const m = 11 { items/line };
    var i, j, k: integer;
    begin
      k := n div m;
      for i := 0 to k − 1 do
        begin
          for j := 1 to m do
            write(a[i*m+j]:5);
          writeln
        end;
      for j := 1 to n mod m do
        write(a[k*m+j]:5);
      writeln
    end;
```

```
begin
   initialize(a);
   sort(a);
   display(a)
end { run };

begin
   writeln('Quicksort tree:',
      ' n = ', n:1, ', p = ', p:1);
   writeln; run
end.
```

17.7   The FFT Tree

The binary FFT tree computes the fast Fourier transform of n complex numbers. The program is discussed in Chaps. 8–9.

Test case: n random complex numbers.

```
program fourier(input, output);
const
   d = 2 { tree depth: log(p+1)−1 };
   p = 7 { tree nodes: 2**(d+1)−1 };
   n = 128 { items: 2power>=2**d };
type
   complex = record re, im: real end;
   table = array [1..n] of complex;

{ complex arithmetic }

function pair(re, im: real): complex;
var a: complex;
begin
   a.re := re; a.im := im;
   pair := a
end;
```

```
function sum(a, b: complex): complex;
begin
  a.re := a.re + b.re;
  a.im := a.im + b.im;
  sum := a
end;

function difference(a, b: complex): complex;
begin
  a.re := a.re − b.re;
  a.im := a.im − b.im;
  difference := a
end;

function product(a, b: complex): complex;
var c: complex;
begin
  c.re := a.re*b.re − a.im*b.im;
  c.im := a.re*b.im + a.im*b.re;
  product := c
end;

{ discrete fourier transform }

procedure dft(var a: table);
type channel = *(complex, integer);
var bottom: channel;

  procedure permute(var a: table);
  type map = array [1..n] of integer;
  var rev: map; half, incr, size,
    j, k: integer; aj: complex;
  begin
    rev[1] := 1;
    half := n div 2;
    size := 1;
    while size <= half do
```

```
  begin
    incr := half div size;
    for j := 1 to size do
        rev[j + size] := rev[j] + incr;
    size := 2*size
  end;
for j := 1 to n do
  begin
    k := rev[j];
    if j < k then
        begin
            aj := a[j]; a[j] := a[k];
            a[k] := aj
        end
  end
end;

procedure combine(var a: table;
  first, last: integer);
const pi = 3.1415926536;
var even, half, odd, j: integer;
  w, wj, x: complex;
begin
  half := (last − first + 1) div 2;
  w := pair(cos(pi/half), sin(pi/half));
  wj := pair(1, 0);
  for j := 0 to half − 1 do
    begin
        even := first + j;
        odd := even + half;
        x := product(wj, a[odd]);
        a[odd] := difference(a[even], x);
        a[even] := sum(a[even], x);
        wj := product(wj, w)
    end
end;
```

```
procedure fft(var a: table;
   first, last: integer);
var size, k, m: integer;
begin
  m := last − first + 1;
  size := 2;
  while size <= m do
    begin
      k := first + size − 1;
      while k <= last do
        begin
          combine(a, k − size + 1, k);
          k := k + size
        end;
      size := 2*size
    end
end;

procedure leaf(bottom: channel);
var a: table; first, last, i: integer;
begin
  receive(bottom, first, last);
  for i := first to last do
    receive(bottom, a[i]);
  fft(a, first, last);
  for i := first to last do
    send(bottom, a[i])
end;

procedure root(bottom, left,
   right: channel);
var a: table; first, last, middle,
   middle2, i: integer;
begin
  receive(bottom, first, last);
  for i := first to last do
    receive(bottom, a[i]);
```

```
    middle := (first + last) div 2;
    send(left, first, middle);
    for i := first to middle do
        send(left, a[i]);
    middle2 := middle + 1;
    send(right, middle2, last);
    for i := middle2 to last do
        send(right, a[i]);
    for i := first to middle do
        receive(left, a[i]);
    for i := middle2 to last do
        receive(right, a[i]);
    combine(a, first, last);
    for i := first to last do
        send(bottom, a[i])
end;

procedure tree(depth: integer;
    bottom: channel);
var left, right: channel;
begin
    if depth > 0 then
        begin
            open(left, right);
            parallel
                tree(depth − 1, left)|
                tree(depth − 1, right)|
                root(bottom, left, right)
            end
        end
    else leaf(bottom)
end;

procedure master(var a: table;
    bottom: channel);
var i: integer;
begin
```

```
      send(bottom, 1, n);
      for i := 1 to n do
        send(bottom, a[i]);
      for i := 1 to n do
        receive(bottom, a[i])
    end;

begin
  permute(a);
  open(bottom);
  parallel
    tree(d, bottom)|
    master(a, bottom)
  end
end { dft};

procedure run;
var a: table; seed: real;

  procedure random(var value: real);
  { 0 <= value <= 1 }
  const a = 16807.0; m = 2147483647.0;
  var temp: real;
  begin
    temp := a*seed;
    seed := temp − m*trunc(temp/m);
    value := seed/m
  end;

  procedure initialize(var a: table);
  var i: integer; re: real;
  begin
    seed := 1.0;
    for i := 1 to n do
      begin
        random(re);
        a[i] := pair(re, 0)
```

```
          end
     end;

     procedure display(a: table);
     const m = 4 { items/line };
     var i, j, k: integer; aij: complex;
     begin
        k := n div m;
        for i := 0 to k − 1 do
           begin
              for j := 1 to m do
                 begin
                    aij :=a[i∗m + j];
                    write(aij.re:8, ' ',
                        aij.im:8, ', ')
                 end;
              writeln
           end;
        writeln
     end;

  begin
     initialize(a);
     dft(a);
     display(a)
  end { run };

  begin
     writeln('FFT tree:',
        ' n = ', n:1, ', p = ', p:1);
     writeln; run
  end.
```

17.8   The Annealing Pipeline

The annealing pipeline uses simulated annealing to find a near-optimal tour of n cities. The program is discussed in Chaps. 11 and 14.

Test case: A square grid of n cities with a shortest tour of length n.

```
program salesperson(input, output);
const
    s = 4 { s*s square, s even };
    n = 16 { s*s cities };
    m = 2 { trials, m mod p = 0 };
    p = 2 { pipeline nodes };
type
    city = record x, y: real end;
    tour = array [1..n] of city;
    table = array [1..m] of tour;


function distance(p, q: city): real;
var dx, dy: real;
begin
    dx := q.x − p.x;
    dy := q.y − p.y;
    distance := sqrt(dx*dx + dy*dy)
end;


procedure solve(a: tour; var b: tour;
    trial: integer);
{ 1 <= trial <= m }
var seed: real; index: integer;



    procedure random(var value: real);
    { 0 <= value <= 1 }
    const a = 16807.0; m = 2147483647.0;
    var temp: real;
    begin
        temp := a*seed;
        seed := temp − m*trunc(temp/m);
        value := seed/m
    end;


    procedure generate(var i, j: integer);
```

```
{ 1 <= i,j <= n }
var x: real;
begin
  random(x);
  i := trunc(x*n) + 1;
  j := index;
  index := index mod n + 1
end;

procedure select(var a: tour;
  var si, j: integer; var dE: real);
var i, sj: integer;
begin
  generate(i, j);
  si := i mod n + 1;
  sj := j mod n + 1;
  if i <> j then
    dE := distance(a[i], a[j])
      + distance(a[si], a[sj])
      − distance(a[i], a[si])
      − distance(a[j], a[sj])
  else dE := 0.0
end;

function accept(dE, T: real): boolean;
begin accept := dE < T end;

procedure swap(var a: tour;
  i, j: integer);
var ai: city;
begin
  ai := a[i]; a[i] := a[j]; a[j] := ai
end;

procedure change(var a: tour;
  i, j: integer);
var k, nij: integer;
```

```
begin
  nij := (j − i + n) mod n + 1;
  for k := 1 to nij div 2 do
    swap(a,
      (i + k − 2) mod n + 1,
      (j − k + n) mod n + 1)
end;

procedure search(var a: tour; T: real;
  attempts, changes: integer);
var i, j, na, nc: integer; dE: real;
begin
  na := 0; nc := 0;
  while (na < attempts)
    and (nc < changes) do
      begin
        select(a, i, j, dE);
        if accept(dE, T) then
          begin
            change(a, i, j);
            nc := nc + 1
          end;
        na := na + 1
      end
end;

procedure anneal(var a: tour;
  Tmax, alpha: real; steps,
  attempts, changes: integer);
var T: real; k: integer;
begin
  T := Tmax;
  for k := 1 to steps do
    begin
      search(a, T, attempts, changes);
      T := alpha*T
    end
```

```
        end;

   procedure permute(var a: tour;
       changes: integer);
   var i, j, k: integer;
   begin
      for k := 1 to changes do
         begin
            generate(i, j);
            swap(a, i, j)
         end
   end;

begin
   seed := trial; index := trial;
   b := a;
   permute(b, n);
   anneal(b, sqrt(n), 0.95,
      trunc(20.0*ln(n)), 100*n, 10*n)
end { solve };

procedure compute(a: tour; var b: table);
type channel = *(tour);

   procedure master(a: tour; var b: table;
       left, right: channel);
   var trial: integer;
   begin
      send(left, a);
      for trial := 1 to m do
         receive(right, b[trial])
   end;

   procedure node(i: integer;
       left, right: channel);
   { 1 <= i <= p }
   var a, b: tour; j, k, q, trial: integer;
```

```
begin
  receive(left, a);
  if i < p then send(right, a);
  q := m div p;
  for j := 1 to q do
    begin
      trial := (i − 1)*q + j;
      solve(a, b, trial);
      send(right, b);
      for k := 1 to i − 1 do
        begin
          receive(left, b);
          send(right, b)
        end
    end
end;

procedure ring(a: tour; var b: table);
type net = array [0..p] of channel;
var c: net; i: integer;
begin
  for i := 0 to p do open(c[i]);
  parallel
    master(a, b, c[0], c[p])|
    forall i := 1 to p do
      node(i, c[i−1], c[i])
  end
end;

begin ring(a, b) end { compute };

procedure run;
var a: tour; b: table;

  procedure initialize(var a: tour);
  { grid of s*s cities }
  var i, j, k: integer;
```

```
begin
  for i := 1 to s do
    for j := 1 to s do
      begin
        k := (i − 1)*s + j;
        a[k].x := i;
        a[k].y := j
      end
end;

function length(a: tour): real;
var i: integer; sum: real;
begin
  sum := distance(a[n], a[1]);
  for i := 1 to n − 1 do
    sum := sum +
      distance(a[i], a[i+1]);
  length := sum
end;

function shortest(b: table): tour;
var Ek, Emin: real;
  k, min: integer;
begin
  min := 1;
  Emin := length(b[min]);
  for k := 2 to m do
    begin
      Ek := length(b[k]);
      if Emin > Ek then
        begin
          min := k; Emin := Ek
        end
    end;
  shortest := b[min]
end;
```

```
      procedure summarize(var b: table);
      var a: tour; i: integer;
      begin
        a := shortest(b);
        for i := 1 to n do
          writeln(a[i].x:11, ' ', a[i].y:11);
        writeln(length(a))
      end;

    begin
      initialize(a);
      compute(a, b);
      summarize(b)
    end { run };

    begin
      writeln('Traveling salesperson: ',
        n:1, ' cities, ', m:1, ' trials, ',
        p:1, ' pipeline nodes');
      writeln; run
    end.
```

17.9 The Primality Testing Pipeline

The primality testing pipeline uses the Miller-Rabin algorithm to test the primality of a natural number with n digits in radix b. The program is discussed in Chaps. 12–14.

Test case: A large decimal prime and a large decimal composite.

```
program primality(input, output);
const
    b = 10 { even radix };
    b1 = 9 { maxdigit b−1 };
    n = 10 { radix test digits };
    w = 20 { max radix digits 2n };
    m = 2 { trials, m mod p = 0 };
    p = 2 { pipeline nodes };
```

```
type
  number = array [0..w] of integer;
  table = array [1..m] of boolean;

function value(x: integer): number;
var y: number; i: integer;
begin
  for i := 0 to w do
    begin
      y[i] := x mod b;
      x := x div b
    end;
  value := y
end;

function length(x: number): integer;
var i, j: integer;
begin
  i := w; j := 0;
  while i <> j do
    if x[i] <> 0 then j := i
    else i := i - 1;
  length := i + 1
end;

procedure writeno(x: number);
{ 1 <= length(x) <= w+1 }
var i, m: integer;
begin
  m := length(x);
  for i := m - 1 downto 0 do
    write(chr(x[i] + ord('0')));
  writeln('(', m:1, ')')
end;

procedure solve(p: number;
  var sure: boolean; trial: integer);
```

```
{ 1 <= trial <= m }
var seed: real; x: number;

  function maxlong: number;
  var x: number; i: integer;
  begin
    for i := 0 to w − 1 do
      x[i] := b1;
    x[w] := 0;
    maxlong := x
  end;

  function min(x, y: integer): integer;
  begin
    if x <= y then min := x
    else min := y
  end;

  function less(x, y: number): boolean;
  var i, j: integer;
  begin
    i := w; j := 0;
    while i <> j do
      if x[i] <> y[i]
        then j := i
        else i := i − 1;
    less := x[i] < y[i]
  end;

  function equal(x, y: number): boolean;
  var i, j: integer;
  begin
    i := w; j := 0;
    while i <> j do
      if x[i] <> y[i]
        then j := i
        else i := i − 1;
```

```
      equal := x[i] = y[i]
    end;

    function greater(x, y: number): boolean;
    var i, j: integer;
    begin
      i := w; j := 0;
      while i <> j do
        if x[i] <> y[i]
          then j := i
          else i := i − 1;
      greater := x[i] > y[i]
    end;

    function odd(x: number): boolean;
    { even radix b }
    begin odd := x[0] mod 2 = 1 end;

    function product(x: number;
      k: integer): number;
    var carry, i, m, temp: integer;
    begin
      m := length(x); carry := 0;
      for i := 0 to m − 1 do
        begin
          temp := x[i]*k + carry;
          x[i] := temp mod b;
          carry := temp div b
        end;
      if m <= w then x[m] := carry
      else assume carry = 0;
      product := x
    end;

    function quotient(x: number;
      k: integer): number;
    var carry, i, m, temp: integer;
```

```
begin
  m := length(x); carry := 0;
  for i := m − 1 downto 0 do
    begin
      temp := carry*b + x[i];
      x[i] := temp div k;
      carry := temp mod k
    end;
  quotient := x
end;

function remainder(x: number;
  k: integer): number;
var carry, i, m: integer;
begin
  m := length(x); carry := 0;
  for i := m − 1 downto 0 do
    carry := (carry*b + x[i]) mod k;
  remainder := value(carry)
end;

function increment(x: number): number;
var i: integer;
begin
  assume less(x, maxlong);
  i := 0;
  while x[i] = b1 do
    begin
      x[i] := 0;
      i := i + 1
    end;
  x[i] := x[i] + 1;
  increment := x
end;

function decrement(x: number): number;
var i: integer;
```

```
begin
  assume greater(x, value(0));
  i := 0;
  while x[i] = 0 do
    begin
      x[i] := b1;
      i := i + 1
    end;
  x[i] := x[i] − 1;
  decrement := x
end;

function half(x: number): number;
begin half := quotient(x, 2) end;

function multiply(x, y: number)
  : number;
var z: number; carry, i, j,
  n, m, temp, yi: integer;
begin
  n := length(x);
  m := length(y);
  assume n + m <= w;
  z := value(0);
  for i := 0 to m − 1 do
    begin
      yi := y[i];
      carry := 0;
      for j := 0 to n − 1 do
        begin
          temp := x[j]*yi +
            z[i+j] + carry;
          z[i+j] := temp mod b;
          carry := temp div b
        end;
      z[i+n] := carry
    end;
```

```
    multiply := z
  end;

  function trialdigit(r, d: number;
     k, m: integer): integer;
  { trialdigit(r,d,k,m) = min(
      r[k+m..k+m−2] div d[m−1..m−2],
        b − 1) }
  var d2, km, r3: integer;
  begin
    { 2 <= m <= k+m <= w }
    km := k + m;
    r3 := (r[km]*b + r[km−1])*b + r[km−2];
    d2 := d[m−1]*b + d[m−2];
    trialdigit := min(r3 div d2, b − 1)
  end;

  function smaller(r, dq: number;
     k, m: integer): boolean
  { r[k+m..k] < dq[m..0] };
  var i, j: integer;
  begin
    { 0 <= k <= k+m <= w }
    i := m; j := 0;
    while i <> j do
      if r[i+k] <> dq[i]
        then j := i
        else i := i − 1;
    smaller := r[i+k] < dq[i]
  end;

  function difference(r, dq: number;
     k, m: integer): number;
  { r[k+m..k] :=
      r[k+m..k] − dq[m..0];
    difference := r }
  var borrow, diff, i: integer;
```

```
begin
  { 0 <= k <= k+m <= w }
  borrow := 0;
  for i := 0 to m do
    begin
      diff := r[i+k] − dq[i]
        − borrow + b;
      r[i+k] := diff mod b;
      borrow := 1 − diff div b
    end;
  assume borrow = 0;
  difference := r
end;

function longmod(x, y: number;
  n, m: integer): number;
{ longmod = x mod y }
var d, dq, r: number;
  f, k, qt: integer;
begin
  { 2 <= m <= n <= w }
  f := b div (y[m−1] + 1);
  r := product(x, f);
  d := product(y, f);
  for k := n − m downto 0 do
    begin
      { 2 <= m <= k+m <= n <= w }
      qt := trialdigit(r, d, k, m);
      dq := product(d, qt);
      if smaller(r, dq, k, m) then
        begin
          qt := qt − 1;
          dq := product(d, qt)
        end;
      r := difference(r, dq, k, m)
    end;
  longmod := quotient(r, f)
```

```
    end;

function modulo(x, y: number): number;
var m, n, y1: integer; r: number;
begin
  m := length(y);
  if m = 1 then
    begin
      y1 := y[m−1];
      assume y1 > 0;
      r := remainder(x, y1)
    end
  else
    begin
      n := length(x);
      if m > n then r := x
      else { 2 <= m <= n <= w }
        r := longmod(x, y, n, m)
    end;
  modulo := r
end;

function square(x: number): number;
begin
  assume 2*length(x) <= w;
  square := multiply(x, x)
end;

procedure random(var no: real);
{ 0 <= no <= 1 }
const a = 16807.0; m = 2147483647.0;
var temp: real;
begin
  temp := a*seed;
  seed := temp − m*trunc(temp/m);
  no := seed/m
end;
```

```
procedure randomno(var no: number;
   max: number);
{ 1 <= no <= max }
var x: number; i, m: integer; f: real;
begin
   x := value(0);
   m := length(max);
   for i := 0 to m − 1 do
      begin
         random(f);
         x[i] := trunc(f*b1)
      end;
   no := increment(modulo(x, max))
end;


function witness(x, p: number): boolean;
var e, m, one, p1, r, y, zero: number;
   sure: boolean;
begin
   { 1 <= x <= p − 1 }
   zero := value(0);
   one := value(1);
   m := one; y := x;
   e := decrement(p);
   p1 := e; sure := false;
   while not sure and greater(e, zero) do
      if odd(e) then
         begin
            m := modulo(multiply(m, y), p);
            e := decrement(e)
         end
      else
         begin
            r := y;
            y := modulo(square(y), p);
            e := half(e);
```

```
            if equal(y, one) then
               sure :=
                  less(one, r) and less(r, p1)
         end;
      witness := sure or not equal(m, one)
   end;

begin
   { trial > 0 }
   seed := trial;
   randomno(x, decrement(p));
   sure := witness(x, p)
end { solve };

procedure compute(a: number; var b: table);
type channel = *(boolean, number);

   procedure master(a: number; var b: table;
      left, right: channel);
   var trial: integer;
   begin
      send(left, a);
      for trial := 1 to m do
         receive(right, b[trial])
   end;

   procedure node(i: integer;
      left, right: channel);
   { 1 <= i <= p }
   var a: number; b: boolean;
      j, k, q, trial: integer;
   begin
      receive(left, a);
      if i < p then send(right, a);
      q := m div p;
      for j := 1 to q do
         begin
```

```
            trial := (i − 1)*q + j;
            solve(a, b, trial);
            send(right, b);
            for k := 1 to i − 1 do
              begin
                 receive(left, b);
                 send(right, b)
              end
        end
  end;

  procedure ring(a: number; var b: table);
  type net = array [0..p] of channel;
  var c: net; i: integer;
  begin
     for i := 0 to p do open(c[i]);
     parallel
        master(a, b, c[0], c[p])|
        forall i := 1 to p do
           node(i, c[i−1], c[i])
     end
  end;

begin ring(a, b) end { compute };

procedure run(a: number);
var b: table;

  procedure summarize(
     a: number; var b: table);
  var cn, i, pn: integer;
  begin
     writeln; writeno(a);
     cn := 0; pn := 0;
     for i := 1 to m do
        if b[i] then cn := cn + 1
        else pn := pn + 1;
```

```
        writeln(cn:1, ' composite votes, ',
            pn:1, ' prime votes')
    end;

begin
    compute(a, b);
    summarize(a, b)
end { run };

begin
    writeln('Primality testing:');
    writeln(n:1, ' digits, ',
        m:1, ' trials, ',
        p:1, ' pipeline nodes');
    run(value(1653701519));
    run(value(1653701518))
end.
```

17.10   The Forest Fire Matrix

The forest fire matrix uses a cellular automaton with $n \times n$ cells to simulate
a forest fire. The program is discussed in Chap. 16.

Test case: A live forest surrounded by a border of dead trees.

```
program forestfire(input, output);
const
    n = 20 { n x n interior grid
        elements, n = q*m };
    q - 2 { q x q processor nodes };
    m = 10 { m x m interior subgrid
        elements, m even };
    m1 = 11 { m+1 };
    steps = n;
    pa = 0.30 { Prob(alive) };
    pb = 0.01 { Prob(burning) };
type
    state = (alive, burning, dead);
```

```
  row = array [1..n] of state;
  grid = array [1..n] of row;

procedure fire(var u: grid;
    u1, u2, u3, u4, u5: state;
    steps: integer);
type
    subrow = array [0..m1] of state;
    subgrid = array [0..m1] of subrow;
    channel = *(state);

    procedure node(qi, qj, steps: integer;
        up, down, left, right: channel);
    var u: subgrid; k: integer; seed: real;

        procedure copy(no: integer;
            inp, out: channel);
        var k: integer; uk: state;
        begin
            for k := 1 to no do
                begin
                    receive(inp, uk);
                    send(out, uk)
                end
        end;

        procedure output(qi, qj: integer;
            inp, out: channel; var u: subgrid);
        var i, j: integer;
        begin
            for i := 1 to m do
                begin
                    for j := 1 to m do
                        send(out, u[i,j]);
                    copy((q − qj)*m, inp, out)
                end;
            copy((q − qi)*m*n, inp, out)
```

```
    end;

    procedure phase1(qi, qj, b: integer;
      up, down, left, right: channel;
      var u: subgrid);
    var k, last: integer;
    begin
      k := 2 - b;
      last := m - b;
      while k <= last do
        begin
          { 1 <= k <= m }
          [sic] parallel
            if qi > 1 then
              receive(up, u[0,k])|
            if qi < q then
              send(down, u[m,k])|
            if qj > 1 then
              receive(left, u[k,0])|
            if qj < q then
              send(right, u[k,m])
          end;
          k := k + 2
        end
    end;

    procedure phase2(qi, qj, b: integer;
      up, down, left, right: channel;
      var u: subgrid);
    var k, last: integer;
    begin
      k := b + 1;
      last := m + b - 1;
      while k <= last do
        begin
          { 1 <= k <= m }
          [sic] parallel
```

```
            if qi > 1 then
                send(up, u[1,k])|
            if qi < q then
                receive(down, u[m+1,k])|
            if qj > 1 then
                send(left, u[k,1])|
            if qj < q then
                receive(right, u[k,m+1])
        end;
        k := k + 2
    end
end;

procedure exchange(qi, qj, b: integer;
    up, down, left, right: channel;
    var u: subgrid);
begin
    phase1(qi, qj, b,
        up, down, left, right, u);
    phase2(qi, qj, b,
        up, down, left, right, u)
end;

function initial(i, j: integer): state;
begin
    if i = 0 then
        initial := u1
    else if i = n + 1 then
        initial := u2
    else if j = n + 1 then
        initial := u3
    else if j = 0 then
        initial := u4
    else
        initial := u5
end;
```

```
procedure random(var no: real);
{ 0 <= no <= 1 }
const a = 16807.0; m = 2147483647.0;
var temp: real;
begin
  temp := a*seed;
  seed := temp − m*trunc(temp/m);
  no := seed/m
end;

procedure nextstate(var u: subgrid;
  i, j: integer);
{ 1 <= i <= m, 1 <= j <= m }
var x: real;
begin
  case u[i,j] of
    alive:
      if
        (u[i−1,j] = burning) or
        (u[i+1,j] = burning) or
        (u[i,j+1] = burning) or
        (u[i,j−1] = burning)
      then u[i,j] := burning
      else
        begin
          random(x);
          if x <= pb then
            u[i,j] := burning
        end;
    burning:
      u[i,j] := dead;
    dead:
      begin
        random(x);
        if x <= pa then
          u[i,j] := alive
      end
```

```
      end
    end;

    procedure newgrid(qi, qj: integer;
      var u: subgrid);
    var i, i0, j, j0: integer;
    begin
      i0 := (qi − 1)∗m;
      j0 := (qj − 1)∗m;
      for i := 0 to m + 1 do
        for j := 0 to m + 1 do
          u[i,j] := initial(i0+i, j0+j)
    end;

    procedure relax(qi, qj: integer;
      up, down, left, right: channel;
      var u: subgrid);
    var b, i, j, k: integer;
    begin
      for b := 0 to 1 do
        begin
          exchange(qi, qj, 1 − b,
            up, down, left, right, u);
          for i := 1 to m do
            begin
              k := (i + b) mod 2;
              j := 2 − k;
              while j <= m − k do
                begin
                  nextstate(u, i, j);
                  j := j + 2
                end
            end
        end
    end;

  begin
```

```
      seed := 1.0;
      newgrid(qi, qj, u);
      for k := 1 to steps do
        relax(qi, qj, up, down,
          left, right, u);
      output(qi, qj, right, left, u)
    end { node };

    procedure master(right: channel;
      var u: grid);
    var i, j: integer;
    begin
      for i := 1 to n do
        for j := 1 to n do
          receive(right, u[i,j])
    end;

    procedure simulate(
      steps: integer; var u: grid);
    type
      line = array [1..q] of channel;
      matrix = array [0..q] of line;
    var h, v: matrix; i, j: integer;
    begin
      open(h[0,q]);
      for i := 1 to q do
        for j := 1 to q do
          open(h[i,j]);
      for i := 0 to q do
        for j := 1 to q do
          open(v[i,j]);
      parallel
        master(h[0,q], u)|
        forall j := 1 to q do
          node(j, 1, steps,
            v[j−1,1], v[j,1],
            h[j−1,q], h[j,1])|
```

```
            forall i := 1 to q do
               forall j := 2 to q do
                  node(i, j, steps,
                       v[i−1,j], v[i,j],
                       h[i,j−1], h[i,j])
         end
      end;

   begin simulate(steps, u) end { fire };

   procedure run;
   var u: grid;

      procedure display(var u: grid);
      var i, j: integer;
      begin
         for i := 1 to n do
            begin
               for j := 1 to n do
                  case u[i,j] of
                     alive: write('+ ');
                     burning: write('* ');
                     dead: write(' ')
                  end;
               writeln
            end
      end;

   begin
      fire(u, dead, dead, dead,
         dead, alive, steps);
      display(u)
   end { run };

begin
   writeln('Forest fire matrix:',
      ' n = ', n:1, ', p = ', q*q:1);
```

writeln; run
end.

17.11   The Laplace Matrix

The Laplace matrix solves Laplace's equation on a square region with $n \times n$ elements. The program is discussed in Chaps. 15–16.

Test case: A square with a constant temperature on each border.

```
program heatequation(input, output);
const
   n = 20 { n x n interior grid
      elements, n = q*m };
   q = 2 { q x q processor nodes };
   m = 10 { m x m interior subgrid
      elements, m even };
   m1 = 11 { m+1 };
   steps = n;
type
   row = array [1..n] of real;
   grid = array [1..n] of row;

procedure laplace(var u: grid;
   u1, u2, u3, u4, u5: real;
   steps: integer);
type
   subrow = array [0..m1] of real;
   subgrid = array [0..m1] of subrow;
   channel = *(real);

   procedure node(qi, qj, steps: integer;
      up, down, left, right: channel);
   const pi = 3.14159265358979;
   var u: subgrid; k: integer; fopt: real;

      procedure copy(no: integer;
         inp, out: channel);
```

```
var k: integer; uk: real;
begin
  for k := 1 to no do
    begin
      receive(inp, uk);
      send(out, uk)
    end
end;

procedure output(qi, qj: integer;
  inp, out: channel; var u: subgrid);
var i, j: integer;
begin
  for i := 1 to m do
    begin
      for j := 1 to m do
        send(out, u[i,j]);
      copy((q − qj)*m, inp, out)
    end;
  copy((q − qi)*m*n, inp, out)
end;

procedure phase1(qi, qj, b: integer;
  up, down, left, right: channel;
  var u: subgrid);
var k, last: integer;
begin
  k := 2 − b;
  last := m − b;
  while k <= last do
    begin
      { 1 <= k <= m }
      [sic] parallel
        if qi > 1 then
          receive(up, u[0,k])|
        if qi < q then
          send(down, u[m,k])|
```

```
            if qj > 1 then
                receive(left, u[k,0])|
            if qj < q then
                send(right, u[k,m])
        end;
        k := k + 2
    end
end;

procedure phase2(qi, qj, b: integer;
    up, down, left, right: channel;
    var u: subgrid);
var k, last: integer;
begin
    k := b + 1;
    last := m + b - 1;
    while k <= last do
        begin
            { 1 <= k <= m }
            [sic] parallel
                if qi > 1 then
                    send(up, u[1,k])|
                if qi < q then
                    receive(down, u[m+1,k])|
                if qj > 1 then
                    send(left, u[k,1])|
                if qj < q then
                    receive(right, u[k,m+1])
            end;
            k := k + 2
        end
end;

procedure exchange(qi, qj, b: integer;
    up, down, left, right: channel;
    var u: subgrid);
begin
```

```
        phase1(qi, qj, b,
           up, down, left, right, u);
        phase2(qi, qj, b,
           up, down, left, right, u)
     end;

     function initial(i, j: integer): real;
     begin
        if i = 0 then
           initial := u1
        else if i = n + 1 then
           initial := u2
        else if j = n + 1 then
           initial := u3
        else if j = 0 then
           initial := u4
        else
           initial := u5
     end;

     procedure nextstate(var u: subgrid;
        i, j: integer);
     { 1 <= i <= m, 1 <= j <= m }
     var res: real;
     begin
        res :=
           (u[i−1,j] + u[i+1,j] +
              u[i,j+1] + u[i,j−1])/4.0
              − u[i,j];
        u[i,j] := u[i,j] + fopt*res
     end;

     procedure newgrid(qi, qj: integer;
        var u: subgrid);
     var i, i0, j, j0: integer;
     begin
        i0 := (qi − 1)*m;
```

```
      j0 := (qj − 1)*m;
      for i := 0 to m + 1 do
        for j := 0 to m + 1 do
          u[i,j] := initial(i0+i, j0+j)
  end;

  procedure relax(qi, qj: integer;
    up, down, left, right: channel;
    var u: subgrid);
  var b, i, j, k: integer;
  begin
    for b := 0 to 1 do
      begin
        exchange(qi, qj, 1 − b,
          up, down, left, right, u);
        for i := 1 to m do
          begin
            k := (i + b) mod 2;
            j := 2 − k;
            while j <= m − k do
              begin
                nextstate(u, i, j);
                j := j + 2
              end
          end
      end
  end;

begin
  fopt := 2.0 − 2.0*pi/n;
  newgrid(qi, qj, u);
  for k := 1 to steps do
    relax(qi, qj, up, down,
      left, right, u);
  output(qi, qj, right, left, u)
end { node };
```

```
procedure master(right: channel;
  var u: grid);
var i, j: integer;
begin
  for i := 1 to n do
    for j := 1 to n do
      receive(right, u[i,j])
end;

procedure simulate(
  steps: integer; var u: grid);
type
  line = array [1..q] of channel;
  matrix = array [0..q] of line;
var h, v: matrix; i, j: integer;
begin
  open(h[0,q]);
  for i := 1 to q do
    for j := 1 to q do
      open(h[i,j]);
  for i := 0 to q do
    for j := 1 to q do
      open(v[i,j]);
  parallel
    master(h[0,q], u)|
    forall j := 1 to q do
      node(j, 1, steps,
          v[j−1,1], v[j,1],
          h[j−1,q], h[j,1])|
    forall i := 1 to q do
      forall j := 2 to q do
        node(i, j, steps,
            v[i−1,j], v[i,j],
            h[i,j−1], h[i,j])
  end
end;
```

```
    begin simulate(steps, u) end { laplace };

procedure run;
var u: grid;

  procedure display(var u: grid);
  var i, j: integer;
  begin
    for i := 1 to n do
      begin
        for j := 1 to n do
          write(round(u[i,j]):2, ' ');
        writeln
      end
  end;

begin
  laplace(u, 0.0, 100.0, 100.0,
      0.0, 50.0, steps);
  display(u)
end { run };

begin
  writeln('Laplace matrix:',
      ' n = ', n:1, ', p = ', q*q:1);
  writeln; run
end.
```

Bibliography

[1] Aarts, E. and Korst, J. (1989), *Simulated Annealing and Boltzmann Machines*, Wiley, New York.

[2] Aho, A.V., Hopcroft, J.E. and Ullman, J.D. (1974) *The Design and Analysis of Computer Algorithms*. Addison-Wesley, Reading, MA.

[3] Aho, A.V., Hopcroft, J.E. and Ullman, J.D. (1983) *Data Structures and Algorithms*. Addison-Wesley, Reading, MA.

[4] Alagić, S. and Arbib, M.A. (1978) *The Design of Well-Structured and Correct Programs*. Springer-Verlag, New York.

[5] Allwright, J.R.A. and Carpenter, D.B. (1989), A distributed implementation of simulated annealing. *Parallel Computing*, **10**, pp. 335–338.

[6] Ambler, A.L., Good, D.I., Browne, J.C., Burger, W.F., Cohen, R.M. and Wells, R.E. (1977) Gypsy: a language for specification and implementation of verifiable programs. *ACM SIGPLAN Notices*, **12** (2), pp. 1–10.

[7] Arbib, M.A. and Robinson, J.A. (eds.) (1990) *Natural and Artificial Parallel Computation*. MIT Press, Cambridge, MA.

[8] Ashenhurst, R.L. and Graham, S. (1987) *ACM Turing Award Lectures: The First Twenty Years, 1966–1985*, ACM Press, New York.

[9] Bak, P. and Tang, C. (1989) Earthquakes as a self-organized critical phenomenon. *Journal of Geophysical Research*, **94** (B11), pp. 15635–15637.

[10] Bak, P. and Chen, K. (1990) A forest-fire model and some thoughts on turbulence. *Physics Letters A*, **147** (5–6), pp. 297–299.

[11] Barlow, R.H. and Evans, D.J. (1982) Parallel algorithms for the iterative solution to linear systems. *Computer Journal*, **25** (1), pp. 56–60.

[12] Barnes, J. and Hut, P. (1986) A hierarchical $O(NlogN)$ force-calculation algorithm. *Nature*, **324**, pp. 446–449.

[13] Bentley, J.L. and Shamos, M.I. (1976) Divide-and-conquer in multidimensional space. *ACM Symposium on Theory of Computation*, pp. 220–230.

[14] Berlekamp, E.R., Conway, J.H. and Guy, R.K. (1982) *Winning Ways for Your Mathematical Plays*. Vol. 2, Academic Press, New York, pp. 817–850.

[15] Brigham, E.O. (1974) *The Fast Fourier Transform.* Prentice Hall, Englewood Cliffs, NJ.

[16] Brinch Hansen, P., and House, R. (1966) The Cobol compiler for the Siemens 3003. *BIT,* **6**, pp. 1–23.

[17] Brinch Hansen, P. (1973) *Operating System Principles.* Prentice Hall, Englewood Cliffs, NJ.

[18] Brinch Hansen, P. (1977) *The Architecture of Concurrent Programs.* Prentice Hall, Englewood Cliffs, NJ.

[19] Brinch Hansen, P. (1985) *Brinch Hansen on Pascal Compilers.* Prentice Hall, Englewood Cliffs, NJ.

[20] Brinch Hansen, P. (1987) Joyce—a programming language for distributed systems. *Software—Practice and Experience,* **17**, pp. 29–50.

[21] Brinch Hansen, P. (1989) A multiprocessor implementation of Joyce. *Software—Practice and Experience,* **19**, pp. 579–592.

[22] Brinch Hansen, P. (1990a) The linear search rediscovered. *Structured Programming,* **11**, pp. 53–55.

[23] Brinch Hansen, P. (1990b) The nature of parallel programming. In Arbib (1990), pp. 31–46.

[24] Brinch Hansen, P. (1990c) Householder reduction of linear equations. School of Computer and Information Science, Syracuse University, Syracuse, NY. Also in *ACM Computing Surveys,* **24**, pp. 185–194, June 1992. Chapter 3 of this book (revised version).

[25] Brinch Hansen, P. (1990d) The all-pairs pipeline. School of Computer and Information Science, Syracuse University, Syracuse, NY. Chapter 4 of this book (revised version).

[26] Brinch Hansen, P. (1990e) Balancing a pipeline by folding. School of Computer and Information Science, Syracuse University, Syracuse, NY. Chapter 5 of this book (revised version).

[27] Brinch Hansen, P. (1991a) The n-body pipeline. School of Computer and Information Science, Syracuse University, Syracuse, NY. Chapter 6 of this book (revised version).

[28] Brinch Hansen, P. (1991b) A generic multiplication pipeline. School of Computer and Information Science, Syracuse University, Syracuse, NY. Chapter 7 of this book (revised version).

[29] Brinch Hansen, P. (1991c) The fast Fourier transform. School of Computer and Information Science, Syracuse University, Syracuse, NY. Chapter 8 of this book (revised version).

[30] Brinch Hansen, P. (1991d) Parallel divide and conquer. School of Computer and Information Science, Syracuse University, Syracuse, NY. Chapter 9 of this book (revised version).

[31] Brinch Hansen, P. (1991e) Do hypercubes sort faster than tree machines? School of Computer and Information Science, Syracuse University, Syracuse, NY. Also in *Concurrency—Practice and Experience,* **6** (2), April 1994, pp. 143–151. Chapter 10 of this book (revised version).

[32] Brinch Hansen, P. (1992a) Simulated annealing. School of Computer and Information Science, Syracuse University, Syracuse, NY. Chapter 11 of this book (revised version).

[33] Brinch Hansen, P. (1992b) Primality testing. School of Computer and Information Science, Syracuse University, Syracuse, NY. Chapter 12 of this book (revised version).

[34] Brinch Hansen, P. (1992c) Multiple-length division revisited: a tour of the minefield. School of Computer and Information Science, Syracuse University, Syracuse, NY. Also in *Software—Practice and Experience*, **24** (6), June 1994, pp. 579–601. Chapter 13 of this book (revised version).

[35] Brinch Hansen, P. (1992d) Parallel Monte Carlo trials. School of Computer and Information Science, Syracuse University, Syracuse, NY. Chapter 14 of this book (revised version).

[36] Brinch Hansen, P. (1992e) Numerical solution of Laplace's equation. School of Computer and Information Science, Syracuse University, Syracuse, NY. Chapter 15 of this book (revised version).

[37] Brinch Hansen, P. (1992f) Parallel cellular automata: a model program for computational science. School of Computer and Information Science, Syracuse University, Syracuse, NY. Also in *Concurrency—Practice and Experience*, **5** (5), August 1993, pp. 425–448. Chapter 16 of this book (revised version).

[38] Brinch Hansen, P. (1992g) Unpublished measurements of Gaussian elimination on the all-pairs folded pipeline. School of Computer and Information Science, Syracuse University, Syracuse, NY.

[39] Brinch Hansen, P. (1993a) Model programs for computational science: a programming methodology for multicomputers. *Concurrency—Practice and Experience*, **5** (5), August 1993, pp. 407–423. Chapter 1 of this book (revised version).

[40] Brinch Hansen, P. (1993b) The programming language SuperPascal. School of Computer and Information Science, Syracuse University, Syracuse, NY. Also in *Software—Practice and Experience*, **24** (5), May 1994, pp. 467–483.

[41] Brinch Hansen, P. (1993c) SuperPascal—a publication language for parallel scientific computing. School of Computer and Information Science, Syracuse University, Syracuse, NY. Also in *Concurrency—Practice and Experience*, **6** (5), August 1994, pp. 461–483. Chapter 2 of this book.

[42] Brinch Hansen, P. (1993d) Interference control in SuperPascal—a block-structured parallel language. School of Computer and Information Science, Syracuse University, Syracuse, NY. Also in *Computer Journal*, **37** (5), 1994, pp. 399–406.

[43] Browning, S.A. (1980) Algorithms for the tree machine. In Mead (1980), pp. 295–313.

[44] Burton, D.M. (1980) *Elementary Number Theory*. Allyn and Bacon, Boston, MA.

[45] Carmichael, R. D. (1912) On composite numbers p which satisfy the Fermat congruence $a^{p-1} = 1 \bmod p$. *American Mathematical Monthly*, **19**, pp. 22–27.

[46] Cayley, A. (1889–97) *The Collected Mathematical Papers*, 13 vols. Cambridge University Press, Johnson Reprint Corp.

[47] Černy, V. (1985) Thermodynamical approach to the traveling salesman problem: an efficient simulation algorithm. *Journal of Optimization Theory and Applications*, **45**, pp. 41–51.

[48] Cok, R.S. (1991) *Parallel Programs for the Transputer*. Prentice Hall, Englewood Cliffs, NJ.

[49] Cole, M.I. (1989) *Algorithmic Skeletons: Structured Management of Parallel Computation*. MIT Press, Cambridge, MA.

[50] Cooley, J.W. and Tukey, J.W. (1965) An algorithm for machine calculation of complex Fourier series. *Mathematics of Computation*, **19**, pp. 297–301.

[51] Cooley, J.W., Lewis, P.A. and Welsh, P.D. (1967) The history of the fast Fourier transform. *Proceedings of the IEEE*, **55**, pp. 1675–1679.

[52] Cormen, T.H., Leiserson, C.E. and Rivest, R.L. (1990) *Introduction to Algorithms*, MIT Press, Cambridge, MA.

[53] Cosnard, M. and Tchuente, M. (1988), Designing systolic algorithms by top-down analysis. *The Third International Conference on Supercomputing*, Vol. 3, International Supercomputing Institute, St. Petersburg, FL, pp. 9–18.

[54] Courant, R. and Robbins, H. (1941) *What is Mathematics?* Oxford University Press, New York.

[55] Courant, R. and John, F. (1989) *Introduction to Calculus and Analysis*. Vols. I & II. Springer-Verlag, New York.

[56] Dahl, O.-J., Dijkstra, E.W. and Hoare, C.A.R. (1972) *Structured Programming*. Academic Press, New York.

[57] Dewdney, A.K. (1984). Sharks and fish wage an ecological war on the toroidal planet Wa-Tor. *Scientific American*, **251** (6), pp. 14–22.

[58] Dijkstra, E.W. (1968) Cooperating sequential processes. In Genuys (1968), pp. 43–112.

[59] Dijkstra, E.W. (1972) Notes on structured programming. In Dahl (1972).

[60] Dijkstra, E.W. (1982) *Selected Writings on Computing: A Personal Perspective*. Springer-Verlag, New York, pp. 334–337.

[61] Dongarra, J.J., Bunch, J.R., Moler, C.B. and Stewart, G.W. (1979) *Linpack Users' Guide*. Society for Industrial and Applied Mathematics, Philadelphia, PA.

[62] Dongarra, J.J. and Sorenson, D.C. (1989) Algorithmic design for different computer architectures. In Sanz (1989), pp. 33–35.

[63] Dunham, C.B. (1982) The necessity of publishing programs. *Computer Journal*, **25**, pp. 61–62.

[64] Eddy, W. (1977) A new convex hull algorithm for planar sets. *ACM Transactions on Mathematical Software*, **3**, pp. 398–403.

[65] Ellingworth, H.R.P. (1988) Transputers and computational chemistry: an application. *The Third International Conference on Supercomputing*, Vol. 1, International Supercomputing Institute, St. Petersburg, FL, pp. 269–274.

[66] Elliott, R. and Hoare, C.A.R. (eds.) (1989) *Scientific Applications of Multiprocessors*. Prentice-Hall, Englewood Cliffs, NJ.

[67] Evans, D.J. (1984) Parallel SOR iterative methods. *Parallel Computing*, **1**, pp. 3–18.

[68] Fermat, P. de (1640) Letter to Bernard Frenicle de Bessy (October 18).

[69] Feynman, R., Leighton, R.B., and Sands, M.L. (1989) *The Feynman Lectures on Physics*. Vol. I, Addison-Wesley, Redwood City, CA.

[70] Floyd, R.W. (1987) The paradigms of programming. In Ashenhurst (1987), pp. 131–142.

[71] Foley, M. and Hoare, C.A.R. (1971) Proof of a recursive program: Quicksort. *Computer Journal*, **14**, pp. 391–395.

[72] Forsythe, G.E. (1966) Algorithms for scientific computing. *Communications of the ACM*, **9**, pp. 255–256.

[73] Fox, G.C., Johnson, M.A., Lyzenga, G.A., Otto, S.W., Salmon, J.K. and Walker, D.W. (1988) *Solving Problems on Concurrent Processors*, Vol. I, Prentice-Hall, Englewood Cliffs, NJ.

[74] Fox, G.C. (1990) Applications of parallel supercomputers: scientific results and computer science lessons. In Arbib (1990), pp. 47–90.

[75] Frisch, U., Hasslacher, B. and Pomeau, Y. (1986) Lattice-gas automata for the Navier-Stokes equation. *Physical Review Letters*, **56** (14), pp. 1505–1508.

[76] Gardner, M. (1970) The fantastic combinations of John Conway's new solitaire game "Life." *Scientific American*, **223** (10), pp. 120–123.

[77] Gardner, M. (1971) On cellular automata, self-reproduction, the Garden of Eden and the game "Life." *Scientific American*, **224** (2), pp. 112–117.

[78] Garey, M.R. and Johnson, D.S. (1979) *Computers and Intractability. A Guide to the Theory of NP-Completeness*. Freeman, New York.

[79] Genuys, F. (ed.) (1968) *Programming Languages*. Academic Press, New York.

[80] Golub, G.H. and van Loan, C.F. (1989) *Matrix Computations*. Johns Hopkins University Press, Baltimore, MD.

[81] Greenfield, J.S. (1994) Distributed programming paradigms with cryptography applications. *Lecture Notes in Computer Science*, **870**.

[82] Gustafson, J.L. (1988) Reevaluating Amdahl's law. *Communications of the ACM*, **31**, pp. 532–533.

[83] Hoare, C.A.R. (1961) Algorithm 64: Quicksort. *Communications of the ACM*, **4**, p. 321.

[84] Hoare, C.A.R. (1971a) Procedures and parameters: an axiomatic approach. *Lecture Notes in Mathematics*, **188**, pp. 102–171.

[85] Hoare, C.A.R. (1971b) Proof of a program: Find. *Communications of the ACM*, **14**, pp. 39–45.

[86] Hoare, C.A.R. and Perrott, R.H. (eds.) (1972a) *Operating Systems Techniques*. Academic Press, New York.

[87] Hoare, C.A.R. (1972b) Towards a theory of parallel programming. In Hoare (1972a), pp. 61–71.

[88] Hoare, C.A.R. (1985) *Communicating Sequential Processes*. Prentice Hall, Englewood Cliffs, NJ.

[89] Hockney, R.W. and Eastwood, J.W. (1988) *Computer Simulation Using Particles*. Adam Hilger, New York.

[90] Hoppensteadt, F.C. (1978) Mathematical aspects of population biology. In Steen (1978), pp. 297–320.

[91] Householder, A.S. (1958) Unitary triangularization of a nonsymmetric matrix. *Journal of the ACM*, **5**, pp. 339–342.

[92] Hwa, T. and Kardar, M. (1989) Dissipative transport in open systems: an investigation of self-organized criticality. *Physical Review Letters*, **62** (16), pp. 1813–1816.

[93] IEEE (1983) *IEEE Standard Pascal Computer Programming Language*. Institute of Electrical and Electronics Engineers, New York.

[94] Ignizio, J.P. (1973) Validating claims for algorithms proposed for publication. *Operations Research*, **21**, pp. 852-854.

[95] Inmos Ltd. (1988) *occam 2 Reference Manual*. Prentice Hall, Englewood Cliffs, NJ.

[96] Jamieson, L.H., Gannon, D. and Douglas, R.J. (eds.) (1987) *The Characteristics of Parallel Algorithms*. MIT Press, Cambridge, MA.

[97] Kerridge, J. (1993) Using occam3 to build large parallel systems: Part 1, occam3 features. *Transputer Communications*, **1** (to appear).

[98] Kirkpatrick, S., Gelatt, C.D. and Vechi, M.P. (1983) Optimization by simulated annealing. *Science*, **220**, pp. 671–680.

[99] Knuth, D. (1969) *The Art of Computer Programming*. Vol. 2: *Seminumerical Algorithms*. Addison-Wesley, Reading, MA.

[100] Kreyszig, E. (1988) *Advanced Engineering Mathematics*. Wiley, New York.

[101] Krishnamurthy, E.V. and Nandi, S.K. (1967) On the normalization requirement of divisors in divide-and-correct methods. *Communications of the ACM*, **12**, pp. 809–813.

[102] Kung, H.T. (1988) Systolic communication. *IEEE International Conference on Systolic Arrays*. San Diego, CA, pp. 695–703.

[103] Kung, H.T. (1989) Computational models for parallel computers. In Elliott (1989), pp. 1–15.

[104] Lampson, B.W., Horning, J.J., London, R.L., Mitchell, J.G. and Popek, G.J. (1977) Report on the programming language Euclid. *ACM SIGPLAN Notices*, **12** (2).

[105] Lawler, E.L. (1976) *Combinatorial Optimization: Networks and Matroids.* Holt, Rinehart and Winston, New York.

[106] Lawler, E.L., Lenstra, J.K., Rinnooy Kan, A.H.G. and Shmoys, D.B. (eds.) (1985) *The Traveling Salesman Problem: A Guided Tour of Combinatorial Optimization.* Wiley, Chichester, England.

[107] Li, J., Brass, A., Ward, D.J. and Robson, B. (1990) A study of parallel molecular dynamics for N-body simulations on a transputer system. *Parallel Computing,* **14,** pp. 211–222.

[108] Lin, S. (1965) Computer solutions of the traveling salesman problem. *Bell System Technical Journal,* **44,** pp. 2245–2269.

[109] McDonald, N. (1991) Meiko Scientific Ltd. In Trew (1991), pp. 165–175.

[110] Macnaghten, A.M. and Hoare, C.A.R. (1977) Fast Fourier transform free from tears. *Computer Journal,* **20** (1), pp. 78–83.

[111] Marciniak, A. (1985) *Numerical Solutions of the N-body Problem.* D. Reidel, Dordrecht, Holland.

[112] May, D. (1988) The influence of VLSI technology on computer architecture. *The Third International Conference on Supercomputing,* Vol. 2, St. Petersburg, FL, pp. 247–256.

[113] May, D. (1989) Discussion. In Elliott (1989), p. 54.

[114] May, D. (1990) Towards general-purpose parallel computers. In Arbib (1990), pp. 91–121.

[115] Mead, C. and Conway, L. (1980) *Introduction to VLSI Systems.* Addison-Wesley, Reading, MA.

[116] Meiko Ltd. (1987) *Computing Surface Technical Specifications.* Meiko Ltd., Bristol, England.

[117] Miller, G.L. (1976) Riemann's hypothesis and tests for primality. *Journal of Computer and System Sciences,* **13,** pp. 300–317.

[118] Mills, H.D. (1988) *Software Productivity.* Dorset House, New York, NY.

[119] Moscato, P. and Fontanari, J.F. (1989) Stochastic vs. deterministic update in simulated annealing. California Institute of Technology, Pasadena, CA.

[120] Nelson, P.A. and Snyder, L. (1987) Programming paradigms for nonshared memory parallel computers. In Jamieson (1987), pp. 3–20.

[121] Ortega, J.M. (1988) *Introduction to Parallel and Vector Solutions of Linear Systems.* Plenum Press, New York.

[122] Park, S.K., and Miller, K.W. (1988) Random number generators: good ones are hard to find. *Communications of the ACM,* **31,** pp. 1192–1201.

[123] Perlis, A.J. (1966) A new policy for algorithms? *Communications of the ACM,* **9,** p. 255.

[124] Pomerance, C. (1981) On the distribution of pseudoprimes. *Mathematics of Computation,* **37,** pp. 587–593.

[125] Press, W.H., Flannery, B.P., Teukolsky, S.A. and Vetterling, W.T. (1989) *Numerical Recipes in Pascal: The Art of Scientific Computing*. Cambridge University Press, Cambridge, MA.

[126] Press, W.H. and Teukolsky, S.A. (1991) Multigrid methods for boundary value problems. I. *Computers in Physics*, **5** (5), pp. 514–519.

[127] Pritchard, D.J., Askew, C.R., Carpenter, D.D., Glendinning, I., Hey, A.J.G. and Nicole, D.A. (1987), Practical parallelism using transputer arrays. *Lecture Notes in Computer Science*, **258**, pp. 278–294.

[128] Rabin, M.O. (1980) Probabilistic algorithms for testing primality. *Journal of Number Theory*, **12**, pp. 128–138.

[129] Riesel, H. (1985) *Prime Numbers and Computer Methods for Factorization*. Birkhäuser, Boston, MA.

[130] Rivest, R.L., Shamir, A. and Adleman, L.M. (1978) A method for obtaining digital signatures and public-key cryptosystems. *Communications of the ACM*, **21**, pp. 120–126.

[131] Sagan, C. (1980) *Cosmos*. Random House, New York, NY.

[132] Salmon, J.K. (1991) Parallel hierarchical *N*-body methods. California Institute of Technology, Pasadena, CA.

[133] Saltz, J.H., Naik, V.K. and Nicol, D.M. (1987) Reduction of the effects of the communication delays in scientific algorithms on message passing MIMD architectures. *SIAM Journal on Scientific and Statistical Computing*, **8** (1), pp. s118–s134.

[134] Sanz, J.L.C. (ed.) (1989) *Opportunities and Constraints of Parallel Computing*. Springer-Verlag, New York.

[135] Sedgewick, R. (1984) *Algorithms*. Addison-Wesley, Reading, MA.

[136] Seitz, C.L. (1985) The Cosmic Cube. *Communications of the ACM*, **28**, pp. 22–33.

[137] Shih, Z., Chen, G. and Lee, R.T.C. (1987) Systolic algorithms to examine all pairs of elements. *Communications of the ACM*, **30**, pp. 161–167.

[138] Smith, D.E. and Ginsburg, J. (1988) From numbers to numerals to computation. In J.R. Newman (ed.), *The World of Mathematics*. Vol. 1. Tempus, Redmond, WA, pp. 433–454.

[139] Smith, R. and Harrison, D.E. (1989) Algorithms for molecular dynamics simulation of keV particle bombardment. *Computers in Physics*, **3**, pp. 68–73.

[140] Steen, L.A. (ed.) (1978) *Mathematics Today: Twelve Informal Essays*. Springer-Verlag, New York.

[141] Strang, G. (1986) *Introduction to Applied Mathematics*. Wellesley-Cambridge Press, Wellesley, MA.

[142] Strassen, V. (1969) Gaussian elimination is not optimal. *Numerische Mathematik*, **13**, pp. 354–356.

[143] Tennent, R.D. (1981) *Principles of Programming Languages*. Prentice Hall, Englewood Cliffs, NJ.

[144] Trew, A. and Wilson, G. (eds.) (1991) *Past, Present, Parallel: A Survey of Available Parallel Computing Systems*. Springer-Verlag, New York.

[145] Ulam, S. (1986) *Science, Computers, and People: From the Tree of Mathematics*, Birkhäuser, Boston, MA.

[146] Valiant, L.G. (1989) Optimally universal parallel computers. In Elliott (1989), pp. 17–20.

[147] van Albada, T.S. (1986) Models of hot stellar systems. *The Use of Supercomputers in Stellar Dynamics*. Springer-Verlag, New York, NY, pp. 23–25.

[148] von Neumann, J. (1966) *Theory of Self-Reproducing Automata*. Edited and completed by A.W. Burks, University of Illinois Press, Urbana, IL.

[149] Welsh, J. and McKeag, M. (1980) *Structured System Programming*. Prentice Hall, Englewood Cliffs, NJ.

[150] Wirth, N. (1971) The programming language Pascal. *Acta Informatica*, **1**, pp. 35–63.

[151] Wirth, N. (1973) *Systematic Programming: An Introduction*. Prentice Hall, Englewood Cliffs, NJ.

[152] Wirth, N. (1976) *Algorithms + Data Structures = Programs*. Prentice Hall, Englewood Cliffs, NJ.

[153] Wood, D. (1984) *Paradigms and Programming with Pascal*. Computer Science Press, Rockville, MD.

[154] Young, D.M. (1954) Iterative methods for solving partial difference equations of elliptic type. *Transactions of the American Mathematical Society*, **76**, pp. 92–111.

[155] Young, D.M. (1971) *Iterative Solution of Large Linear Systems*. Academic Press, New York.